This Affair of Louisiana

THIS AFFAIR
OF
LOUISIANA

Alexander DeConde

LOUISIANA STATE UNIVERSITY PRESS
Baton Rouge and London

LIBRARY OF CONGRESS CATALOGING IN PUBLICATION DATA

DeConde, Alexander
  This affair of Louisiana

  Bibliography: p. 279
  Includes index.
  1. Louisiana Purchase. 2. United States—
Territorial expansion. I. Title
E333.D42   973.4'6   76–12468
ISBN 0–684–14687–8 Cloth
ISBN 0–8071–0497–3 Paper

Contents

Preface / ix

I. Exploration and Settlement / 3

II. Stake of Empire / 21

III. Peaceful Penetration / 41

IV. Economic Dominion / 57

V. Enduring Dream / 75

VI. Transforming the Dream / 91

VII. Mississippi Crisis / 107

VIII. The President's Dilemma / 127

IX. Shattered Dream / 147

X. Paris / 161

XI. The Constitutional Sanction / 177

XII. Ineffectual Protest / 193

XIII. Elastic Boundaries / 209

XIV. Persisting Coercion / 227

XV. The Imperial Thrust / 241

Notes / 257

Bibliographical Essay / 279

Index / 315

Acknowledgment

While researching and writing this book I benefited from a grant out of the Penrose Fund of the American Philosophical Society, from support given by the Rockefeller Foundation for a period of residence early in 1975 at the Villa Serbelloni, Bellagio, Italy, where I wrote one of my last drafts, and from continuing grants from the Research Council of the University of California, Santa Barbara. Professors Thomas A. Bailey, Wilbur Jacobs, Abraham Nasatir, Albert H. Bowman, and my wife, Glace, read the manuscript and offered perceptive suggestions for improvement. Several student assistants, namely Timothy Matthewson, Joseph Navarro, Sharon Akridge, Rolfe Buzzell, Patricia Raabe, and James McCarthy, helped me in tracking down sources, with typing, and with other chores. The librarians in the inter-library loan department of the University of California, Santa Barbara, library were particularly gracious in obtaining books, journals, newspapers, and copies of manuscript material for my use. I thank them, and all the others who kindly assisted me in this venture.

—A.D.

Preface

❧

*A*lthough the literature on the Louisiana Purchase is voluminous, no serious modern scholar has produced an interpretive synthesis based on that literature and on the documentary sources. So this history offers speculative analysis as well as a chronological narrative. My thesis is that of an expansionist Anglo-American ethos, rooted in the colonial experience, that continues into the first years of the new American nation and emerges during the Louisiana affair as a kind of pious imperialism. Some call it the American sense of mission.

In keeping with this thesis, I recount much that is familiar but concentrate on a theme that has not yet been fully exploited by other scholars—the tradition as well as the fact of expansion in the Jeffersonian era. While I do not conceive of expansion as the only important theme of the early national period, I do regard it as central then and throughout much of the American experience. I try also to correlate the ideology of expansionism, despite its vagaries and inconsistencies, with national policy.

This approach, and the evidence itself as I have analyzed it, has also caused me to differ with other aspects of the conventional wisdom on the subject. For example, instead of viewing the acquisition of Louisiana as a stroke of good fortune made possible by Europe's misfortune or as the culmination of an inexorable pressure of frontiersmen moving westward or even as the work of an inevitable destiny, I see it as the result of a conscious expansionism or of an imperial creed promoting action. In other words, Americans obtained Louisiana because they desired it and worked to get it. Their determination, their rhetoric, and their activity developed logically out of an already old Anglo-American imperial tradition. In addition, thanks to the perspective of hindsight, I see the Louisiana affair as perpetuating that tradition.

Since I employ frequently three key terms that are open to a number of definitions, the reader should know immediately what they mean. In this study *imperialism* connotes the advocacy of taking territory as well as the actual acquiring through use or threatened use of power. *Expansion,* as a synonym, refers to the same process. *Empire* embodies the result of that process, though its meaning may vary from this definition according to its context.

—Alexander DeConde
Santa Barbara, California

This Affair of Louisiana

Chapter I

⚜

Exploration and Settlement

The principal purpose of Sieur de la Salle in making this discovery [of the Mississippi] was to find a port on the Gulf of Mexico on which could be formed a French settlement to serve as a base for conquests upon the Spaniards at the first outbreak of hostilities.

— *Marquis de Seigneley, 1684* [1]

*A*t one time or another four nations—Spain, France, England, and the United States—vied for Louisiana or parts of it. Those who held the best title to that empire, essentially the great valley watered by the Mississippi River and its tributaries and land stretching west to the Rocky Mountains, were the native American Indians who lived there long before Europeans set eyes on it. The Europeans came; they explored; they settled. They made good their claims to the land because they had the power to enforce them. For the aboriginal inhabitants it made no difference who from among the white imperialists emerged victorious. The result was the same—native American dispossession. As Tatooed Serpent, a war chief of the Natchez Indians, put it, "Why did the French come into our country? We did not go to seek them; they asked for land of us." [2]

3

Although populous before the coming of the whites, the native peoples of Louisiana did not repel the Europeans. Nor were they savages, deserving to be displaced by civilized, conquering whites. Some aboriginal groups, such as the Natchez on the banks of the Mississippi, created cultures more elaborate than practically any other north of Mexico. Regardless of their accomplishments, the Indians did not impart political unity to Louisiana or leave a written history of consequence of their region.

The first Europeans to traverse Louisiana, *conquistadores* from Spain, did not stay long enough to bring unity to the region either. But the Spaniards kept written records, and so the history of the struggle for that continental empire usually begins with them.

In 1519 the earliest of these Spaniards, an experienced sea captain named Alonso Alvárez de Piñeda, explored the coast of the Gulf of Mexico. He and his men were the first whites to sight the mouth of the Mississippi River. Piñeda's reports prompted Pánfilo de Narváez, a veteran of soldiering in North America, in April 1528 to lead an expedition of some three hundred men inland from the coast of Florida. Narváez encountered heartbreaking hardships. When he attempted to sail for Mexico, he wrecked his ships. Eight years later, after wandering through southern Louisiana and throughout the Southwest, Álvar Núñez Cabeza de Vaca, the treasurer of the expedition, and three other emaciated survivors reached a Spanish settlement in Mexico.

In recording his experiences, Cabeza de Vaca gave the impression that Florida and adjacent territory contained untapped riches. His accounts inspired Hernando de Soto, a newly appointed governor of Cuba, to organize an expedition of six hundred soldiers and plunge into Louisiana. This force crossed the Mississippi in May 1541, the first whites to do so, but found no wealth. De Soto died the following year of yellow fever. Reduced by hunger, disease, and Indian attacks to about half its original size, the expedition then sailed down the Mississippi to safety. The disastrous results of these first European probings probably kept the Spaniards from occupying the Gulf region. In any case, while Spain came to claim the Mississippi Valley at this time she left no settlements.

Louisiana's first European settlers, the French, moved into the Mississippi Valley from the north rather than from the Gulf of Mexico. Samuel de Champlain, a colonizer as well as explorer, who became governor of New France in 1633, encouraged his countrymen to expand into the interior of North America. Seeking natives to convert to Christianity, French Jesuit missionaries were among the first to roam and chart the region. In 1634 Jean Nicolet, an experienced explorer sponsored by Champlain, journeyed as far west as Green Bay, Wisconsin, and picked up tales from Indians about a great river, the Mississippi, to the south. In 1659 Médard Chouart, sieur des Groseilliers, a fur trapper, penetrated the region of the upper Great Lakes. He, too, reported the existence of a large river nearby.

Two years later Louis XIV, the Sun King, assumed personal rule of France. Under the influence of his capable minister of finance, Jean Baptiste Colbert, Louis tried to shut the Spaniards out of the heart of North America and curb British imperial expansion. English officials and colonists seeking to tap the fur country of the interior were asserting rights in the great valley that the Spaniards claimed as their own and that the French desired. To carry out his North American policy, Louis in 1663 appointed Jean Talon, an energetic expansionist, intendant of New France. Talon's arrival in North America set in motion a great Anglo-French rivalry for control of the Mississippi Valley.

As intendant, or the king's personal representative who could often act independently of the governor, Talon for a time dominated the government of New France. He concluded that

France's North American colonies needed more French people. He estimated that there were fewer than thirty-five hundred whites in New France, whereas English colonies to the south contained about twenty-five thousand. To strengthen the French position, he made alliances with Indian peoples, pushed exploration of the interior, and founded settlements there. He also believed that possession of the Mississippi River would provide New France with a natural frontier and a passage to the South Sea, or Pacific Ocean. In 1672 he organized an expedition to be headed by Louis Jolliet, trader, explorer, and cartographer, and Père Jacques Marquette, a Jesuit missionary familiar with the customs of American Indians.

In that year Louis de Buade, comte de Frontenac, took over as governor of New France, replacing Talon as the most powerful Frenchman in America. Frontenac approved the Jolliet-Marquette expedition, which set out in 1673. The two explorers sailed into the Mississippi in July, the first authenticated Frenchmen to reach the great river.

Robert Cavelier, sieur de La Salle, a young adventurer from Rouen, saw a map Jolliet had made of the Mississippi and linked it with de Soto's discovery. La Salle then conceived a scheme for connecting Louisiana with Canada by a chain of posts and for expanding France's empire into the interior of North America. He assumed that if French soldiers and settlers fortified the shores of Lake Ontario, made treaties of friendship with the native Americans along the way, and erected a string of forts along the Mississippi to the Gulf, they could hold the heart of North America against either Spanish or English attacks. La Salle presented his idea to the court at Versailles. In 1678 Colbert finally authorized him to explore western Canada and to establish military posts there.

Encountering trouble with Indians, La Salle put aside his plan to build forts but persisted in his explorations. He sailed down the Illinois River into the Mississippi and descended that

6

stream to its mouth. He named the territory he had traversed Louisiana, after his sovereign. On April 9, 1682, La Salle planted a column and a cross painted with "the arms of France" and "in the name of His Majesty and his successors to his crown" took possession "of this country of Louisiana, the seas, harbors, ports, bays, adjacent straits, and all the nations, people, provinces, cities, towns, villages, mines, minerals, fisheries, streams and rivers comprised in the extent of said Louisiana." [3]

La Salle then formulated another project, colonization of the lower Mississippi Valley. Trade and settlement by way of the Gulf, he was convinced, would be less difficult for the French than travel through the Great Lakes southward. He returned to Quebec and then to France in 1683, leaving his lieutenant, Henry de Tonti, in charge of the western country at an outpost on the Illinois River called Fort Saint Louis.

La Salle quickly realized that Louis XIV, then at war with Spain, was more interested in seizing gold and silver mines in Mexico than in colonization. So La Salle linked his plan with the idea of building a base on the Gulf Coast for attacking New Spain. In April 1684 Louis named him governor of Louisiana. In July, with four ships loaded with soldiers, mechanics, and colonists totaling 280 people, La Salle sailed to occupy the mouth of the Mississippi. Failing to find the entrance to the river, he landed his expedition at Matagorda Bay, Texas. In March 1687, after trying for two years to reach the river by foot, La Salle at age forty-three was murdered by two of his own men before he could fulfill his dream to establish a French settlement at the mouth of the Mississippi.

In the summer of 1684, shortly after La Salle had sailed for North America, France had made peace with Spain in the Treaty of Ratisbon. This peace, followed by La Salle's failure, led the French government to abandon immediate plans for striking at New Spain by colonizing the lower Mississippi.

La Salle's explorations nonetheless had far-reaching results in the imperial rivalry of France, Spain, and England. They gave birth to the first French settlement in middle America, a small post established by Tonti in 1686 on the Arkansas River, about fifteen miles from its juncture with the Mississippi, and thereafter known as Tonty's Fort. Members of the La Salle expeditions wrote accounts of their travels that familiarized many in Europe with the possibilities of developing Louisiana.

Dreading the idea of French colonization, the government in Madrid considered La Salle's intrusion into the Gulf of Mexico a threat to Florida, Texas, and the rest of its North American empire. So the Spaniards took measures to defend lands they held or claimed. They sent eleven expeditions in search of La Salle and his men. Although the Spaniards failed to find him, the French danger caused Spain to plant settlements throughout the Southwest and to reassert her claim to Louisiana.

La Salle's expeditions served ultimately as the basis for France's title to Louisiana and even to Texas. This claim, which made use of a European legal concept called the doctrine of discovery that gave ownership of allegedly unoccupied land to the white discoverers, kept France in active imperial rivalry with Spain and England. Since exploration and settlement in Louisiana were costly, the French maintained their interest in the region not for immediate economic reasons but mainly for political ones. They recognized in the Mississippi a vital waterway connecting Canada with the interior of North America and the Gulf. By controlling the Mississippi as well as the Saint Lawrence River, they assumed that they could keep the English and the Spaniards out of the heart of North America and that they might themselves come to dominate the entire continent.

Soon, as Anglo-American traders infiltrated the Mississippi Valley, the French downgraded their imperial rivalry with Spain and concerned themselves more with the English challenge. If the English took over Louisiana, they would not only gain an

8

empire the French had yet to occupy but also would make France's position in Canada untenable.

The first clash between England and France that involved empire in the New World, the War of the League of Augsburg, broke out in Europe in 1688. Within a year it spread to North America, where the English colonists called it King William's War. The French and their Indian allies invaded Maine, New Hampshire, and New York. In 1690 an expedition of New Englanders captured Port Royal in French Acadia. In the Treaty of Ryswick, signed near The Hague in September 1697, the belligerents restored their North American conquests. This imperial war, as far as America was concerned, ended indecisively.

With peace, French activity in Louisiana picked up. It received additional stimulus after publication in 1697 of a partly fraudulent narrative, *Nouvelle Découverte,* by Louis Hennepin, a Franciscan missionary who explored with La Salle. Hennepin urged the British king, whom he knew and whose favor he sought, to occupy the mouth of the Mississippi and establish a colony in the area. A year later an English physician and land proprietor in New Jersey, Daniel Coxe, actually organized an expedition for founding such a settlement. Nothing came of the effort because the French were already there.

In 1697 also the possibility of making money through land speculation prompted a group of French merchants to form the Louisiana Company and to request a tract of land from the crown. Fearing that the private venture could not succeed in the face of Spanish and English opposition, Louis de Phélypeaux, comte de Pontchartrain, the minister of marine, refused the charter. To protect French interests and to fight against imperial rivals if necessary, he organized a government force to occupy Louisiana.

Pontchartrain chose a thirty-eight-year-old Canadian naval officer, Pierre Lemoyne, sieur d'Iberville, to head the expedition. With forty-eight of his men, Iberville entered the Missis-

XIV considered abandoning Louisiana. Suffering from neglect and flood, the settlers evacuated Fort Saint Louis in 1710 for another site, and somehow Louisiana as a colony survived.

With the Treaty of Utrecht of April 1713, which ended the War of the Spanish Succession, French power in the New World began to decline. For the first time France yielded to England lands in North America—Newfoundland, Acadia, and Hudson Bay—that she had long claimed and held and for which she had fought. Louisiana remained intact and in French possession, but nominally so. France's failure to define its boundaries and to colonize it left it open to further dispute with England.

Drained of resources by constant wars, the French crown decided meanwhile to turn over Louisiana to a private company for organized development. In September 1712 the king granted Antoine Crozat, a wealthy merchant to whom he was indebted, exclusive right to trade in Louisiana for fifteen years. The grant attempted, in a general way, to define the extent of Louisiana. It gave Crozat jurisdiction over territory between New Mexico and the Carolinas and from the Gulf of Mexico to the Great Lakes. He had only one obligation, to send two ships a year to Louisiana with twenty-five men or women of his choice. He hoped to profit from his monopoly with minimum investment, mainly by establishing trade between Louisiana and Spain's American colonies and by the mining of gold and silver.

Crozat's representatives along with Louisiana's new governor, Antoine de la Mothe Cadillac, arrived at Mobile Bay in 1713. They found the colony there in miserable condition. Since Cadillac too was more interested in swift profits than in the welfare of the colonists or the Indians, the new officials brought more dissension rather than stability to Louisiana.

Cadillac failed to find gold and silver, but in his quest for trade he opened an overland route to Spanish settlements west of the Mississippi. In August 1714 he placed a Canadian officer, Louis Juchereau de St. Denis, in charge of a party of Frenchmen and Indians and of merchandise destined for Mexico. On the Red River, St. Denis founded Natchitoches, the first French post in western Louisiana. Then he traveled south, reaching the Spanish presidio of San Juan Bautista on the Rio Grande. From there he journeyed to Mexico City, arriving in June 1715, only to be imprisoned.

The St. Denis expedition so alarmed Spanish officials that they fortified eastern Texas with missions and presidios and then strengthened their position in Florida. The French, in turn, fortified Natchitoches, making it their westernmost permanent settlement in Louisiana.

Crozat's agents also wanted to build up Louisiana's fur trade and stimulate the cultivation of indigo and tobacco. Crozat was convinced that this program required new settlements northward to Ohio. While unwilling to finance such economic expansion, the crown furnished two hundred soldiers to block English incursions from the Carolinas. Anglo-Americans had been striking at Indian territory west of the Appalachians in an effort to drive a wedge between Canada and Louisiana.

As part of this effort against English expansion, Jean Baptiste Lemoyne, sieur de Bienville, a brother of Iberville, in 1716 built Fort Rosalie, on the site of the later city of Natchez. It became the most important trading center on the lower Mississippi. By the end of the year Crozat's people had established posts on the important rivers and had linked Louisiana and Canada. Louisiana then took on new importance as a barrier to Anglo-American advances on France's entire North American empire. The French now committed themselves to keeping open the line of communication between Louisiana and Canada.

During these years Crozat's hopes for profit from his monopoly faded. He could not meet the competition from English traders who, despite French defenses, had entered eastern Louisiana. Explaining that he had failed to find the gold and silver he had expected, to attract workers for plantations, or to stimulate a solid commerce with Spain's colonies, he remitted his charter to the crown in August 1717.

Two years earlier, in September 1715, after a reign of seventy-two years, Louis XIV had died. He left France and her empire bankrupt by years of war on a global scale. If Canada and Louisiana were to grow, or even survive, under the French flag, they needed peace and new support from the mother country.

At this time there appeared in France a young Scottish economist named John Law. Considered by some a financial genius and by others a reckless gambler, he would make Louisiana famous, or infamous, in France and in all of Europe. In May 1716 the regent, Philippe II, duc d'Orleans, ruling in the name of Louis XV, was persuaded to put into practice Law's theory that the wealth of a country exists in its supply of money. Law's system, operating through a private bank he controlled, seemed to work. So when he became attracted to Louisiana, the prince regent granted him control of that empire in August 1717. Hoping to settle the colony and squeeze profit from it, Law organized the *Compagnie de la Louisiane ou d'Occident.* In return for a monopoly of twenty-five years on terms similar to those given Crozat, this company obligated itself to defend the colony and generally to make it prosper. Law envisaged the development of Louisiana as a national effort, so he tried to gain as many shareholders as possible for the company's stock. To attract clients, he revived the idea of quick riches from mines, yet he especially desired to make Louisiana a place of settlement where profit might come from agriculture.

Bienville, who became governor-general of Louisiana in February 1718, also had ideas for stimulating growth. As one of his first tasks he took on the building of a new town on the Mississippi River. He chose his site on the east bank of a bend in the river about 107 miles from the sea that could command river and ocean traffic and named it New Orleans, after the prince regent. Four years later, after the center of settlement shifted from the coastal area to the Mississippi, this town became the capital of Louisiana.

Through shrewd advertising depicting the colony in unrealistically favorable terms, Law aroused interest in Louisiana. Everyone in France with funds to invest, it seemed, wanted to share in the wealth of the colony. They talked of "nothing else but Louisiana and its wonders." In 1719 Law enlarged his enterprise by absorbing other firms and changed its name to the *Compagnie des Indes.* Speculation in the company's stock became a national pastime.

In his efforts to populate Louisiana, Law rounded up vagrants, prostitutes, criminals, and other social outcasts. The colony became a dumping ground also for political exiles. In 1720 Law's company gained a monopoly of the French slave trade and began transporting several thousand blacks to Louisiana.

By this time, as the company continued to push colonization and stock speculators enriched themselves, investors began learning of the realities of Louisiana. Stories of hardships, starvation, and death reached France. The colony's reputation plummeted. Speculators sold their inflated stock; depositors started runs on banks; the public's confidence in the economy sank; and paper money lost its value. Before the end of 1720 the bloated enterprise collapsed. Law, who had become France's minister of finance, resigned and fled the country.

The bursting of the Mississippi Bubble, as John Law's get-rich-quick scheme was called, plunged France into another bankruptcy. But it did not sink Louisiana or destroy the Company of the Indies. Law's activity gave the colony its first substantial growth. When he took over, Louisiana had only four hundred French people; by 1721 the European population had climbed to at least eight thousand. Lumbering and agriculture, mainly the planting of indigo, corn, rice, and tobacco, became established. With Law's failure, Louisiana as a land of promise fell into disgrace and lost its brief tenure as the focus of attention in France's overseas empire.

Although shorn of many privileges, the Company of the Indies continued to control Louisiana's economy. Like its predecessors, it placed the quest for profit above the welfare of the colonists. Yet for a decade, from 1721 to 1731, the province continued to grow. New Orleans, the Natchez area, and the Illinois region became small centers of population and commerce.

At the same time the rivalry between England and France for mastery of the Mississippi Valley picked up momentum. The French claimed the entire Ohio Valley and considered the Appalachians the eastern limit of Louisiana. They were determined "to prevent the English from establishing themselves there, which would render them too powerful, for it is certain," according to a contemporary report, "that once in Louisiana, they would soon go on to seize both new and old Mexico." [5]

English leaders viewed Louisiana, along with Canada, as a wall confining their colonies to the Atlantic seaboard. Various colonial officials, such as Lieutenant Governor Alexander Spotswood of Virginia, urged the government in London to sponsor projects that would weaken, if not destroy, French control of the interior. They viewed the Mississippi Valley as the field for expansion and wanted to prevent the French from strengthening their settlements and from recruiting more Indian allies.

The British government did not send troops on organized invasions into the Mississippi Valley. Instead, private individuals—fur trappers, land speculators, and settlers—pressed into the Ohio country on their own, threatening Louisiana's line of communication with Canada. These Anglo-Americans of the southwestern frontier, who used the concept of French encirclement as an excuse for their own expansionism, were among the more ardent of British imperialists.

To thwart the Anglo-American advance, the French continued to rely on their old policy of building alliances with Indian peoples. They succeeded in winning native Americans to their side in large numbers, and they buttressed their claims to a Louisiana with an eastern boundary at the Alleghenies by building fortifications at strategic points on that frontier. Despite these efforts, as before, they found themselves unable to prevent the western penetration of the Anglo-Americans. In comparison to the Anglo-Americans, the French in North America were weak, and especially so in Louisiana. That province grew slowly and did not prosper as did the English colonies.

Étienne de Périer, a young naval officer who took over as governor-general in March 1727, continued Bienville's basic policies. Périer began public works projects, mainly canals and levees, to protect New Orleans from floods. He left colonists in other areas, such as those beyond Natchez, to fend for themselves. In the Illinois country, essentially the region north of the Arkansas River watered by the Mississippi and its tributaries, the Fox Indians had been fighting since 1718 to destroy the French and their native allies. Even though the Fox failed in that goal, the French virtually abandoned the Illinois country. In 1731, a year after the end of the Fox War, the Company of the Indies went into the region and erected a fort at the confluence of the Ohio and Wabash rivers. It dominated travel north and south and protected the link between Louisiana and New France.

In the south another Indian uprising shook the foundation of French policy toward the native peoples. The ineptitude of the French commander at Fort Rosalie brought on the trouble. He ordered the powerful Natchez Indians to give up, against their will, an important village and religious shrines. On November 28, 1729, the Natchez secretly attacked Fort Rosalie and slaughtered most of the settlers. Only about twenty-five men escaped. In February of the following year Périer organized

16

an expedition that drove the Natchez Indians across the Mississippi.

The Natchez War drained Louisiana's French manpower, ruined crops, and depleted the company's limited finances. The Company of the Indies therefore decided to cut its losses. It petitioned the king to take back the colony, which Louis XV agreed to do in January 1731. In July the company surrendered its charter and Louisiana became a royal colony. Bienville again became governor.

Indian hostility persisted. Since the French were often unable to supply the Louisiana tribes with goods at prices they desired, the native peoples turned to Anglo-American traders, giving them the best furs and pelts. This English economic hold on the Indians exacerbated Anglo-French rivalry.

In the Illinois region Foxes in the north and Chickasaws in the south, used as allies by the English in their westward penetration, made communication between Canada and Louisiana difficult. Periodically the Chickasaws, who lived at the head of the Mobile River, would raid French settlements. So in 1736 Bienville launched a major campaign against them. Chickasaw fortifications backed by British artillery and troops, combined with Bienville's inadequate planning and poor tactics, defeated the French. Three years later, after assembling a force of twelve hundred white troops and more than twenty-four hundred Indian and black auxiliaries, Bienville again marched into Chickasaw territory. This massive show of force persuaded the Chickasaws to request peace in April 1740.

Imperial rivalry also bedeviled French settlement in western Louisiana. Spanish officialdom continued to view any French movement in the direction of Texas and New Mexico as dangerous. Much to the consternation of the Spaniards, in 1739 a small Canadian trading party led by two brothers, Pierre and Paul Mallet, made its way through hostile Comanche country to Taos and Santa Fe and opened what came to be the Santa Fe

Trail. Resenting the intrusion, the Spanish authorities detained the party for seven months. Nonetheless, the Mallets managed to return to Illinois with news that the people of New Mexico desired commerce. Others from Louisiana followed the Mallet example, risking imprisonment and confiscation of their goods by the Spanish officials.

The confrontations with the English were more dangerous. Punitive expeditions, such as Bienville's against the Chickasaws and the British, were expensive, a drain the government in Paris could not readily accept. Moreover, Indian attacks in eastern Louisiana, supported by Anglo-Americans, continued, as did the failure of efforts by the French to lure European settlers to Louisiana. For a while the white population of Louisiana even declined. An estimate in 1731 showed 5,000 whites, 2,000 blacks, and unnumbered Indians; another in 1745 placed the whites at 3,200 and the blacks at 2,020.

Bienville gave up the governorship in May 1743 to Pierre de Rigaud, marquis de Vaudreuil-Cavagnial, a Canadian and son of a former governor of New France. In that year England and France again clashed. So Vaudreuil followed a policy of strengthening Louisiana's defenses in anticipation of British attacks. In the following year hostilities did spread to North America, where the conflict became known as King George's War.

Anglo-American leaders of the time, such as Governor William Shirley of Massachusetts, held to a sweeping vision of western empire. They wanted to conquer all of France's territory in North America. "The French aim at nothing less than to have the whole Continent," one of them maintained. "I think we ought to have the same views and prosecute them." [6]

Alarmed by Anglo-American aggressiveness, Vaudreuil fortified the entrances to the Mississippi and obtained two thousand additional troops from France. Yet lower Louisiana did little to help upper Louisiana, essentially the Illinois country, or hard-pressed Canada during the conflict. As a result of this war, which ended inconclusively in 1748 with the Treaty of Aix-la-Chapelle, and of Vaudreuil's policies, Louisiana's cost to the crown greatly increased.

In North America the peace amounted to little more than a pause in the clash of empires. The French held the western end of the Ohio Valley and claimed the eastern portion by right of the doctrine of discovery. The English based their claims to the upper basin on their colonial charters. In them the king, oblivious to the rights of Indians and others, granted proprietors or companies land from sea to sea, the right of discovery in it, and the power to negotiate treaties with native Americans such as the Iroquois. Early proprietors, held back mainly by France's Indian allies, did not try to exploit their western claims. But Anglo-American traders and some settlers, as has been seen, had long been active in the Ohio Valley. The French had always resented their activities. When by 1748 the population of the English colonies had markedly increased, the Ohio Company, made up of land speculators from Virginia, Maryland, and Pennsylvania, acquired grants in the Ohio region. Settlers then attempted to cut through the Allegheny passes into the valley, and the French became more alarmed than ever. This new phase of Anglo-American imperialism endangered the entire French domain in North America.

While aware of this threat from the east, Vaudreuil wanted to strengthen France's hold on all of Louisiana, on frontiers facing Spanish lands as well as on those contested by the Anglo-Americans. He sent exploring and trading expeditions into New Mexico, where, as in the past, Spanish authorities treated them harshly. His traders nevertheless built up an indirect contraband commerce with Spanish merchants in the area. In 1751 the viceroy in New Spain, fearful of an attack from Louisiana, resolved some of the border difficulties through direct negotiation with French colonial authorities.

French explorers and traders also penetrated the upper reaches of the Missouri River in search of a route to the Pacific Ocean. They made known to whites the watershed of the Mississippi and Missouri rivers, or most of the trans-Mississippi west. By 1752 their efforts brought the flag of France to the foot of the Rocky Mountains, made French influence dominant above the Red River, and extended the claimed borders of Louisiana far into the west.

These western explorations stopped because of conflict with the Anglo-Americans in the east. During the tenuous peace the English and the French each hardened their determination to destroy the power of the other in the Mississippi Valley. In this looming collision of New World empires, unlike past wars, French leaders were convinced that they would have to fight within a weak and still thinly settled Louisiana.

Chapter II

✣

Stake of Empire

The Almighty . . . had made Choice of the present Generation to erect the American Empire.
—*William Henry Drayton, 1776* [1]

*A*mong Frenchmen immediately concerned with the British penetrations of the Ohio Valley, Roland-Mîchel Barrin, comte de La Galissonière, governor of Canada, stands out as one willing to draw a line and to fight. In 1749 he sent about 250 men commanded by Captain Pierre-Joseph de Cèleron de Blainville, a frontier soldier and fur trader, to the Ohio to proclaim French ownership of the valley and to warn the Anglo-Americans to stay out. If the English gained control of the area, Detroit would become defenseless, opening the way for them to take Canada, the Illinois country, and lower Louisiana. Finding the Anglo-American infiltration more extensive than anticipated, the French did not at this time fortify the upper Ohio Valley.

Earlier the colonial wars in America between Britain and

France, although important in the struggle for empire, had been secondary to the conflicts in Europe. After 1750 the colonial antagonism became in itself a major concern of the rivals. For a few years the French managed to check the Anglo-American probings into the Ohio region, but with difficulty.

The French and the English both sought assistance from native peoples in the Ohio Valley. Usually the Indians preferred the Anglo-Americans as traders and the French as allies, but basically they resented all white intrusions. Why, the Indians appeared to reason, should they have to choose sides in a quarrel between white invaders over their ancestral land? Regardless of such feelings or how they were expressed, the native Americans became unmourned expendables in the imperial rivalry.

Not just policy makers in London but also Anglo-American expansionists such as Benjamin Franklin believed that neither the Indians nor the French should stand in the path of expanding empire. Franklin praised "the Prince that acquires new Territory, if he finds it vacant, or removes the Natives to give his own People Room." [2] He envisioned the Anglo-Americans pushing westward across the Mississippi, uprooting Indians, multiplying, and eventually outnumbering the people of mother England.

The French, concerned with their own vision of empire in North America, now became more determined than ever to stop Anglo-American expansion. Officials in America believed that England, in addition to seeking Canada, "now plans the invasion of Florida and Louisiana." Galissonière urged his home government to build up Canada's defense and fortify her link with Louisiana, saying that Canada "will serve as the outwork of Louisiana." [3] In 1752 the French government reaffirmed Galissonière's frontier policy and made preparations to drive the Anglo-Americans from the Ohio country.

In the following year Canada's new governor, Ange de Menneville, marquis de Duquesne, mobilized the colony's mili-

sippi in March 1699; in April he planted a temporary settlement, Fort Maurepas, on Biloxi Bay. He thus carried out French imperial policy, for as Pontchartrain explained, "the King does not intend to form an establishment at the mouth of the Mississippi, but only to complete the discovery in order to hinder the English from taking possession there." [4] When Iberville went back to France, he urged a change in policy, arguing that if the government did not act more decisively the English would seize Louisiana and eventually all of North America. He recommended building permanent settlements in Louisiana.

When Iberville returned to Louisiana in December 1699, he learned that Coxe's ships had entered the Mississippi. So he constructed a small post on the river, about fifty-four miles from its mouth. This outpost, Fort La Boulaye, could provide only a token defense against the English, but with it France at last fortified the gateway to the Mississippi. Iberville then explored farther up the river and formulated plans for alliances with the Indians to block Anglo-American penetration of the Mississippi Valley. He also concluded that the French had to compete economically if Louisiana were to be kept out of English hands. On his return to France he pleaded for aid to Louisiana, stressing the strategic importance of keeping it linked to Canada.

Fort Maurepas had to be abandoned. On his third voyage to Louisiana, Iberville planted a new post on Mobile Bay, which he hoped to make the heart of his colony. This town, called Fort Saint Louis, became a small trading center. The War of the Spanish Succession, beginning in Europe in 1701 and spreading in the next year to North America as Queen Anne's War, however, kept the French government from supporting the settlers adequately. So Iberville, considered by historians to be the founder of French Louisiana and the prime mover in its colonization, left only a small settlement barely subsisting. Yet its defense cost more than the crown could afford. In 1707 Louis

tary resources and began constructing a series of forts from Lake Erie to the headwaters of the Ohio River. The Anglo-Americans decided to thwart this preemptive policy. Robert Dinwiddie, the lieutenant governor of Virginia and an imperialist who believed that the colony had no western limits except the Pacific Ocean, took the counteraction. He sent George Washington, a twenty-one-year-old major of militia, to warn French officers they were trespassing on English land. Denying the charge, the French refused to withdraw. Within the following year Dinwiddie provided Washington with about one hundred men and ordered him to return to the frontier to build a fort at the forks of the Ohio where the Allegheny and Monongahela rivers join. A larger party of French and Indians forced the Anglo-Americans to retreat over the crest of the Alleghenies, which the French said marked the border of the English colonies. Then French troops built their own structure, Fort Duquesne, at the forks.

Washington came back with more militia and attacked a small French party, killing ten. Reacting swiftly, the French sent a larger force against the Anglo-Americans and compelled Washington to capitulate. These skirmishes, like the prologue to an epic, introduced the large-scale hostilities known in North America as the French and Indian War.

After Washington's setback the Virginia authorities asked London for help against the French. The Anglo-Americans alluded to the old encirclement argument, saying that the French were the aggressors who sought to push them into the sea. Previously, jealousies among the English colonies had prevented concerted action, but in the summer of 1754 Anglo-American leaders felt that they had enough in common so that they could meet in Albany, New York, to discuss the situation. They proposed a plan of union that the British government opposed.

Although speaking in the language of defense against French imperialism, Anglo-American expansionists desired unity more for offensive purposes than for defense. They said they wished to prevent the "dreaded junction of the French settlements in Canada with those of Louisiana," but they also admitted eagerness to open the west to their own expansion.[4] A New England writer of popular almanacs expressed one aspect of expansionist thinking. He pictured the land west of the Appalachians as "capable of producing Food and Physick, and all Things necessary for the Conveniency and Delight of Life: In fine, the Garden of the World!" To attain "this inestimable Prize" for which "two mighty Kings contend," he warned, the colonies must unite.[5]

While rejecting the plan of union, the policy makers in London did undertake military action in support of western expansion. They built up British forces in North America and placed Major General Edward Braddock in command. In July 1755, as English soldiers and Anglo-American militia advanced toward Fort Duquesne, a smaller force of French and Indians decisively defeated Braddock's army.

These colonial clashes, combined with developments in Europe, led to a shift of alliances and to declarations of war. This conflict, which Europeans called the Seven Years' War, had as its stake the destiny of most of North America. Historians sometimes refer to it as the Great War for Empire.

Policy makers in France, realizing that they had neither a strong enough navy nor a large enough population in their American colonies to do more than merely defend them, did not expect in the North American fighting to expand their holdings. They assumed they would suffer some loss but counted on victories in Europe to restore the empire. Despite this policy of Europe first and despite the odds against them, the French colonial leaders in America clung to the hope of somehow fighting well enough so they would not have to give up territory. Under the leadership of Marquis Louis Joseph de Montcalm de Saint-Véran, the French in North America, along with Indian allies, in the first two years of hostilities won victories or held their own. Thus for a while their hopes appeared justified.

Most of the fighting took place in Canada. Although the hostilities did not engulf Louisiana, the French always feared that they would. In February 1753, when Louis Billouart, chevalier de Kerlérec, a naval officer, took over as governor, Louisiana's people expected war and tried to prepare for it. Kerlérec told his superiors that the colony was virtually defenseless and would fall before the first English assault. If native American allies deserted, the French had no hope of holding on anyway. So Kerlérec tried to retain and strengthen Indian friendship. His policy did not achieve much, but it may have saved a weakened Louisiana from a major Indian attack inspired by the British.

The English blockaded the Gulf of Mexico from Cape San Antonio, Cuba, to the Yucatàn coast and virtually isolated Louisiana from France. In July 1754 Kerlérec reported that the English were moving as they pleased in Louisiana and were threatening to interrupt communications with Illinois. He attempted to fortify the mouth of the Mississippi and managed to send some supplies from the Illinois region to the battle areas in Ohio and Canada, but Louisiana contributed little to the embattled north. For all practical purposes upper Louisiana, close to the fighting, became a dependency of Canada.

Suffering from its isolation and from internal weaknesses, lower Louisiana by 1756 found itself almost destitute. Yet the Creoles, using their own meager resources and help from friendly Indians, kept Louisiana functioning. At times survival seemed doubtful because England's Cherokee allies tried to provoke other tribes into attacking and driving the French from the land.

By 1758, as the tide of war turned and British forces captured fort after fort, the French were forced to withdraw from the Ohio Valley. Illinois became the only French district north of the Ohio River to maintain itself free of foreign control to the end of the war. When news of the northern collapse filtered south, the people of lower Louisiana became convinced they would soon come under attack. Anglo-American expansionists favored conquest, but the British never invaded the province.

Nonetheless, Louisiana's plight still verged on the desperate. Owing to a food shortage in 1759, troops went on half rations. Prices climbed, bringing disastrous inflation. Unable to offer direct assistance, the French government allowed the Creoles to trade with Mexico. Kerlérec even sought powder and ammunition from the Spaniards at Veracruz.

By 1760 the war in America had ended in all but technicalities. The British had destroyed French power. Louisiana still remained in French hands, but with a future clouded by uncertainty. Early in 1761 the French ambassador to Spain admitted that his government had not sent supplies to Louisiana for four years. France's foreign minister, Duc Étienne François de Choiseul, called for peace negotiations on the condition that territory occupied by each side should remain in the hands of the immediate possessor. On this basis Canada would go to England, but unconquered Louisiana seemed likely to remain a French colony. In March the British welcomed Choiseul's proposal.

At this time of uncertainty French policy makers considered Louisiana expendable for acceptable peace terms elsewhere. This opportunism upset Spanish leaders. Spain had never recognized French title to Louisiana and still voiced a hazy claim to it. In practice Spain accepted French control and in at least one way benefited from it. The Spaniards feared English domination of North America more than they did the French. Louisiana in French hands served as a buffer shielding New Spain from the Anglo-Americans. Earlier, when Spain's Carlos III thought that England might grasp the province, he said that "after the peace I must arrange with France for Louisiana, perhaps by giving

France something in exchange." [6] He and his advisers desired Louisiana for strategic reasons, not because they saw any intrinsic value in it. They wanted it in order to keep the Anglo-Americans from taking it. Spain's apprehensions were sound. Policy makers in London argued that in the peacemaking Louisiana ought "to be insisted on to make a part of the British dominions together with all the Rivers that the French possessed or occupied in the Gulph of Mexico." [7]

Knowing the Spanish attitude, Choiseul followed a double policy. He tried to use the colony either to gain an alliance with Spain or a favorable peace with England. In the summer of 1761 he held out Louisiana as a possible reward if Spain would aid France. For this reason, among others, Spain in August concluded an alliance, the second Bourbon Family Compact, with France. The treaty committed France to cede Louisiana to Spain for a loan or for an immediate declaration of war against England.

Choiseul's willingness to part with Louisiana stemmed from necessity. In a memorial in October the French government admitted it could no longer protect Louisiana. For the colony to remain out of the British empire, even to survive in time of war, it needed goods and assistance from Spain.

England's reaction to the new Family Compact came in January 1762 with a declaration of war against Spain. The expanded hostilities ended Choiseul's tactic of using Louisiana as a war bribe but did not help the French much. Spain proved an ineffective ally. Choiseul therefore continued his efforts to obtain peace. In negotiations in June the English demanded eastern Louisiana, essentially the territory west of the Alleghenies to the Mississippi, in order to gain a mainland port on the Gulf of Mexico. Choiseul agreed, so long as France could retain her sugar and other islands in the Caribbean—St. Domingue, Martinique, Guadeloupe, and Saint Barthélemy.

The French minister's willingness to give up Louisiana east

of the Mississippi contradicted a promise he had made to Spain to keep the English out of the Gulf. The Spaniards therefore protested. To appease them, Choiseul planned to cede the remainder of Louisiana west of the Mississippi, including New Orleans, which was then considered an island, to Spain. Still disliking the terms, the Spaniards reiterated their old claim to Louisiana, insisting that France could not dispose of any part of it without their consent. So they blocked agreement with the English.

In August 1762 British forces captured Havana, a key to Spain's power in the Gulf of Mexico. When the news reached Madrid, Spain's attitude toward peace changed. To regain Havana, she was willing to give England what she truly desired—Florida.

Still anxious to secure a peace treaty, Choiseul now had his sovereign, Louis XV, offer Carlos III of Spain the remainder of Louisiana. In an effort to save Florida for Spain, Choiseul was even willing to cede all of Louisiana to England. Considering Florida more valuable, the British would not consider the French plan. Finally, to prevent Louisiana or what remained of it from going to the British, the Spaniards accepted the French offer. With western Louisiana they would have actual if not legal control of the Mississippi; they might even block Anglo-American expansion into the heart of the continent; and they could perhaps check smuggling into New Spain.

In November 1762, in the secret Treaty of Fontainebleau, Louis ceded New Orleans and Louisiana west of the Mississippi to his "brother and cousin" Carlos, ostensibly as compensation for Spain's sacrifice of Florida. At first Carlos protested, saying, "No, no. My cousin is losing altogether too much." [8] But Carlos took the colony. On that day the warring powers signed a preliminary peace draft. Choiseul was so eager to win Spain's consent to these articles and to preserve France's Caribbean islands that he paid for it with an empire.

The terms of the peace preliminaries were essentially those of the Treaty of Paris concluded in February 1763. They gave that part of Louisiana lying east of the Mississippi River, except New Orleans, to England. So Louisiana as the French had held it or claimed it was broken up, and the English secured ports on the Gulf. England also gained the right of free navigation on the Mississippi to the sea. Spain ceded Florida to England and regained Cuba and the Philippines, which the British had also captured.

The Seven Years' War thus destroyed France's North American empire and opened to Anglo-Americans the prospect "of a vast growth of power and wealth with an amazing westward expansion." [9] France lost Canada in battle but gave up Louisiana because she valued peace in Europe more than she did a colony that had always been a liability and that she had therefore neglected. Nonetheless, many Frenchmen opposed the cession. Some never forgave Choiseul for what they considered a betrayal of king and country. [10]

France did not reveal the gift to Spain until October 1763 when she transferred the eastern portion of Louisiana to the British. Although anxious to rid itself of responsibility for western Louisiana too, the French government retained control because the Spaniards were unprepared for prompt possession. For a while French rule and even French settlement continued. In February 1764 a French merchant from New Orleans, Pierre Laclède Liguest, founded a trading post just below the junction of the Missouri and Mississippi rivers and called it Saint Louis. It became the commercial center of that region and a gateway to all of Louisiana.

In that same month Major Arthur Loftus, commanding about 350 Anglo-American soldiers, attempted to supplant the French in posts on the upper Mississippi and to extend British hegemony to the west bank. He tried to ascend the river from New Orleans in a convoy of twelve vessels, but Indian attacks forced him to retreat. Loftus and other British officials believed that the French had secretly instigated the assaults in order to stymie further Anglo-American expansion in Louisiana.

France and Spain did not make the cession of Louisiana public in Europe until April 1764. Then they sent word to the Creoles. Finally, in October, Spain accepted nominal possession. Even then she moved slowly in occupying her new province; she lacked the manpower necessary for actual control.

When news of the colony's cession reached New Orleans, it set off a protest movement led by planters, merchants, and civil administrators. Those Creoles petitioned the king not to surrender the province to Spain. Choiseul blocked the petition, explaining that France could not afford the expense of Louisiana. "Is it not better, then," he asked, "that Louisiana should be given away to a friend and faithful ally, than be wrested from us by an hereditary foe?" [11]

At this time also some Indian ambassadors from Pontiac, the chief of the Ottawas, who was organizing the western tribes to combat Anglo-American expansion, arrived in New Orleans to seek guns, powder, troops, and other help from the French. When these Indians first learned of France's defeat and of Louisiana's transfer, according to historian Francis Parkman, they refused to believe and reacted bitterly. "These red dogs [red-coated British soldiers] have crowded upon us more and more," their spokesman, a Shawnee chief, explained, "and when we ask them by what right they come, they tell us that you, our French fathers, have given them our lands. We know that they lie. These lands are neither yours nor theirs, and no man shall give or sell them without our consent." [12] Despite these brave words, Pontiac and his allies, like the French, failed to stem the advance of the Anglo-Americans.

The Spanish crown meanwhile commissioned Antonio de Ulloa, a scientist and naval officer, to assume control of Louisiana. He arrived in New Orleans in March 1766, accompanied by three civil officers and a force of only ninety soldiers. Without troops for occupation and defense, Ulloa could not govern. So the French governor, Charles Philippe de Aubry, agreed to a collaboration. Ulloa would defer actual possession in the name of Spain until he had enough troops to garrison the various posts. He would, however, raise the Spanish flag outside New Orleans while Aubry continued to run the colony through French administrators.

Spanish officials conciliated the Creoles by allowing them to retain French customs and laws. The Spaniards did not even attempt to integrate Louisiana into their imperial administrative system, keeping it a separate entity under the direct control of the king. Insensitive to this effort to pacify them, the Creoles resented the Spanish presence. Nothing Ulloa did seemed to satisfy them. In 1768 a Spanish decree that cut off trade with France sparked a rebellion. On the morning of October 28 Creole rebels took over New Orleans and expelled Ulloa and other Spaniards. Ulloa then fled to Havana.

The colonists again petitioned the French king, asking him to reverse the cession to Spain. He refused to interfere. Choiseul assured the Spanish government that France would cooperate, not interfere, with the transfer of Louisiana. Some Creoles then thought of converting Louisiana into an independent republic guaranteed by both France and Spain. It would thus remain a buffer between the Anglo-American settlements and Mexico without either France or Spain being drained by its administrative costs. Nothing came of this or other separatist schemes.

The uprising did, however, change Spanish policy toward Louisiana. If the crown did nothing, the king's ministers reasoned, Spain's other colonies might follow the example of New Orleans and cripple if not destroy the empire. So the government decided to crush the rebels and to occupy Louisiana in force. The king chose one of his favorite generals, an Irish soldier of fortune named Alexander O'Reilly, to carry out this project.

O'Reilly arrived at New Orleans in July 1769 with twenty-one ships and more than two thousand men. He took possession of the colony in the name of Spain on August 18. Then he arrested the leaders of the revolt and ordered them tried for treason under Spanish law. To forestall violent protest, he proclaimed an amnesty for all rebels except the leaders, who were convicted. The court ordered five executed and six imprisoned for long periods. The general then tried to build a solid foundation for Spanish rule by making the colony profitable, by bringing it into harmony with the rest of Spanish America, and by trying to block Anglo-American encroachments.

Spain continued the French policy of protective friendship with Indian tribes because she believed it would help to keep the Anglo-Americans on the eastern side of the Mississippi River. After the Seven Years' War the Anglo-Americans had stepped up their westward movement, flowing into lands the French had evacuated. They searched for furs, traded with Indians, settled on the land, built forts, and founded towns. Within a few years they appeared poised for large-scale expansion across the Mississippi. By 1767 Anglo-Americans were diverting trade from Illinois down the Mississippi River to the towns they controlled along the Gulf. On the Mississippi they turned Natchez and Baton Rouge into fortified settlements; on the Gulf they made Pensacola the hub of their interests.

When the Spaniards took possession of Louisiana, they barred Anglo-American traders and settlers and other "illicit intruders." Spanish administrators could not enforce this policy because they had no money for maintaining strong defenses. They managed to construct a few forts along the Mississippi, and in place of an army they created a citizens' militia, which in 1769 contained slightly more than one thousand men. Spanish soldiers failed, however, to stop incursions across the Mississippi or to prevent smuggling by Anglo-American traders based in Missouri. Anglo-Americans penetrated as far west as Texas and captured much of Louisiana's commerce. They even supplied New Orleans with the greater part of its food.

During these transitional years British policy makers considered attacking Louisiana, and in 1770 their menaces led to a war scare. In that year Britain and Spain almost stumbled into war in a dispute over the Falkland Islands. British planners then outlined more conquest in North America. They reinforced Pensacola with one thousand men, and in 1771 General Thomas Gage, the British commander in the west, mobilized his army for an invasion of Louisiana. Even though in the previous year another military man, Don Luis de Unzaga y Amezaga, succeeded O'Reilly and took over as Spain's first governor of Louisiana, the Spaniards knew they could not match British power. If the British crossed the Mississippi in force, the Spanish troops there planned to retreat to Mexico and to leave Louisiana's fate to be settled at a peace conference. When Spain backed down in the global confrontation, the war scare passed. In Louisiana fear of Anglo-American power just over the border always influenced the thinking of Spanish officialdom.

A few years later, as unrest and then rebellion broke out in the English colonies, the Spanish government decided secretly to aid the rebels in order to fragment Anglo-American power and enhance Louisiana's security. In line with this policy, in August 1776 Oliver Pollock, a wealthy Anglo-American merchant residing in New Orleans, arranged with Governor Unzaga for the sale of ten thousand pounds of powder from Spanish arsenals for use by rebels in Virginia.

In the following January Don Bernardo de Gálvez, another soldier, became governor of Louisiana. In keeping with policy from Madrid, he allowed French agents aiding the American rebels to operate from Louisiana. He also continued aid to Pollock, especially in procuring supplies and loans for rebel mili-

33

tary expeditions up the Mississippi and Ohio rivers. Gálvez permitted New Orleans to become a base for various operations against the British. American privateers, for example, brought their prizes there and sold them. He funneled Spanish money and munitions to George Rogers Clark, the Virginian who campaigned against the British in the west. Gálvez viewed the British subjects in the Floridas, especially those who had prospered around Mobile and Pensacola and had remained loyal to their mother country, as a menace to Louisiana. So early in 1778, after Americans had raided West Florida, his officials permitted them to pass through Louisiana.

In June 1779 Spain, expecting to regain the Floridas as well as Gibraltar and Minorca, entered the war against England. The British in Illinois and the Floridas then formulated plans for attacking Louisiana. Thus, as the Spaniards expected, Louisiana became an open theater of conflict. Aware of British intentions, Gálvez, under the guise of preparing to defend New Orleans, worked out an offensive of his own. Using regular Spanish troops and Louisiana militia, he sprang surprise attacks in August 1779 against Natchez and Baton Rouge and took them. In March 1780 he also captured Mobile. In that same year his lieutenant governor repulsed an attack on Saint Louis. Gálvez gained his greatest victory in May of the following year when at the head of an army from Havana he forced the British to surrender Pensacola.

By the end of the war Spain had not only maintained herself in Louisiana but had also expelled the British from the Gulf of Mexico and had extended her possessions eastward. Through conquest or diplomacy her soldiers held the Floridas and adjacent territory at least as far north as the Tennessee River. Spain, it seemed, had attained the major North American objectives for which she had fought.

For Louisiana new disadvantages offset these successes. The Americans of the newly created United States were the same

aggressive people who under the British flag had pushed west-
ward and threatened to take over the colony. In both their mili-
tary strategy and diplomacy the American patriot leaders
showed a determined expansionism. The Continental Congress
quickly supported an invasion of Canada and appealed to the
people of Quebec to join an expanding empire. "Seize the op-
portunity presented to you by Providence itself," it said. "You
have been conquered into liberty, if you act as you ought." [13]

Aggressive patriots viewed the American Revolution itself
as a war of conquest. "The Unanimous Voice of the Continent is
Canada must be ours," John Adams wrote; "Quebec must be
taken." [14] Benjamin Franklin accompanied a rebel army that
invaded Canada, and he tried to persuade the Canadians to join
the new American nation. Even after the failure of this effort to
conquer in the spring of 1776, the expansionist fervor among
American leaders for Canada and other neighboring territory
persisted. "We shall never be upon a solid Footing till Britain
cedes to us what Nature designs we should have," Samuel
Adams said, "or till we wrest it from her." [15]

Some American expansionists assumed that the United
States alliance with France in February 1778 enhanced their op-
portunity to gain territory. William Ellery, a Rhode Island pol-
itician, described the expanded vision apparently common
among his friends. "I think it absolutely necessary to a future,
lasting peace," he wrote, "that we should be possessed of Can-
ada, Nova Scotia and the Floridas, which we cannot effect with-
out the open assistance of France." [16]

Southerners harbored even greater ambitions. They aspired
to the acquisition of the entire Mississippi Valley, as well as the
Floridas, but muffled some of their aggressiveness in order not
to lose Spanish help. Oliver Pollock, for example, urged George
Rogers Clark to capture West Florida before Spain should de-
clare war against England; otherwise, the United States would
lose a valuable conquest. Thomas Jefferson, then governor of

Virginia, explained to Clark that he should treat the people well in the land he conquered. "We wish them to consider us as brothers, and to participate with us in the benefits [of] our rights and Laws," Jefferson said. They should willingly become a part of the United States.[17] In general, the lust for lands such as Louisiana, as well as Canada, stimulated the enthusiasm of western frontier regions for the American Revolution.

Acutely aware of American expansionism, Spain fought on the side of the United States mainly to weaken a common enemy. She refused to do anything consciously that would add to American strength. Despite pressure exerted on her by France to join, Spain refused to become a party to the Franco-American alliance. Even though Spanish money helped George Rogers Clark, Spanish officials saw in his conquests in the Illinois country evidence of the new nation's imperial desires, an implicit coveting of Louisiana. In 1780 this concern for her possessions led Spain to rebuff overtures from the United States for an alliance. She even refused to recognize the United States as independent until after the signing of the peace. Spain's policy makers perceived Americans as a people of limitless territorial ambition.

Few contemporaries expressed the American attitude toward western expansion as clearly as did Benjamin Franklin shortly before the peace negotiations. When he heard that Spain wished to "coop up" the United States east of the Appalachians, he prophesied a future wherein his country would expand and grow rich. Speaking of the Spaniards, he said, "I would rather agree with them to buy at a great price the whole of their right on the Mississippi than sell a drop of its waters. A neighbour might as well ask me to sell my street door." [18] During the preliminary peace negotiations in Paris in the spring of 1782 Franklin and the other American commissioners advanced claims to Canada, the Floridas, and western lands.

To the Spaniards these territorial claims of Americans and

their despoiling of Indians seemed proof enough of a ruthless land hunger. In August John Jay, one of the American peace commissioners, and Pedro Pablo Abarca y Bolea, conde de Aranda, Spain's ambassador to the court at Versailles, conferred over the western boundary of the United States. The American insisted upon drawing the line at the Mississippi River, thus including within the United States old eastern Louisiana, or land that had never been part of the thirteen English colonies. "That territory belongs to free and independent nations of Indians," Aranda said, "and you have no right to it."

"These are points to be discussed and settled between the Indians and ourselves," Jay responded. "With respect to the Indians we claim the right of pre-emption; with respect to all other nations, we claim the sovereignty over the territory." [19] Spain consistently opposed such a frontier because she believed Americans would use it as "an avenue of penetration into Louisiana." [20]

The French, too, viewed Americans as an expansionist people and considered their claim to eastern Louisiana as shady. This American thrust for empire convinced French leaders that they had helped give birth to another imperialist power. "The Americans in pushing their possessions as far as the Lake of the Woods," one of them observed, "are preparing for their remote posterity a communication with the Pacific." [21]

Some historians, notably Henry Adams and Frederick Jackson Turner, maintained that France sided with Spain on the issue of the western boundary because she wished to regain Louisiana for herself. Charles Gravier, comte de Vergennes, France's minister for foreign affairs, the story goes, wanted Louisiana as France had once claimed it, with an eastern boundary at the Allegheny Mountains. He is said to have offered to buy the province from Spain. Available evidence, based on a document of dubious authenticity, fails to support this theory. Yet the French desire for Louisiana may have been real enough.

When British observers learned of the preliminary peace provisions, some of them also remarked about the expansionist appetite of Americans. The United States, one of them commented, is *"not content with Independence, it aims at conquest."* They predicted an imperialist future for the new American nation. "The pride of empire will awaken and conquests will be multiplied on neighboring borders," a London observer forecast. "Florida and all the Spanish possessions on the banks of the Mississippi will fall before them; and as they increase in power, that power will reach the limits of the Southern Ocean, and dispossess the Europeans of every hold upon the great continent of America." [22]

As agreed upon in the preliminary settlement and in the definitive treaty of peace with England signed in Paris in September 1783, the United States acquired eastern Louisiana, essentially the territory between the Appalachians and the Mississippi. England also agreed to share her right to navigate the Mississippi, "from its source to the ocean," with the United States. This arrangement, to which Spain was not a party, aggravated Spain's distrust of the United States and affected her control of Louisiana proper.

During the war Spain had allowed Americans free use of the river as a favor without granting or recognizing any privilege on the waterway through Spanish territory. The Spaniards argued correctly that England could not give or share her right of navigation with a third nation. Moreover, England's privilege had ended technically in 1779 when she and Spain had gone to war.

Regardless of the niceties of international obligations, the crux of the problem was access to the Gulf of Mexico. Now that eastern Louisiana had become American territory, the Mississippi formed the boundary between the United States and Spanish Louisiana. As an international waterway whose banks had different owners, it lay open on equal terms to Americans and to the subjects of Spain. Both could use it freely. But the river did not serve as an international boundary for its full length. As it flowed to the sea on its last two hundred miles or so, Spain controlled both banks and claimed dominion over the eastern bank as far north as the confluence of the Ohio and the Mississippi. No one, therefore, could navigate the lower Mississippi, any more than one could travel by land across Spanish territory, without permission from Spain.

The treaty of 1783 also fixed the boundary between West Florida and the United States at the thirty-first parallel. In the preliminary agreement, however, the British had inserted a secret article saying that if West Florida remained in their possession its boundary would be more than a hundred miles farther north, to latitude 32°25' at the mouth of the Yazoo River. That line had formed the frontier of West Florida in the twenty years the British had held it.

In her treaty of peace with Spain in 1783 England ceded the Floridas with indefinite boundaries. Spain contended rightly that she was not bound by the terms of the final Anglo-American treaty. Her extreme claim, based on right of conquest, went far north of the thirty-first parallel to the Tennessee and Ohio rivers. It included parts of Georgia, Tennessee, Kentucky, and most of Alabama and Mississippi.

Spain held on to this territory in the old Southwest, known as the Yazoo Strip, with military posts in Alabama, Mississippi, and Tennessee and with treaties that established protectorates over Indian tribes in the region. She hoped that these native allies, in fighting for their lands, would shield her possessions against advancing American frontiersmen.

Spain's security measures did little to diminish her uneasiness over the protection of Louisiana. On her Louisiana and Florida borders she now faced an aggressive new nation, more threatening than Britain had been. Americans belligerently asserted the right to free navigation of the lower Mississippi, were

39

land hungry, held Spanish culture in contempt, were hostile to Spaniards as a people, and were led by men who espoused an expansionist credo. To Martín de Navarro, Louisiana's intendant, they were the "new enemies." [23] So in 1784 Spain closed the lower Mississippi to Americans. When that order became known in the American Southwest, it brought the smoldering hostility between Spain and the United States to the surface and touched off a crisis. The pivot was Louisiana.

Chapter III

✣

Peaceful Penetration

We cannot but anticipate the period, as not far distant, when the AMERICAN EMPIRE will comprehend millions of souls, west of the Mississippi.

Jedidiah Morse, 1789 [1]

*D*uring the Revolutionary War, as though continuing and expanding Britain's imperial thrust, American frontiersmen pushed southward and westward well beyond the Appalachians into lands that Spain guarded jealously but ineffectively. "Notwithstanding the pressure of the present war on our people," Thomas Jefferson wrote approvingly to the governor of Louisiana, "they are lately beginning to extend their Settlements rapidly on the Waters of the Mississippi." So he sought a "close Connection" between his own state of Virginia and Louisiana.[2]

For a while Spanish officials permitted some closeness beyond that required for military purposes. Early in the struggle patriot refugees from British West Florida obtained sanctuary in Louisiana. In 1779 they even founded a small village, Gálveztown, on the Iberville River sixty miles northwest of

41

New Orleans. This became the first essentially American town in Spanish Louisiana. Many Americans moved into New Orleans. After Spain conquered West Florida, she permitted those Americans who lived there to remain if they took an oath of allegiance to the crown. Her officials also allowed other Americans to take up residence there and in Louisiana.

Esteban Miró, who became acting governor of Louisiana in 1782, persuaded the government in Madrid that if it allowed American immigration the colony would develop more rapidly and gain needed strength. He assumed that in time the Americans could become assimilated and would turn into loyal subjects of the crown. Need rather than cold analysis produced this rationalization. The crown had tried to attract various Europeans to Louisiana by subsidizing their immigration. This experiment turned out both costly and ineffective. Even though Americans might prove dangerous, they could be settled in Louisiana at no cost to the government. Moreover, Miró considered this policy of open immigration preferable to running the risk of invasion by trying to exclude Americans. With this policy Spain reluctantly tried to accommodate herself to what she could not prevent.

Spanish policy makers were aware that with peace the Anglo-American westward movement had picked up momentum. Like bees swarming after a new home, Americans rushed through the Cumberland Gap into the Ohio Valley. They populated Kentucky and Tennessee, the main settlements in the trans-Appalachian west. These settlers cleared the land and produced from it tobacco, hemp, wheat, corn, whiskey, beef, and pork. They exported their crops through Natchez or New Orleans. From these ports they sometimes imported manufactured goods, though they usually obtained such items as needed from eastern cities via land routes across the Allegheny Mountains. This overland trade seldom satisfied western farmers because of its high transportation costs. Westerners felt that the lack of secure, inexpensive portals of trade impeded their region's economic growth. These Americans considered the ports across the border in Louisiana and West Florida natural outlets for their products.

Spanish officials were acutely aware of the attitude of the western Americans and they also realized that their territories bordering the United States were just about defenseless. So the protection of these borderlands as a defensive barrier in depth for Mexico became a key to Spain's policy in Louisiana.

Except for a few settlements such as at Pensacola, Saint Mary's River, and Saint Augustine and scattered Indian villages, the Floridas east of Mobile Bay consisted of wilderness. Small contingents of Spanish troops held territory to the north.

As for Louisiana, it contained few settlements north of the Red River. The banks of the Mississippi were dotted with people, mainly Indians, some Americans, and a few groups of French, but settlements elsewhere were sparse. Although wide open to infiltration by American hunters, traders, farmers, and armed adventurers, this northern region of the colony was not easily accessible to Spanish authorities. Spaniards did not settle there in large numbers, and even when they had come as traders, they had lost out to Anglo-American competitors. It appeared obvious, at least on the basis of proximity and the desire to do so, that Americans could more readily exploit this territory than could the subjects of Spain. In the 1780s, like a young stream slowly picking up volume, westward-moving Americans began that exploitation. They crossed the Mississippi and Missouri rivers, plunged into upper Louisiana, and used Saint Louis as a door to the outside world.

The American penetration of lower Louisiana and West Florida followed a different pattern. This region contained most of the white population, and here the Spaniards concentrated their commerce, administration, and defense. Here the settlements were compact and within reach of Spanish sea power.

43

Other powers, particularly the United States, coveted this part of Louisiana more than any other. With its port of New Orleans, now a prosperous city accessible to trade from all areas of the Western world, it dominated the economic life of the Mississippi Valley. The wealth of the region now came mainly from sugar plantations. Its population, commerce, and other economic activity were all on the upswing. Lower Louisiana in the 1780s was a booming frontier land of uneasy stability, precarious peace, and international intrigue.

While stronger than the rest of the province, lower Louisiana could not really protect itself. Any well-armed invasion force could have broken through the fortifications at New Orleans, though it probably would have encountered tough resistance from Spain's saltwater navy, still a formidable force. Spain also supplemented her few posts along the Mississippi with a freshwater navy. Its vessels patrolled the river and searched for smugglers, but they could not properly guard a fifteen-hundred-mile frontier against invasion.

Spain tried to use Indians to hold back American expansion. Through treaties concluded in Mobile and Pensacola in 1784, she attempted to act as the protector of the Creek, Chickasaw, and Choctaw native American tribes in the old Southwest.

Authorities in Louisiana also resorted to various economic tactics to block infiltrating foreign traders but not legitimate immigrants. They tried to monopolize the trade with Indians and to compete with Americans by organizing a Spanish fur company. These efforts failed because the Spaniards could not handle the commerce of their own colonies. Nor could they stop American trappers and merchants, who were more numerous, active, and better prepared for business than they were, from getting a hold on Louisiana's economy.

Mostly, though, Spain tried to maintain a tight grip on Louisiana's economy not through beating out foreign competition but by decree. When she closed the lower Mississippi to foreigners in 1784, she hoped to profit from her monopoly and at the same time to stifle the growth of American settlements in the trans-Appalachian west.

Spain's economic policy did not work out as desired, mainly because the people of Louisiana needed American goods and services and connived at smuggling to get them. When Spain took possession, the province lost its considerable overseas commerce with France and with French colonies. This loss struck hard at the Creoles. They preferred French goods and French capital to all others and could not obtain acceptable substitutes from Spain. Even the *cabildo,* or municipal council, in New Orleans became a party to this illegal trade. It imported American flour because it could not readily pay for the more expensive product. Without the easily available American supply, people in the city might starve. So necessity, as much as anything else, forced them to buy basic products, such as flour, from Americans.

The people of Louisiana as well as Americans suffered from the closure of the lower Mississippi, but the farmers in the Southwest were enraged by it. For twenty years, first as Anglo-Americans and then as citizens of the United States, these settlers had enjoyed free use of the river. They had come to look upon such navigation as a right, not a privilege. Supported by politicians from the southern states, they demanded that Congress force Spain to reopen the Mississippi. The politicians maintained that "the interest of the whole western country within the United States, from the northern extremity of Lake Erie to the Mississippi, depended on the free navigation of that river." [3]

This insistence upon free use of another country's land and water resources reflected a feeling that Spain's land and its use really should belong to Americans as a natural right. The "Geographer of the United States," for example, rephrased but did

45

not change this old Anglo-American expansionist ideology. He maintained that the natural resources of the North American continent promised to support a power greater than any in the past. "If we want it," meaning Louisiana, he said, "I warrant it will soon be ours." [4] Our people, the "lords of America," will dominate its commerce.

Congressional delegates from the Northeast, representing merchants and ship-owning interests, were not as easily aroused over problems of the Mississippi frontier as were southerners and westerners. What northeasterners wanted most immediately from Spain was a commercial treaty allowing them to trade in her New World colonies. They had enjoyed such a commerce briefly during the Revolutionary War, but Spain had ended the trading privilege with the coming of peace. This concern for commerce did not mean that the leaders in the Northeast opposed expansion. They, too, assumed that Americans would someday populate the continent. As one of their most influential spokesmen, John Adams, boasted in 1785, the United States was "destined beyond a doubt to be the greatest power on earth, and that within the life of man." [5]

Fearing that American frontiersmen might try to settle by force what Congress could not resolve by diplomacy, Carlos III's first minister, Don José Moñino y Redondo, conde de Floridablanca, took the initiative in seeking a settlement of grievances with the new republic. He was prepared to make limited concessions, but not without what he considered vital equivalents. In return for recognition of Spain's exclusive right to control the lower reaches of the Mississippi, he was willing to modify her most extensive boundary claims affecting the United States and to offer trading privileges in several of Spain's homeland ports to Americans. He also desired a defensive alliance and a mutual guarantee of territories in America. Essentially, these were the instructions Floridablanca gave Don Diego de Gardoqui, Spain's first envoy to the United States, who arrived in New York in May 1785 to negotiate.

Gardoqui, an astute and polished diplomat who spoke excellent English, considered his bargaining position reasonable and relatively strong. For, as Floridablanca himself pointed out, the terms Spain now offered were essentially what John Jay, as unofficial envoy to Madrid, had proposed in 1781 in return for Spanish recognition of American independence. At that time he had offered to hold back American expansionism, to Spain's advantage, saying "that the United States shall guarantee to his Catholic Majesty all his dominions in North America." [6]

For other reasons, too, at this time Gardoqui's terms, on the surface at least, appeared especially attractive. Spanish trade concessions could help alleviate the woes of a depression that had settled upon the United States. Some Americans thought that even continued restrictions on the use of the Mississippi would bring some benefit. It could slow the growth of the trans-Appalachian west and keep it from breaking away from the Union. Meanwhile the mutual territorial guarantee could contribute to a cementing of this region to the Union. That guarantee need not impair the inexorable westward thrust of Americans. Time was on their side, so why hurry?

Congress authorized John Jay, then secretary for foreign affairs, to negotiate with Gardoqui. But it imposed the proviso that any agreement he reached must assure Americans free navigation of the lower Mississippi and a settlement of the Florida boundary at the thirty-first parallel. Gardoqui could not yield on both these points. As instructed, he offered the commercial concessions in Spain, desired mostly by northern seaboard merchants, in a package deal that required a temporary closing of the Mississippi. After almost a year of fruitless negotiation, Jay, a New Yorker attuned to coastal interests, decided to act on these terms.

47

In August 1786 Jay asked Congress for a change of instructions so that he could conclude a treaty wherein the United States would "forbear" use of the Spanish portion of the Mississippi for thirty years but without surrendering the "right" or principle of free navigation. He argued that the United States could gain immediate navigation only by a war for which it was unprepared. "Why, therefore," he asked, "should we not (for valuable consideration, too) consent to forbear to use what we know is not in our power to use?" [7]

By a simple majority of seven to five, Delaware being absent, Jay won the revision of instructions he desired. But Congress had split along a sectional line. All the delegates from the southern states voted against him.

When the arrangement became public, it convinced southerners that Jay was willing to sacrifice the welfare of the Southwest to the immediate interests of the Northeast. Furious westerners talked of separating from the Union, even of seeking British protection, if Jay went ahead with a treaty on such terms. "To sell us and make us vassals to the merciless Spaniards is a grievance not to be borne," one disgruntled Kentuckian wrote. "Preparations are now making here (if necessary) to drive the Spaniards from their settlements at the mouth of the Mississippi." If the American government would not help them, they would turn elsewhere. "Great Britain stands ready with open arms to receive and support us." [8]

Since approval of nine states in Congress was necessary for ratification of any treaty and the southern states stood fast in opposition, Jay did not pursue the negotiations further. Even when the Spaniards retreated and offered new concessions for a treaty, Jay would not buck the public clamor. Southern distrust of the North remained an important factor in matters concerning Louisiana. Southerners and westerners assumed that northerners would place their desire for commerce before what they

48

conceived as in the national interest—ahead of westward migration and expansion.

Actually, northern and southern leaders at this time generally assessed the national interest from a similar perspective. Both disliked giving any firm guarantee for Spanish territory and both believed in the idea of mission, or that Providence had destined Americans to expand at the expense of Spaniards and, of course, Indians. Jefferson expressed the concept well. "Our confederacy," he wrote, "must be viewed as the nest from which all America, North and South is to be peopled. We should take care too not to think it for the interest of that great continent to press too soon on the Spaniards. Those countries cannot be in better hands." He feared only that the Spaniards were "too feeble" to hold Louisiana until the population of the United States became "sufficiently advanced to gain it from them piece by piece." [9]

Like Jefferson, policy makers in the new American government thought of Louisiana and the Floridas as being held by the Spaniards in a kind of trusteeship. Ultimately those territories, like fruit when ripe, would fall under the domination of the United States. So American leaders not only opposed any transfer of ownership from Spain, they also responded with alarm even to mere rumors of a change in status. In 1786 John Jay, for example, sharply questioned Louis Guillaume Otto, France's *chargé* in the United States, about a rumored retrocession. Although the French denied any possibility of a reacquisition, American suspicion lingered.

Constantly aware of this American covetousness, Spanish authorities experimented with various tactics toward their neighbor in efforts to protect Louisiana. They continued to subsidize Indians who were as anxious as they were to block American expansion. One of these agents, a Creek chieftain with Scottish blood, Alexander McGillivray, tried to create a confederation of southern Indian tribes that would roll back the American tide. Beginning in 1786, he set the frontier from George to Kentucky ablaze with attacks on American settlers. McGillivray's resistance did not save Indian lands; it gained them only a brief respite. The westward-moving whites kept coming.

Spanish policy makers meantime decided to try honeyed guile rather than open resistance in dealing with the American frontiersmen. Spain manipulated its rules for use of the lower Mississippi and encouraged separatist sentiments in the American West. This tactic began taking form in August 1786 when James White, a delegate to Congress from North Carolina, told Gardoqui that westerners were so disgruntled they would consider severing their bonds to the Union and placing themselves under Spain's protection.

This separatist sentiment persuaded another American, James Wilkinson, a twenty-nine-year-old former brigadier general in the Continental army who had turned to trading and land speculation in Kentucky, that he could squeeze big profits from the frontier troubles. He arrived in New Orleans in July 1787 and quickly won the confidence of Governor Miró. He induced Miró and Martín de Navarro, the intendant, to support a scheme for separating Kentucky from the Union and attaching it to Louisiana. Pointing to the multiplying American settlements west of the Appalachians, Wilkinson played on the Hispanic dread of American imperialism. If Spain did not go along with his plan, he intimated, she would surely lose Louisiana to the advancing Americans.

What Wilkinson proposed gained a favorable reception because it agreed with the thinking of the colonial officials. Navarro was still convinced that "the powerful enemies we have to fear in this province are . . . the Americans, whom we must oppose by active and sufficient means." Like Wilkinson, he also wished to encourage trade and immigration, for without it "this country would have been a desert." Yet in the face of American expansion he contemplated the future with despair, saying, "I see clouds rising and threatening us with a storm that will soon burst upon this province." [10]

Miró apparently saw in Wilkinson's scheme a chance to help shape the future instead of just awaiting it. He thought that the desire of westerners for free navigation of the Mississippi was strong enough to make the plan acceptable to them. He asumed that secession would weaken the United States and make it a less dangerous neighbor to Louisiana and that Spain would also benefit from increased trade between Kentucky and New Orleans. Wilkinson and his friends expected to amass wealth through a monopoly of trade privileges with Louisiana that they assumed Spain would grant them.

In this plan, known to ethnocentric Americans as the "Spanish Conspiracy," Wilkinson became "No. 13," a Spanish agent and pensioner. He even signed a formal declaration of intent to transfer his allegiance from the United States to Spain. He and his associates took their commitment to Spain lightly. Playing on two sides, they also plotted to revolutionize the Floridas and Louisiana and then use them as bases for overthrowing royal government in the rest of Spanish America.

The government in Madrid used Wilkinson's information and debated his recommendations but ultimately declined to go along with his scheme. Rather than incite rebellion in Kentucky, Spain decided to promote commerce with the United States. In December 1788 it issued a royal decree allowing Americans to ship and sell goods in New Orleans subject to moderate export and import duties, essentially a tariff of 15 percent. Yet Gardoqui paid and used a number of Americans, such as John Sevier, a Tennessee frontiersman, land speculator, and politician, in efforts to separate the western territories from the Union.

Acting on the theory that a populous colony would be the

best defense against American encroachments, Spain in her December decree opened Louisiana to all comers. Spanish authorities actually invited Americans to settle in the province. On entering, the immigrants had to swear allegiance to the Spanish crown. As subjects of Spain they could acquire tracts of land free of charge proportionate in size to the number of people they brought to work their farms.

This liberal immigration and land-grant policy did not stimulate a massive migration into Louisiana. But it did attract speculators who advertised for immigrants and it pleased the expansionists who held office in a new federal American government established in 1789. "I wish a hundred thousand of our inhabitants would accept the invitation," the new secretary of state, Thomas Jefferson, said. "It will be the means of delivering to us peaceably, what may otherwise cost us a war." But he did not want the government to appear to the Spaniards as delighted with their policy. "In the meantime," he suggested to the president, "we may complain of this seduction of our inhabitants just enough to make them [the Spaniards] believe we think it a very wise policy for them, & confirm them in it." [11]

Such tact was not only prudent but necessary. Colonial officials eyed the immigrants with suspicion, convinced that the oath to the crown meant nothing to Americans who were bent on "conquest by colonization." What the Spanish authorities saw around them seemed convincing evidence of a peaceful conquest. Wherever Americans went in Louisiana they appeared to take over. They worked their way into much of the colony's economic life. Fleets of boats carrying great quantities of provisions from Cumberland, Kentucky, and elsewhere covered the Mississippi. Clashes between American rivermen and Spanish authorities erupted frequently. In one instance twenty-four Kentuckians, according to the American version, battled fifty Spanish soldiers, killing five and wounding twelve. The Spaniards called the Kentuckians "white savages" because they handled "the tomahawk pretty freely." [12] Understandably, suspicious government servants viewed American settlers and businessmen as subversives who would turn against Spain in the first crisis with the United States.

Such a crisis appeared imminent after Spaniards and Englishmen in 1789 quarreled over trading rights at Nootka Sound, an outpost of empire on the remote west coast of Vancouver Island. Anticipating war, William Pitt, England's prime minister, made plans to strike at Spanish territory in North America. President George Washington, who assumed the existence of such a strategy, asked his cabinet officers for guidance if the British should attack and conquer Louisiana. He considered the very idea "of having so formidable and enterprizing a people as the British on both our flanks and rear" alarming. [13]

All the president's advisers shared his concern. Alexander Hamilton, his secretary of the treasury, regarded control of the Mississippi "as essential to the unity of the Empire." He suggested that when the United States grew in strength and "we are able to make good our pretensions, we ought not to leave in the possession of any foreign power, the *territories* at the mouth of the Mississippi, which are to be regarded as the key to it." [14]

While expressing hope for neutrality, Jefferson suggested intervention in the war if necessary to prevent the "calamity" of "Louisiana and the Floridas be[ing] added to the British empire." He even favored the use of French assistance in forcing Spain to surrender New Orleans and the Floridas to the United States. "We have a right" to a port in Spanish territory "for our commerce," he said, by "nature" and "by Treaty. It is *necessary* to us." In exchange for territory and the port he was willing to offer Spain a guarantee of some duration for Louisiana west of the Mississippi. [15]

When the Spaniards found themselves without an ally, they recognized their weakness, backed down from their confrontation with the British, and the crisis passed. The crisis also reminded them of what they had long known: the seriousness of the possessive attitude of American leaders toward Louisiana.

The Spanish rulers commissioned spies to roam through American settlements south of the Ohio River to measure the depth of anti-Spanish prejudice, which was strong throughout the region. These agents reported that Americans talked of war, of taking over Louisiana, and of sweeping on to Mexico. The authorities in New Orleans learned in 1790, for example, that James O'Fallon, a promoter and land speculator in the American West, had worked out a filibustering scheme to conquer Louisiana. Regardless of whether or not these reports were exaggerated, the number of Americans in the colony, their boasting, and their aggressiveness, as well as their hatred of Spain, made the rulers increasingly apprehensive about the safety of the province.

Some officials within Louisiana, as a consequence, took issue with policies emanating from Madrid. They denounced liberal immigration, for instance, as suicidal, comparing it to inviting the fox into the chicken coop. So Miró's successor, Barón Francisco Luis Héctor Carondelet, a Belgian in the service of Spain who began his administration in January 1792, changed that policy. He tried to keep Americans out and once again to attract Catholic European immigrants to Louisiana. He also revived the old French policy of arranging alliances with Indian tribes to protect Louisiana's northeast frontier against the American "menace." Indian attacks on the American frontier increased, but ultimately this strategy failed.

In 1793, after Spain went to war against France, she again had to modify her defensive policies in Louisiana. Then she opened channels of economic activity. At the same time Spanish policy makers hoped that Americans would be so eager to share in this commerce that they would willingly pay a price for it, essentially a moderation of boundary claims and of demands for free navigation of the Mississippi. This tactic failed to elicit concessions from the American government, mainly because Louisiana needed American foodstuffs and her people were determined to have them regardless of policy in Madrid. The United States now provided the only market for the colony's products and the main source for its food and other necessities.

Carondelet was convinced that if his officials attempted to block trade with the United States the people of Louisiana would revolt. Colonial authorities therefore not only tolerated this trade but also encouraged it by reducing the duty on imports and relaxing commercial restrictions for Americans. As Carondelet assumed, this contraband commerce eased the pressure from westerners on the American government to do something about the Mississippi. While never approving of this illegal trade, the government in Madrid did nothing to stop it. So the wars of the French Revolution opened Louisiana more widely than ever to precisely what Spanish policy makers had striven to prevent—American economic penetration.

Chapter IV

✤

Economic Dominion

This prestigious and restless population, continually forcing the Indian nations backward and upon us, is attempting to get possession of all the vast continent those nations are occupying between the Ohio and Mississippi Rivers, the Gulf of Mexico and the Appalachian Mountains. . . . If they obtain their purpose, their ambitions will not be limited to this part of the Mississippi. . . . Their method of spreading themselves and their policy are so much to be feared by Spain as are their arms.

Barón de Carondelet, 1794 [1]

*I*n 1793 Spanish rule in Louisiana was menaced not only from westward-moving Americans but also from a new enemy—republican France. Barón de Carondelet, the governor, knew that France's revolutionary emissary to the United States, Edmond C. Genêt, was gathering forces to attack Louisiana and that the province could not repel invasion if it came. Since the governor could not rely on support from the French Creoles, he pleaded with his superiors for military reinforcements. On his own he organized and drilled two companies of militia and strengthened fortifications around New Orleans. Creole Jacobins also threatened revolution from within and at times disrupted civil stability. On one occasion in 1794 Carondelet even summoned Anglo-Americans settled in Natchez to help police New Orleans.

Deeply concerned with other pressing foreign and domestic problems, the American government did not attempt to derive benefit from such unrest. In fact, at this time it wished to discourage attacks against Louisiana, whether under American or French auspices. Now that Spain had allied herself with Britain against France, the Federalist government wished to avoid hostilities with Spain. Yet Spanish officials, such as Carondelet, believed that "Genêt's coup against Louisiana . . . failed only because of lack of money." [2]

In carrying out this policy of restraint, the federal government had to move cautiously because of the fluid situation in the West. In political persuasion frontiersmen of the Ohio Valley were generally Republicans friendly to French revolutionary ideals and hostile to the pro-British Federalists who controlled the central government and determined its policies. These westerners disliked the government's foreign policy, its Indian policy, its economic policy, especially its tax on whiskey, and its failure to obtain free navigation of the lower Mississippi.

Regardless of the nature of government policy, the westerners regarded unobstructed use of the lower Mississippi as "a right which must be obtained." Dissatisfied with the precarious nature of their navigational privileges, they especially resented the Spanish duties on their goods deposited in New Orleans for transshipment elsewhere. Restless and prone to take action when aggrieved, they appeared eager to cooperate with French adventurers or to take matters in their own hands against Spanish Louisiana in defiance of a distrusted central government.

Although other Americans did not feel so keenly the western sense of grievance, many shared in western expansionist attitudes. Even among conservative New Englanders there were those who openly praised expansionism. One of them put the imperialist credo into verse.

All hail, thou western world! by heaven design'd
Th' example bright, to renovate mankind.

Soon shall thy sons across the mainland roam;
And claim on far Pacific shores, their home;
Their rule, religion, manners, arts, convey,
And spread their freedom to the Asian sea.[3]

Knowing of this attitude, the captain general of Louisiana and the Floridas prognosticated that Americans "will absorb Louisiana." Carondelet, too, warned his superiors of the "unmeasured ambition" of this "new and vigorous people . . . advancing and multiplying in the silence of peace." These Americans, he said, lusted after the Indian lands between the Appalachians and the Mississippi. Once in control, they would assault Louisiana and "the very kingdom of Mexico [*Mégico*]. Their method of spreading themselves and their policy are so much to be feared by Spain as are their arms." [4] To hold back the American tide, he urged the government in Madrid to send military reinforcements, build up Louisiana's defenses in general, and subsidize Indian attacks on American frontier settlements. He also thought, as had other colonial officials, that if Spain would encourage westerners to secede from the Union this would also enhance Louisiana's security.

Despite its sensitivity to American expansionism, Spain until this time had refused to negotiate an agreement to replace the abortive Jay-Gardoqui Treaty. Now events in Europe in combination with the American pressure on the Louisiana-Florida frontiers persuaded the Spanish government that it could benefit from an arrangement that would ease friction with the United States.

This change in policy began taking form early in 1794 when Spain's leaders realized that their alliance with England was bringing them more harm than good. French forces were invading Spain at both ends of the Pyrenees, and the distant British were unable to help. In Louisiana, too, the British were unavailable or unwilling to do anything to counter American threats. In the spring of that year, for example, Carondelet sent a courier to John G. Simcoe, the governor of Upper Canada,

THIS AFFAIR OF LOUISIANA

proposing common action against Americans and French in case they attacked Louisiana. Simcoe replied that he hoped the English-Spanish alliance would be strengthened but that he could not then give Carondelet any assistance.

So Manuel de Godoy, the twenty-eight-year-old duque de la Alcudia, the king's first minister of state, and the king's other high advisers reversed the direction of Spain's foreign policy. They decided to abandon the alliance with England and to conciliate the United States. In making this shift, Godoy was willing to use Louisiana for whatever advantage it might bring to Spain's new international orientation.

Before Godoy could acquire anticipated benefits, he had to ward off expected dangers. Resenting the reversal, Britain would probably attack Spain. Engaged at the time in negotiations with the American government over old grievances, Britain might also conclude an alliance and join forces with the United States to invade Spanish America. Godoy at this point assumed that by giving Americans something they had long desired without having to fight for it he might be able to keep them at least neutral if Spain and Britain fought. In addition to easing the threat of an American invasion, this reorientation of policy had the virtue of reducing Louisiana's burdensome defense costs.

In the summer of 1794, therefore, the Spanish crown asked the American government to renew the long disrupted negotiations over differences between them. In response in November, President George Washington nominated Thomas Pinckney of South Carolina, then his minister to Britain, for the post in Madrid. Pinckney arrived on June 28, 1795, just as Godoy was secretly concluding an agreement whereby Spain deserted England and gained peace with France. This treaty, signed at Basel on July 22, was ratified by both France and Spain within two weeks, and on August 7 Madrid announced the end of the war with France. As a reward for securing this settlement of Basel, King Carlos IV conferred on Godoy the title Prince of the Peace.

When Godoy began his negotiations with Pinckney, therefore, the success flowing from Basel placed him in a good mood and fortified his willingness to offer important concessions for American friendship. At first, though, Godoy tried to induce the United States to join Spain and France in a triple alliance designed to protect Spanish territory in North America. Seeking a guarantee against American expansionism had been a principle of Spanish diplomacy since the independence of the United States. Although Americans had several times considered making such a guarantee, it became a principle of American policy to resist a commitment. "You should not, by any clause of treaty, bind us to guarantee any of the Spanish colonies," Jefferson as secretary of state had instructed commissioners to Spain a few years earlier. He explained that during the Nootka Sound crisis "when we thought we might guarantee Louisiana on their [the Spaniards'] ceding the Floridas to us, we apprehended it would be seized by Great Britain, who would thus completely encircle us with her colonies & fleets." [5]

In 1795 no such danger seemed imminent, so the American negotiators in Madrid flatly refused any kind of territorial guarantee. Because Godoy believed that John Jay, an American diplomat negotiating in London, might conclude an alliance with the British and trigger an Anglo-American assault on Louisiana, he gave in to American demands.

On October 27, 1795, at the summer palace of the Spanish court in the village of San Lorenzo de Escorial, Pinckney and Godoy signed an agreement known either as the Treaty of San Lorenzo or Pinckney's Treaty. With it Spain retreated—but did not abandon her overall strategy—in her policy of using lands on Louisiana's frontier as part of her defense in depth against Americans. By recognizing the thirty-first parallel as the southern boundary of the United States and thereby surrendering good claims to sovereignty over considerable territory in the Old Southwest, Spain accepted a restricted eastern boundary for Louisiana. She admitted in effect that she could not maintain her position in the Ohio Valley in the face of American expansionism. She retreated only because she felt compelled to do so, and she did so as gracefully as circumstances would permit.

Almost as important as the territorial settlement, as far as westerners were concerned, was the concession on the Mississippi River. Spain now allowed Americans to navigate the lower Mississippi and to deposit goods at New Orleans, free of duty, for transshipment to distant ports. She granted these privileges for only three years, but she agreed to renew them or to permit the free deposit elsewhere. In the treaty the Spaniards also promised to stop inciting Indians on the frontier against the United States.

The American government was delighted with the results of the Pinckney negotiation. Without war it gained recognition of its supremacy in the Ohio Valley and achieved a major objective in an implicit program of continuing territorial expansion. When news of the treaty became known, it placated westerners, quashed what remained of most separatist schemes, and dealt a blow to Wilkinson and others involved in the "Spanish Conspiracy."

French leaders were amazed by the privileges that the Treaty of San Lorenzo granted to Americans. The terms seemed so disadvantageous to Spain that many assumed Godoy had acted in bad faith and had no intention of carrying them out. Even Timothy Pickering, the American secretary of state, shared this feeling. They failed to understand Spanish policy. Godoy had no reason for negotiating a treaty merely to sabotage it. Even though he moved slowly, at first he acted in good faith in carrying out Pinckney's Treaty. In June 1796 he ordered Carondelet to execute the terms as they applied to Louisiana. The governor did so, but regretfully.

Carondelet could work up no enthusiasm for the strategy of seeking American friendship. Crises on Louisiana's frontiers, even if sparked by others, seemed somehow always to involve Americans. Spaniards and Americans watched each other's military movements with suspicion, with Spanish officials fearing assaults all along the thinly defended Mississippi frontier. For protection against surprise attack Carondelet relied on the inadequate patrols of his freshwater navy.

The so-called Blount Conspiracy added to the frontier uneasiness. In 1796 Colonel William Blount, a senator and speculator from Tennessee, plotted to seize land in Louisiana with an army of frontiersmen and Indians. Carlos Martínez de Irujo, Spain's minister in Philadelphia, charged that the British had a hand in the scheme. They had promised, according to available evidence, to supply ships as well as troops for Blount's invasion. Exposure of the plot added to Spanish feelings of defenselessness in Louisiana. Some Americans, such as James Madison, saw the Blount Conspiracy not as a problem in American relations with Spain but as an aspect of French-British rivalry. They viewed it as a British effort to forestall any French move to take Louisiana from Spain.

This rivalry between the great powers compelled Carondelet to suppress his distrust of Americans and to turn to them for support. He assumed that when war broke out again between Spain and Britain, which it did after Spain allied herself with France in the Treaty of San Ildefonso in August 1796, the British would invade Louisiana from Canada. So did some American leaders. But the British government denied plans for any such invasion.

To Carondelet the danger of a British assault seemed real enough to cause him to take measures for the defense of upper Louisiana and at least temporarily to reverse the policy on immigration. He now encouraged American settlers to come in, believing they would help protect the province. This desperate expedient again stimulated a flow of Americans into Louisiana and West Florida. As before, critics likened their coming to the settling of the Goths at the gates of Rome. After 1796 practically all the new settlers in Louisiana were Americans. They helped tighten the American grip on the province's economy.

West Florida underwent a faster and more intensive process of Americanization because it had a substantial English-speaking population when Spain acquired it. Incoming Americans brought no feeling of security to the Spanish authorities. As in Louisiana, they were unassimilable and a threat to Spanish rule.

Godoy, meanwhile, also realized that to seek and to rely on an artificially inspired American friendship was to pursue an illusion. Not only did the Treaty of San Lorenzo fail to acquire for Spain the good will he desired, but also the Federalist government seemed to him a tool of the British. Even those Americans friendly to France remained hostile to Spain. So in October 1796 he put aside his policy of conciliating the United States, mainly by suspending compliance with the Treaty of San Lorenzo. He ordered Louisiana's governor not to run the boundary as agreed upon by the treaty and to retain until further notice several posts above that line.

This continuing Spanish presence on the east bank of the Mississippi provoked angry protests from westerners. They particularly resented the prolonged occupation of Natchez, about forty miles north of the thirty-first parallel; according to American estimates, seven-eighths of the town's inhabitants were American by birth or sympathy. In June 1797 Americans in Natchez rebelled and threatened to storm the fort there and to set up a government of their own. Manuel Luis Gayoso de Lemos y Amorín, the governor of the Natchez district, negotiated with the rebels and settled the conflict on generous terms. Nonetheless, this episode placed additional strain on relations between Spaniards and Americans on the Louisiana frontier. It also intensified the quarrel between Secretary of State Pickering and Irujo, that insolent "Spanish puppy" who had been bickering for almost a year over the terms of the Spanish withdrawal in the Old Southwest.

In that June also President John Adams complained to the Senate that the Spaniards were blocking demarcation of the southern boundary. "Gracious Heaven! insulted by a Spaniard!" This was just what could be expected, a biased nationalist said, "from a tawny-pelted nation, which Americans have ever been taught to despise!" [6] Expansionists and other Americans, too, again muttered threats of war and spoke of assaulting Louisiana.

These threats, as well as the Natchez affair, apparently influenced Godoy. They reminded him of Louisiana's defenselessness. Spain alone could not block an American invasion, but with French help she could probably put up strong resistance. Without abandoning Spain's attachment to France, therefore, Godoy again took measures to placate the United States. In September 1797 he rescinded orders to Louisiana's governor to hold on to the forts north of the thirty-first parallel and directed the evacuation to proceed as originally planned. So in 1798 Lemos, who had recently become governor of the entire province, finally withdrew the Spanish troops from Natchez and the other posts in what was now American territory. Pickering thought that this action "may have resulted from Spain's seeing or fearing the necessity of ceding Louisiana to France, and hence concluding that she might as well do a grateful thing to us before surrender." [7]

In any case, in February 1799 the United States took possession of the Natchez region. It then organized this acquisition, extending from the Mississippi to the Chattahoochee River, as the Mississippi Territory. Some Americans thought that Natchez could be built into a major port that would rival New Orleans in importance.

Meanwhile the dependence of the western United States on

New Orleans increased. The benefits flowing from the Treaty of San Lorenzo set off a commercial revolution in the Mississippi Valley. The farmers of the American West sent more and more of their produce down the Mississippi to New Orleans and from there to the West Indies, to the Atlantic states, and to Europe. Perhaps a dozen American flatboats had floated down the river to New Orleans in 1792. Within a few years they numbered in the hundreds. This commerce, along with the flow of immigrants, was turning Louisiana into a sphere of American influence.

In the late 1790s Americans already comprised a majority in the government of Baton Rouge and were increasingly visible in New Orleans. The extent of American trade and influence throughout eastern Louisiana alarmed Spanish officials and also those French leaders who hoped to regain the province. As in West Florida the Americans in Louisiana remained unassimilable, an alien element within an alien culture. The bishop of Louisiana considered them "a gang of adventurers who have no religion and acknowledge no God," who were contaminating the colony, and who were eager to wrench it from Spain.[8]

Despite their economic power and the liberal terms of the Treaty of San Lorenzo, Americans trading in Louisiana continued to dislike their status. The Spanish authorities did not put the privilege of deposit in New Orleans into effect until April 1798. Americans felt that their "right" to use New Orleans was inadequately protected, being subject to the whim of the Spanish king. The American government could not appoint a resident agent to look after their interests in New Orleans. Nor did it have the privilege of sharing in the selection of an "equivalent establishment" if the right of deposit at New Orleans were cancelled. The treaty allowed American trade to flow through New Orleans without restriction in one direction only—outwardly.

The situation improved later in the year. Daniel Clark,

Jr., an American merchant who represented a Philadelphia firm and who acted unofficially in a consular capacity in New Orleans, obtained important concessions for Americans trading there. Colonial officials agreed to permit American ships to carry goods to and from New Orleans on the same terms as Spanish vessels, subject only to a duty of 6 percent. They also allowed exporters to ship goods from New Orleans to American territory on the Mississippi without payment of any duty. Louisiana's governor hoped that these concessions would increase the volume of trade and give New Orleans control of markets in the interior.

The more important reason for this commercial liberality, however, was Spain's war with England. Cut off from their normal sources of supply, Louisiana and other Spanish border provinces needed American products more than ever. So great was the need that when Madrid ordered colonial officials to revoke the trade concessions, they refused. They defied the crown because if they could not have access to American goods they knew from past experience that economic ruin or rebellion would probably follow.

Even without the new concessions Spain's commercial restrictions in Louisiana did not injure basic trade much. Although irksome, the regulations were designed mainly to protect Spain's own interests rather than to cripple Americans. Sensitive to any kind of restriction, westerners tended to exaggerate their need for an open river. Those in a position to use the Mississippi had rarely found it closed.

Some Americans, such as James Wilkinson and his friends, nonetheless sought to benefit from this western concern over the river commerce and from turmoil in Louisiana. They were eager to exploit both fellow Americans and Spaniards. Now, in 1798, Wilkinson held high office, commander of the army in the West, and had considerable influence in the American government. Aware of Wilkinson's intrigues, Daniel Clark informed the government in Philadelphia about them. These revelations brought no action, for various Federalist leaders were friendly to Wilkinson. Alexander Hamilton considered him "a man of more than ordinary talent, courage, and enterprise" and wished to use him in plans to conquer Louisiana.[9]

The United States was then involved in the naval hostilities of the Quasi-War with France. Expecting the conflict to expand, President John Adams and the Federalists in Congress were trying to arm the country. Hamilton gained command of a provisional army intended for defense against a French invasion. But if it ever became more than a force on paper, he planned to use this army offensively to invade the Floridas and Louisiana. He rationalized this contemplated aggression with the theory that Spain, though at peace with the United States, as an ally of France deserved to be despoiled and that France planned to seize the provinces for herself. We should take "possession of those countries for ourselves, to obviate the mischief of their falling into the hands of an active foreign power, and at the same time to secure to the United States the advantage of keeping the key of the western country," he said. "I have been long in the habit of considering the acquisition of those countries as essential to the permanency of the Union, which I consider as very important to the welfare of the whole." [10] Hamilton discussed such ideas, essentially his imperial design, with Wilkinson.

Other Federalist leaders, too, were expansionists. Although John Adams and his wing of the party differed with Hamiltonians over the politics of the Quasi-War, they also desired Louisiana and the Floridas. Federalists of various persuasions, therefore, liked Hamilton's project. If he seized Louisiana, they reasoned, the federal government could crush secessionist sentiment in the West, eradicate the enthusiasm of westerners for France and Jeffersonian Republicanism, and solidify the Union.

Louisiana also provided Federalists with a concrete, seemingly achievable war objective. "A war with Spain," a pro-Federalist gazetteer had written earlier, "is absolutely necessary to the salvation of this country, if a war with France takes place, or if the Spaniards have ceded Louisiana to France. They must both be driven into the Gulf of Mexico, or we shall never sleep in peace. Besides, a war with Spain would be so convenient!" The wealth gained from Spanish America "would be the cream of the War." [11]

Federalist war hawks readily accepted such arguments and were convinced of the necessity for action because they believed that Spain intended to cede Louisiana and the Floridas to France. Pickering, for instance, was convinced that the French had been pressing Spain to cede Louisiana and that the pressure was so urgent that the Spaniards could not resist much longer.

These Federalists were alarmed by the mere idea of the French as neighbors. They believed that once the French established themselves in Louisiana they would exploit discontent in the West to promote secession. So strong were the anti-French sentiments of Americans during the Quasi-War that Irujo, the Spanish minister in Philadelphia, advised his government to make certain that any negotiations with the French concerning Louisiana were kept secret, especially from the Federalist government in Philadelphia. American leaders, he warned, would rather go to war than to allow Spain to transfer Louisiana to France.

Such a war was what Francisco Miranda, a soldier of fortune and revolutionary born in Venezuela who devoted himself to freeing his homeland from Spain, desired. Miranda's plan, as he explained it to Hamilton, to other Americans, and to British officials early in 1798, called for an alliance of Britain, the United States, and the Hispanic colonies against France and Spain. He wished to merge the Anglo-French war and the Quasi-War and use the enlarged conflict to liberate Spain's American possessions. He desired an Anglo-American expedition against Hispanic America, with Britain furnishing the ships and the United States the troops. For Americans the reward would be Louisiana and the Floridas.

The British were willing to go along. Prime Minister William Pitt told Miranda, "we should much enjoy operating jointly with the United States in this enterprise." [12] Rufus King, the American minister in London, also liked the plan. So did Secretary of State Pickering. A hispanophobe and an anglophile, he was eager for a rupture with Spain and an alliance with England. Hamilton, too, urged cooperation on the Miranda project and made his ideas known to President John Adams.

Anxious to have the Americans join them in an alliance against the French, the British now expressed approval of American imperial designs if they could themselves acquire Santo Domingo. "The Conquest of Louisiana and Florida by the United States," William Wyndham Grenville, Britain's foreign minister, explained, "instead of any Cause of Jealousy, would certainly be Matter of Satisfaction to this Government." [13]

While faced with hostilities with France, President Adams wished to cultivate Spanish neutrality. So in October 1798 he rejected both the Miranda proposal and the British suggestion of an alliance. In the matter of Louisiana he believed that the United States should pursue an independent course.

Westerners, on whose bellicosity and hatred of Spain the Hamiltonians had counted, also proved less eager for war than these Federalist expansionists had presumed. Many westerners remained loyal to the Republican party, which opposed the war with France, and others who were benefiting from the state of Louisiana's economy feared that war with Spain would destroy their export privilege through New Orleans. Albert Gallatin, one of their spokesmen and a prominent Republican politician, summed up their position. Any attempt at this point to conquer Louisiana, he said, would carry grave risks and would bring westerners no new privileges. Instead, it would deprive them of the Spanish and French markets they now held.

Federalist truculence, which was much more obvious than the Republican restraint in the West, particularly alarmed the Spanish authorities in Louisiana. On their own, with virtually no help or guidance from Madrid, they tightened the restrictions on American immigration. Governor Lemos was more adamant in his opposition to Americans than Carondelet had been. In 1799 the acting intendant, Juan Ventura Morales, issued new regulations designed to keep out Americans. A short time later the king forbade the granting of any land whatsoever in Louisiana to American citizens. These measures came too late to be effective. American settlers continued to enter the province illegally because they were land-hungry expansionists who felt that Spain's trusteeship of those lands was temporary. They felt able to remain in Louisiana because the Spaniards were weak and had insufficient power to enforce their own immigration laws.

Despite the seriousness of the American threat and the defenselessness of Louisiana, officials there continued efforts to incite rebellion in the American West. This was a futile policy. Regardless of their grievance against the federal government and their opposition to Federalist military ventures during the Quasi-War, Westerners never lost their hatred of Spaniards or their desire to conquer Louisiana.

By the end of the eighteenth century it was obvious not only to American expansionists but also to other interested observers, such as the French, that Spain's days in Louisiana were numbered. The frontier infiltrations and the legal and illegal settlements by Americans had made defense of the colony against the United States difficult if not impossible. The Spanish crown, which had never provided adequate defenses, found the cost of maintaining the province so great that it stationed only enough troops there to control the Creoles and to with-

71

stand incursions by freebooters, but not enough to resist a strong invader. Madrid, for example, did nothing concrete, despite pleas from officials in Louisiana, to combat the expected assaults from Blount and Hamilton.

Policy makers in Madrid even resented pleas from Louisiana for help. They felt that the colony was sucking Spain into rivalries she did not need and should avoid. They were convinced that the province had become a dangerous liability and more trouble than it was worth. Mariano Luis de Urquijo, secretary of state for foreign affairs, analyzed its various costs and concluded that they were too high. The colony was a parasite; its revenues covered only one-fifth of what the mother country expended on it.

Profit from increased trade also proved disappointing. Much of that commerce went untaxed, mainly by passing through the American deposit in New Orleans. Even the effort of the ruling establishment in Madrid to placate the Creoles by making exceptions for Louisiana in Spain's colonial system added to administrative costs. Officials in Louisiana went further than this; they tolerated smuggling by American traders through New Orleans to other Spanish colonies. Rarely did those officials enforce Spain's commercial laws to the letter.

With their limited resources for policing, the Spanish authorities would have been unable to prevent smuggling, even if they had tried to do so wholeheartedly. When they did attempt more than perfunctory regulation, American traders complained of harassment. Such charges were sometimes justified, especially when Spanish guards boarded flatboats, molested crews, and exacted excessive fees. These were, however, capricious actions that annoyed more than they injured American commerce.

Americans engaged in such extensive smuggling that it became an important part of New Orleans's economy. Moreover, as Louisiana planters specialized more and more in cash crops

such as sugar and cotton, the most populous part of the colony
became even more dependent on American food than it had
been in the previous decade. Hundreds of flatboats loaded with
whiskey, flour, and other products flowed down the river to
provision New Orleans and to fill the holds of ships that waited
in the port. American boatmen, saltwater sailors, legitimate
traders, and smugglers streamed through the city. In 1801, ac-
cording to available estimates, well over three thousand of them
passed through. More than half the ships entering New Orleans
flew the American flag. Many others, although under Spanish
registry, were owned by Americans. Frequently American ships
hoisted Spanish colors only as they hove into sight of the look-
out at the mouth of the Mississippi. By this time, the begin-
ning of the nineteenth century, the United States had absorbed
the larger part of Louisiana's commerce.

A change in the attitude of political and business leaders in
the Northeast toward use of the lower Mississippi accompanied
American economic penetration. Eastern merchants, many of
whom helped finance the Louisiana commerce and profited from
it, came to look more favorably than they had in earlier years
upon the westerners' demands for secure privileges on the lower
Mississippi. American interest in the fate of Louisiana, which
had always been strong among policy makers and westerners,
ceased to be elitist or mainly sectional. By the turn of the cen-
tury the desire for acquisition of Louisiana, or at least part of it,
had behind it a broad geographical constituency and had be-
come an important factor in national politics.

In 1801 American names on Spanish land grants in Loui-
siana exceeded those of all others, and more than half of the
white population in upper Louisiana was American. Although
still a minority in lower Louisiana, Americans were firmly en-
trenched in West Florida. They were establishing themselves
west of the Mississippi in increasing numbers, especially in the
Missouri country. By 1802 the first wave of Americans had al-

73

ready crossed Louisiana and settled in Texas. American traders and others who found cattle ranching profitable had reconnoitered and even mapped this western country all the way to the borders of Mexico. So, while American merchants were capturing Louisiana's economy, American settlers were moving their frontier into Louisiana. The next step, seemingly invited by Louisiana and Spain's weakness, appeared to be conquest.

Chapter V

✤

Enduring Dream

There are no other means of putting an end to the ambition of
the Americans than that of shutting them up within the limits
which Nature seems to have traced for them; but Spain is not in
a condition to do this work alone.

Talleyrand, 1798 [1]

*F*rom the end of the Seven Years' War to the time of the
American Revolution sentimental Frenchmen, especially those
living in North America, dreamed of someday regaining Loui-
siana. These dreamers did not make policy, and France's monar-
chical government did not attempt to rebuild an American em-
pire. In their treaty of alliance with the United States in
February 1778 the men of the old regime not only agreed to
fight for American independence but also renounced any desire
to repossess Canada. They did not, however, extend this renun-
ciation to Louisiana. Charles Gravier, comte de Vergennes,
France's foreign minister at the time, denied rumors circulating
among his American allies that in aiding the United States his
government was seeking to regain Louisiana.

This dream of a resurrected French empire in North

America had behind it some elements of logic. Those who were not burdened with the costs of defending and administering Louisiana saw it as an area of great commercial potential. Moreover, Frenchmen in North America often viewed repossession differently from the policy makers in Paris. In March 1778, for example, a French trade commissioner in New Orleans, Villars de Brevil, argued that if the United States should win its independence then France should recover Louisiana, and he repeated the suggestion in 1781 when independence had been virtually achieved. He believed that Americans posed a greater threat to the colony's security than had the English.

The desire of such French agents apparently led to rumors in 1786 "that Louisiana was to be exchanged for a French possession in some other part of the world." Knowledgeable Americans realized that if Louisiana again belonged to France "she would put a complete stop to the plans of conquest which the new states of the union have for the western bank of the Mississippi." American expansionists did not have to worry at this point because Vergennes put the rumors to rest. "There has never been a question of an exchange of Louisiana for a French possession in the West Indies," he told his representative in New York, "and, if it is again mentioned to you, you will formally deny it." [2]

Yet in the following summer another French trader, Barthélemi Tardiveau, who lived in Kentucky, took up the theme of the rumors. He wrote a memoir urging the French government to repossess Louisiana and reap the profits from the trade with the American West that such possession would bring. He argued that Spain, living in dread of American expansionism, looked upon Louisiana as a burden and therefore France could easily regain the colony. Once in control, France could win over American westerners with commercial concessions. "Happy my native land should she not pass by this opportunity," he wrote, "one of those which does not occur twice!" [3]

Tardiveau submitted his memoir to Comte Éléonore François Élie Moustier, at the time France's minister to the United States and a man who was himself intensely interested in Louisiana. Moustier not only forwarded Tardiveau's memorial to the French foreign office but also incorporated much of it into a report of his own.

Other governments, too, viewed Tardiveau's ideas with considerable interest. George Beckwith, a British secret agent in New York, obtained a copy of the document and sent it to the governor of Canada who forwarded it to London. The governor hinted that in view of schemes such as Tardiveau's, Britain should take over Louisiana. The contents of the memoir also got into the hands of Don Diego de Gardoqui. After assessing Tardiveau's views and becoming alarmed, he sent them on to Madrid. This concern by agents of France, England, and Spain over America's inland empire formed the basis for numerous rumors about a possible change in status for Louisiana.

Moustier's memoir, composed in 1789, had a special significance because he was one of the first important officials to advance the idea of reacquisition in a carefully reasoned paper. Despite the record of loss during France's possession of the colony, he maintained that Louisiana in French hands for the second time would increase in wealth and population and would become the hub of a considerable commerce. He pointed out that Americans were rapidly settling the trans-Allegheny region and that this thrust of population westward would contribute to Louisiana's prosperity. Louisiana would complement Santo Domingo and France's other Caribbean possessions and could become the foundation of a profitable and economically and militarily self-sufficient western empire. The Caribbean islands would exchange sugar, coffee, molasses, and rum for Louisiana's timber and anticipated food surpluses.

To regain Louisiana, Moustier suggested, French leaders should convince Spain that it was a burden and a source of danger in her relations with the United States. Under France the colony could, like a shield, protect Spain's other North American possessions from the aggressive Americans without cost to her.

Moustier's plan gained no immediate support in France, but apparently it influenced the thinking of important people on the subject of Louisiana. In the United States, where Moustier frequently talked about his ideas for France's recovery of Louisiana, his views aroused antagonism. Secretary of State Thomas Jefferson, for one, saw them as hostile to the expansion of the American empire.

In these years Louisiana's Creoles also wanted to see France's western empire revived. Several times they made secret overtures or sent petitions to Paris for reunion with France. The revolution in France in 1789, which overthrew the old regime, brought to power men who considered Louisiana's cession to Spain a crime. They scrutinized and sympathized with the petitions for repossession coming from enthusiastic revolutionaries in New Orleans. They also realized that to regain Louisiana, France must act before Americans peopled the Mississippi Valley and wrenched control of the lower Mississippi from Spain. So in 1790, when France's leaders suggested a new alliance to replace the old Family Compact, they asked Spain to seal the agreement with the retrocession of Louisiana. Distrustful of the revolutionaries, the Spanish crown rejected the proposal.

In September 1792 moderate revolutionaries, the Girondins, abolished the monarchy and declared France a republic. Expansionists among them considered various schemes for retaking Louisiana by force. At this point they did not look upon Americans as adversaries in a struggle for empire but as allies and fellow republicans. So the Girondin government did not talk about reannexing Louisiana but referred vaguely to the idea of liberation. It assumed that the American government would join French republicans in an invasion, even though Spain was at peace with both countries, and would perceive mutual benefit in the emancipation of the province from the yoke of monarchism.

On this assumption the Girondins instructed their minister to the United States, Edmond C. Genêt, appointed in November, to "germinate the principles of liberty and independence in Louisiana," essentially to conquer it.[4] In January 1793 the government sent Constantin François de Chasseboeuf, comte de Volney, to Louisiana on the pretext of conducting a scientific expedition but in fact to investigate political conditions as a prelude to "liberation."

France and Spain went to war in March, shortly after Genêt had left France for his mission. He arrived in the United States in April and immediately launched his project to detach Louisiana from Spain. Believing that he had Secretary of State Jefferson's support, he organized an expedition under the tricolor of republican France made up of American volunteers. A number of prominent Americans favored the planned invasion, among them George Rogers Clark. He offered to take all of Louisiana for France with an army of one thousand two hundred whites supported by Indian allies.

Genêt's plot against Louisiana failed because his conduct alienated President George Washington, other influential Federalists, and even some Republicans, such as Jefferson. The American government asked for Genêt's recall, and his own government, taken over by Jacobins in June 1793, disavowed his project.

Regardless of the repudiation of Genêt, French statesmen continued to think seriously of finding means to reestablish French power in the Mississippi Valley. Genêt's successor, Jean Antoine Joseph Fauchet, became a warm advocate of the reacquisition of Louisiana, especially after consummation of the Jay Treaty in November 1794. French leaders concluded that the agreement, whose contents were secret, had brought into being the Anglo-American alliance they had long feared. Sharing this assumption, Fauchet urged his government to regain Louisiana, either through peaceful diplomacy or through war. "Louisiana extends her arms to us," he wrote.[5] Its possession would counterbalance the Jay Treaty and would make the United States dependent on France rather than England. Unless France acted or a revolution occurred in Spanish policy, he predicted, the force of events would give Louisiana to the United States.

As peace between France and Spain approached, policy makers in Paris abandoned their plans to use force but not their desire to regain Louisiana. Recovery of the province now became one of their major foreign policy objectives. They even hoped to use the Jay Treaty as a lever in prying the colony from Spain's grip.

In the peace negotiations at Basel the French diplomats tried to recover Louisiana, relying on Spain's dread of American aggression to facilitate retrocession. If Spain returned the province, these negotiators pointed out, France would close the Mississippi to Americans and check their westward expansion. Since Manuel de Godoy, the Spanish negotiator, apparently thought such a cession at this point would bring on war with the United States, Spain resisted. Occupied mainly with war against Austria, France did not attempt to force the issue by insisting upon Louisiana. So in the Treaty of Basel, Spain gave up her half of Santo Domingo, or the eastern section of the island, to France but held on to Louisiana.

After Godoy failed to obtain the American guarantee for the territorial integrity of Louisiana that he sought in the Treaty of San Lorenzo, he saw no further value in the province and assumed that the French, as they themselves persistently pointed out, could guard it more effectively than could Spain. So in December he reversed the position he had taken at Basel six months earlier by offering to exchange Louisiana for eastern Santo Domingo. Considering the price too high, France refused the offer but continued negotiations for a later transfer of Louisiana on better terms.

Believing that Spain could not resist French pressure, those who made policy in the United States assumed that the Treaty of Basel contained a secret clause promising Louisiana to France. They were convinced that France had never abandoned aspirations for empire in North America and that it was merely a matter of time before she attempted to occupy Louisiana. Her possession of that colony, they reasoned, could destroy the Union. Once France acquired Louisiana and the Floridas, she would try "to sever Canada from England, unite with those provinces," American leaders believed, "and invite the western parts of our union to separate from it and join this new power which was thus to be reared in that quarter." [6]

France's dream of empire, moreover, clashed with the imperial desires of the Federalist establishment. If France gained a foothold in Louisiana, a Federalist newspaper argued, "the United States would be encircled by an artful, insinuating, active nation, and must forever renounce the hope of obtaining by purchase or amicable means, the territory west of the Mississippi, to the ocean." Then, "nothing short of conquest will ever enable the Americans to secure the property and jurisdiction of that vast country, which would otherwise naturally and easily fall into their range of settlements."

When entrenched in Louisiana, France would also be in a position to dominate Mexico and other Spanish possessions in the Americas. "In the hands of the plodding Spaniards they do no harm and little good to the world at large, but in the hands of an active nation, Mexico would be a dangerous engine of power." Taking for granted American westward expansion and prognosticating the Monroe Doctrine, the journalist explained that it "is our interest" to "prevent any powerful nation from making establishments in our neighbourhood." [7]

Some Federalist officials, such as Treasury Secretary Oliver Wolcott, Jr., echoed these sentiments. He was convinced that the French would be "the worst and most dangerous neighbours we could have." They would "be like ants and weasels in our barns and granaries." [8]

These anxieties elicited pained denials from French officials of any aggressive designs in the New World. If France took action in Louisiana, they asserted, it would be mainly to keep the British out and not to reacquire the province.

France's new revolutionary government, the Directory, which had come to power in October 1795, did not even pretend to adhere to such a policy. Charles Delacroix, the Directory's minister of foreign relations, desired Louisiana not only as an imperial possession but also as an instrument for exerting influence over the American government. Like the Spaniards, he considered infiltrating Americans a menace to the colony. Like other contemporary imperialists, he believed that when France regained possession she would stop the American penetration and could use Louisiana to counterbalance any Anglo-American alliance.

Delacroix sought both Louisiana and an alliance from Spain. Although Godoy considered Louisiana a liability to Spain, he was reluctant to part with it without obtaining something substantial in return. The Directory kept exerting pressure on him, arguing repeatedly that in France's hands Louisiana would protect the rest of Spanish America from England and the United States, "whose population increases with a rapidity truly disturbing for her neighbors." "We alone," the directors claimed, "can trace with [a] strong and respected hand the bounds of the power of the United States and the limits of their territory." [9]

As part of Delacroix's Louisiana policy the French minister in Philadelphia, Pierre Auguste Adet, in March 1796 commissioned General Georges Henri Victor Collot, a former governor of Guadeloupe, to reconnoiter the Ohio and Mississippi valleys. Collot traveled to New Orleans and St. Louis and roamed through what he called "the Western *imperium* of the American continent." Although he urged cooperation with Spain for its defense, he maintained that only French control of this heartland could hold back "the American phalanx." So frightened were the Spaniards of American expansionism he believed, that "as long as Spain remained in possession of Louisiana, one of her chief objects was to hide from the Americans whatever attractions the country might have for them." [10]

Collot outlined plans for the possible defense of Louisiana, once in French possession, against the Americans at the line of the Alleghenies. He envisioned a Louisiana as it had been claimed by the old regime, an empire stretching from the Alleghenies to the Rockies that included territory now belonging to the United States as well as to Spain. He concluded "that the Western states of the North American republic must unite themselves with Louisiana and form in the future one single compact nation" or else the United States would devour Louisiana. [11]

Insofar as it touched upon the future of Louisiana, Collot's reconnaissance had two significant results. It intensified American suspicions of French designs on the colony, and as embodied in his report, it served as a work of reference for French officials. Policy makers were to refer often to Collot's ideas as the basis for their own views on Louisiana.

Collot's venture also coincided with events in Europe that spurred hope among French leaders that their dream of western empire might soon be transformed into reality. On June 26, 1796, Godoy concluded negotiations with the French minister in Madrid for a treaty of alliance whereby Spain would cede Louisiana in exchange for Gibraltar and for fishing rights off Newfoundland. Again the Directory considered the price too high and refused to ratify the agreement. Moreover, England, being in possession of what Spain desired, stood in the way of such a transaction.

So in August at San Ildefonso, when Spain and France agreed to an alliance against England, Louisiana was not mentioned. Yet the Directory was still eager to reacquire the colony. In separate negotiations it offered the Spanish crown territory in Italy for the realm of the duke of Parma, a brother of Queen María Luisa, in exchange for Louisiana and the Floridas. Despite the alliance and the need to unload Louisiana, Godoy, a former lover of the queen, distrusted the Directory. He and other Spanish officials felt that France in an effort to gain peace might, after reacquisition, turn over Louisiana to England and thereby place the rest of Spanish America in jeopardy. At the same time Delacroix thought that England was preparing to invade Louisiana and that Spain therefore needed French support. He wished, consequently, to keep negotiations over Louisiana alive and vital.

Unaware of Spain's hesitation in agreeing to a retrocession, many in the United States were convinced that as a result of the new French-Spanish alliance Louisiana had changed hands. "There is every reason to believe, indeed with me the fact is certain," an anti-French journalist wrote, "that Spain has ceded Louisiana to France." [12]

While expressing concern over these rumors, Secretary of State Timothy Pickering summarized American policy toward Louisiana in these years. "We have often heard," he said, "that the French government contemplated the repossession of Louisiana; and it has been conjectured that in their negotiations with Spain the cession of Louisiana & the Floridas may have been agreed on. You will see all the mischief to be apprehended from such an event. The Spaniards will certainly be more safe, quiet and useful neighbors. For her own sake Spain should absolutely refuse to make these cessions." [13]

As though privy to Delacroix's thoughts, Pickering felt

that France was trying to acquire Louisiana in order to dominate the United States. So he instructed David Humphreys, the new American minister in Madrid, to cut through the rumors and to ascertain Louisiana's true status. If Spain had not ceded the colony, Humphreys was to do all that he could to prevent any transfer. Pickering also attempted to warn the French that reacquiring Louisiana would bring on a clash with the United States, which "could not fail to associate themselves with Great Britain, and make common cause against France." [14] He and other Federalist leaders believed, almost as a matter of faith, "that France means to regain Louisiana, and to renew the ancient plan of her monarchs of *circumscribing* and encircling what now constitute the Atlantic states." [15]

Meanwhile Spain's suspicions that the Directory might use Louisiana in bargaining with England proved sound. Late in 1796 France and England undertook peace talks, and their negotiators discussed the question of the colonial spoils Britain had taken from France and her allies. Although William Pitt, Britain's prime minister, did not demand Louisiana, he desired it. He instructed James Harris, Lord Malmesbury, the English envoy who resumed the negotiations at Lille in July 1797, that no colony under discussion would offer greater advantage to England's "interests as *the town and port of New Orleans with a sufficient territory to be annexed to it.*" [16] This gain would offset France's reacquisition of Santo Domingo in the previous year. Godoy was willing to cede both Louisiana and the Floridas for Gibraltar. But when Lord Malmesbury suggested the exchange to Pitt, he refused to pay that price. The British government could use Louisiana as a tool in its diplomatic maneuvering, but apparently its desire was not deep enough to warrant a strategic concession for the province. In October the peace talks collapsed.

This long war with England made France's relations with the United States, strained by conflicting maritime policies, increasingly bitter. The Directory feared, as Pickering had threatened, that the United States would ally itself with Britain, invade Louisiana and the Floridas, and destroy France's chance to recover Louisiana. So in the summer of 1797, while also discussing peace at Lille, they instructed Dominique Catherine Pérignon, their ambassador in Madrid, to apply pressure on the Spaniards for a prompt cession of Louisiana and to stress the danger of an Anglo-American assault as a reason for their doing so.

At this juncture also a ministerial crisis with important repercussions for Louisiana occurred in Paris. In July Charles Maurice de Talleyrand-Périgord replaced Delacroix as the Directory's minister of foreign relations. This pleasure-loving former aristocrat, a one-time Catholic bishop who had turned his hand to diplomacy, had a clear vision of western empire. He had lived in exile in the United States for more than two years as a land speculator and had returned to France with a fixed view of Americans as an expansionist people. In a paper he read before the *Institut national,* a society of learned men in the arts and sciences, in the preceding April he had suggested that France should regain Louisiana as a means of stifling American expansionism. He explained, as Moustier had suggested, that Louisiana could bring France substantial commercial benefits and could supply her West Indies with the provisions they required.

Although Talleyrand did not shape the Directory's foreign policy—he called himself "the editor responsible for other people's works"—he frequently influenced policy. For example, in March 1798 he succeeded in helping to drive Godoy from office because he was not sufficiently pro-French. Talleyrand urged the Spaniards to surrender Louisiana, using the well-worn argument that they needed France there to build a barrier between Mexico and American imperialists. Like Delacroix, he wanted France to reacquire Louisiana before American or Anglo-American

invaders wrenched it from Spain's feeble grip. This concern mo-
tivated much of Talleyrand's conduct in his dealings with
Americans. His attitude assumed a crucial importance because
he became a key figure in France's relations with the United
States during the hostilities of the Quasi-War.

During that conflict Americans heard all kinds of rumors
to the effect that France would take over the Spanish posts on
the Mississippi, become master of Louisiana, and even invade
the United States. The French, on the other hand, worried
about an American invasion of Louisiana sparked by Federalist
war hawks. Joseph Philippe Létombe, the French consul general
in Philadelphia, warned Talleyrand in April 1798 that "already
they talk about the conquest of Louisiana" and of alliance with
Britain.[17] Like others, Létombe suggested the barrier theory,
that France place herself between Spain's provinces and the
United States.

Talleyrand himself again sang the barrier refrain in May
while playing on Spain's anxiety over American imperialism.
He instructed France's new ambassador to Spain, Ferdinand
Pierre Guillemardet, to inform the Spaniards that the United
States planned to make itself lord of the North American conti-
nent. As had his predecessors, Talleyrand believed that there
were "no other means of putting an end to the ambition of
Americans than that of shutting them up" behind the Appala-
chians. Since Spain could not "do this great work alone," he
explained, she should allow France to take over Louisiana and
the Floridas. France would make these territories "a wall of
brass forever impenetrable to the combined efforts of England
and America." [18]

With Louisiana as the main objective of his mission, Guil-
lemardet arrived in Madrid in June 1798. Prodded by Tal-
leyrand and by knowledge that the American Congress was
passing war measures against France, he moved with a sense of

urgency. If the Quasi-War expanded into a full-scale conflict, his diplomacy could become meaningless. The Americans would most likely block the retrocession.

In July Spain gave in partially to this pressure. She agreed to allow French troops to go to Louisiana to help repel expected British and American invasions.

At this time Létombe, the highest-ranking French diplomat remaining in the United States, submitted a report to the Directory containing some of Collot's recommendations. The consul general advised the Directory not to declare war against the United States but to concentrate on acquiring Louisiana and the Floridas through negotiation and to use force only against Canada. He believed that this strategy would conciliate the United States, sever its ties to England, and secure France's desired western empire against American attack. In sum, it would permit France to recover without excessive struggle that preponderance in the New World "which the nature of things gives to us." [19]

Godoy, who now wielded power behind the scenes, moved cautiously in response to the French pressure for Louisiana. Sensitive to the sentiments of expansionists and war hawks in the United States, he and his advisers realized that if the Americans learned with certainty that he was bargaining for the sale of the colony to France they would probably seize it, either on their own or with British help. No one interested in Louisiana could ignore England's position. Britain's new foreign minister, Lord Hawkesbury, believed with "no doubt that France had obtained a cession of it." Nonetheless, he said that at present England wanted no additional colonies and "had no thoughts of an expedition to the Mississippi." She might, however, in the future seize Louisiana as a war measure, "with a view of holding something to give up at peace." [20]

Godoy wished to keep Louisiana out of both American and

British hands. But he also wanted still to retain control of it while negotiating with the French for a good price.

For the French the politics of the Quasi-War complicated those negotiations. Talleyrand contributed to the intensification of that conflict by seeking bribes from American diplomats. Then, when a bigger war with the United States appeared imminent, he sought to contain the Quasi-War because if it expanded it would endanger his efforts to regain Louisiana. Tainted with scandal and apparently sensing the collapse of the Directory, Talleyrand resigned from office in July 1799, with Louisiana still desired but still beyond France's grasp.

Chapter VI

⚜

Transforming the Dream

France since the Revolution had not thought of that possession [Louisiana], and that even on representations made by the United States she had momentarily sacrificed the project of seizing it to the desire to live on friendly terms with the United States.

James Madison, 1801 [1]

*I*n November 1799 Napoleon Bonaparte overthrew the Directory and replaced it with a new government headed by three consuls and hence called the Consulate. As First Consul he wielded the real power. He readily took over the Directory's plan for Louisiana, seeing in it apparently compensatory achievement for his recent failure to hold on to Egypt and empire in the east. He was also aware of the old French dream of restoring empire in the west, and that imperial vision, too, attracted him. Bonaparte even reappointed Talleyrand minister of foreign relations in place of Karl Friedrich Reinhard, a blunt man who had little time to pursue the Louisiana quest, in part because Talleyrand was a known and sophisticated champion of the idea of a revived empire in North America. Since both the general and the former bishop shared in the vision of western empire, both considered quick repossession of Louisiana a matter of first importance. So under the Consulate France's relations with Spain promptly improved, and as they did so, the dream of reacquiring Louisiana appeared to verge on a transformation into reality.

Bonaparte understood that Louisiana's Creoles, despite their long separation, still held France in great affection and wished to return to her rule. He also believed that he could defeat Britain and then consolidate France's empire in North America with Creole support. In any case, he immediately infused new life into the efforts to regain Louisiana. In July 1800 he ordered Talleyrand to reopen negotiations in Madrid. Spain's secretary of state for foreign affairs, Mariano Luis de Urquijo, expressed willingness to give up the colony for territory in Italy, as the Directory had earlier offered, if the other European powers involved would consent. He did not wish to have the retrocession drag Spain into a war she could not handle. "Between ourselves," Urquijo wrote, "Louisiana costs us more than it is worth." [2] King Carlos IV, who admired Bonaparte, went along, especially because his queen was eager to see her brother Fernando, the duke of Parma, seated on a throne in central Italy.

To speed up negotiations, the First Consul decided to send a new special envoy, General Louis Alexandre Berthier, to Madrid. He instructed the general to offer a territory of indefinite size in Italy for the duke of Parma in exchange for Louisiana, the Floridas, and ten warships. Bonaparte wanted the Floridas as well as Louisiana because with a combination of those territories France would acquire four hundred miles of coast on the Atlantic as well as a coastline that would permit him to exert considerable influence in the Gulf of Mexico and in much of the Caribbean.

While one group of the Premier Consul's diplomats was bargaining in Madrid, another had been and was continuing to negotiate with Americans in Paris to terminate the Quasi-War. His conciliatory attitude toward the United States stemmed, in part at least, from his desire to overcome American resentment toward French policy and to keep Americans from seizing Louisiana before he could occupy it. Although he and Talleyrand realized that any accommodation with the United States could not long survive once France took over Louisiana, they tried to play down whatever might arouse American suspicions or might otherwise jeopardize realization of the dream of a restored western empire. Most of all in this regard, the Consulate wanted to keep the naval war with the United States from flaring up again just as the negotiations in Madrid were about to bear fruit.

Despite Bonaparte's precautions, the sensitiveness of Americans to the fate of Louisiana threatened to ruin his plan of empire before he could get it moving. In August 1800 the American minister in Madrid, David Humphreys, saw a brief item in a Paris newspaper announcing Berthier's mission. Humphreys immediately became upset. French and Spanish officials calmed him by denying they were negotiating over the retrocession of Louisiana to France. The American government did not press the matter.

This touchiness and Bonaparte's own sensitivity toward the American reaction toughened his determination to regain Louisiana quickly. Like his immediate predecessors, he attempted to use the Spanish dread of United States expansionism as a means of forcing Carlos IV to speed up the treaty making. He warned the Spanish monarch that the close relationship between the United States and England "may and must some day bring these two powers to concert together the conquest of the Spanish colonies." Carlos should therefore cede Louisiana to France "at once." [3]

This continuing concern over the American threat to Louisiana reflected a general attitude among Spaniards and Frenchmen familiar with the colony's status. Almost from the beginning of his rule the First Consul tried to gain some substantive understanding of the problem. He asked his ministers to gather whatever information they could uncover relating to Louisiana. So they looked into Victor Collot's recommendations, and when he returned to Paris early in October 1800, they immediately asked him to prepare an exhaustive report on Louisiana. They also commissioned Joseph Xavier Delfau de Pontalba, a wealthy Creole who had resided in the colony for eighteen years and had been "employed by the government in a superior office," to prepare a memoir for Bonaparte's use.

Commenting on Americans, Pontalba pointed out "that Louisiana can never cease to be the object of their ambition . . . [that] their position, the number of their population, and their other means, will enable them to invade this province whenever they may choose to do so, and that, to preserve her, it is necessary to conciliate and control them by keeping up intelligence with the most influential men among them, and to grant them privileges until this province be sufficiently strong to defend herself with her own resources against the torrent which threatens her."

Pontalba believed that westerners "would sweep everything on their passage" and could easily take New Orleans. He observed, moreover, that American expansionists filled the newspapers with their "bold schemes . . . designating Louisiana as the high road to the conquest of Mexico." *"Louisiana is the key of America,"* he said, and so it had "for a long time past, been the object of the ambition of the United States." Americans, therefore, he warned, "would be deeply disgusted if they saw her pass into the hands of so preponderating a power as France; and they would have invaded her long ago if they had foreseen such an event." [4] This warning did not reach Bonaparte until after Berthier had consummated the first agreement in the retrocession of Louisiana.

Berthier arrived in Madrid in September 1800, at about

the time Pontalba was completing his memoir. The negotiations went well, but Carlos refused to cede the Floridas and would give only six instead of the ten warships the First Consul demanded. According to Urquijo, "The King had pronounced himself so strongly against the cession of any portion whatever of Florida as to make it both useless and impolitic to talk with him about it." [5] Carlos still wished to unload Louisiana but would not do so in panic. In order to complete the transaction, the French for the present yielded on the Floridas.

On October 1, 1800, the day after American and French negotiators in Paris concluded the Convention of Môrtefontaine that ended the Quasi-War, Berthier signed a secret treaty at San Ildefonso. With it Spain promised to cede Louisiana and pledged six warships as well to France. In exchange, Bonaparte would provide a kingdom in Italy for the duke of Parma. Both parties desired secrecy in order not to affront the United States or Great Britain and thereby forestall a possible Anglo-American invasion before Bonaparte could send troops to defend Louisiana.

This second Treaty of San Ildefonso was provisional. It stipulated that France should not take possession of Louisiana until the First Consul had delivered the Italian kingdom to the duke of Parma and had gained general recognition of his sovereignty there. This minor delay did not at this point upset Bonaparte's plan of empire. He was still at war with England, and the United States had yet to ratify the Treaty of Môrtefontaine. Even though he was eager to occupy his new empire, he realized that if he attempted to do so prematurely he might still drive the United States into an alliance with England and revive the hostilities of the Quasi-War, but on a larger scale.

In verbal agreements accompanying this second Treaty of San Ildefonso, Bonaparte promised Carlos that France would not sell, give, or otherwise dispose of Louisiana to any third country. Historians have long conjectured over Bonaparte's true purpose in making this pledge. Some believe he had no intention of keeping his promise to Carlos. Others feel that he did and that he planned to make Louisiana the heart of a permanent empire from the moment he began negotiations.

Carlos did not at the time question the pledge. He thought he had struck a good bargain, and from his own perspective he had. He had traded "the vast wildernesses of the Mississippi and of the Missouri" for Tuscany, the flower of Italy, "the beautiful and learned home of Galileo, of Dante, of Petrarch, and other great men of letters and science." His brother-in-law, he explained, would rule over a highly civilized, "humane and gentle people" in "the classical land of the arts and sciences." [6]

Before Bonaparte could barter Tuscany, occupy Louisiana, and make his dream of western empire a reality, he needed to end hostilities with France's enemies. He had taken the first step toward a general peace with the Treaty of Môrtefontaine. He followed it with the Treaty of Lunéville of February 9, 1801, which forced peace upon Austria and gave possession of the Grand Duchy of Tuscany to France. The Premier Consul changed the duchy's name to the Kingdom of Etruria. Since he disliked the duke of Parma, he now proposed giving Tuscany to Fernando's son, Luis, the prince of Parma, rather than to Fernando himself. Lucien Bonaparte, Napoleon's younger brother who had become the French ambassador in Madrid, persuaded Carlos to accept the change.

On March 21 Lucien concluded the Convention of Aranjuez which confirmed and slightly altered the preliminary agreement of San Ildefonso. In it the First Consul promised to seat Luis, who had married Queen María Luisa's daughter and therefore was her son-in-law as well as nephew, on the throne of Etruria. The Spanish crown gave France the island of Elba and restated its intention to cede Louisiana to her. Godoy, who now influenced policy through his kinsman Pedro de Cevallos, who held the position of minister of foreign affairs, did not resist the arrangement. Despite French efforts to maintain secrecy, Americans quickly learned that they had made some kind of an agreement. "I fear that we have another iron in the fire—" a young American diplomat in Holland reported not quite correctly, "that France is to have the Floridas and Louisiana!!! I am endeavoring to ascertain the truth, but think, now, that there is great reason to believe it." [7]

Regardless of the leaks, Bonaparte went ahead with his imperial program. Next he moved to make peace with England. On October 1, 1801, his agent in London signed preliminary articles of peace, which freed him from the menace of the British fleet as he proceeded with preparations to take possession of Louisiana. He planned first to garrison the province and then to populate and use it as a granary for France's islands in the Caribbean. He hoped his plan would end the dependence of those islands, as well as Louisiana itself, on the United States for food supplies and make them less vulnerable than in the recent past to blockade in time of war. This design, based on the thinking of earlier dreamers such as Moustier, also assumed that once Louisiana had become populous and prosperous it would be able to defend itself even if cut off from France by a hostile naval power such as England.

The Premier Consul and his advisers also realized that time, which favored the Americans and not the French, was an enemy of this grand design. Realistically they knew that the tide of American western settlements, particularly in upper Louisiana, was so great that if France now hesitated she might never be able to rebuild her New World empire. She must move more swiftly. Bonaparte decided, therefore, after his strategy had been set in motion, to risk American resentment by occupying Louisiana as soon as he could gather sufficient force. He hoped to soften resistance by assuring Americans that France would not interfere with their control of old eastern Louisiana and by offering them commercial privileges on the lower Mississippi. So he ordered Talleyrand to demand from the Spanish crown the authority to take possession of Louisiana regardless of Etruria's status.

Like Bonaparte, Talleyrand wanted to put the old barrier theory of containing American expansionism into practice by occupying Louisiana without unnecessary delay. Yet he also felt apprehensive about moving too soon. If France pursued her Louisiana policy openly before carefully preparing for all foreseeable contingencies, she might even at this late hour still drive the United States and Britain into an alliance. Then, despite all the careful planning, the whole dream of western empire would vanish.

Regardless of this difference over timing and Bonaparte's desire for quick possession, before he could occupy Louisiana he felt he had to restore French rule in the West Indies possession, especially Santo Domingo,* the jewel of France's colonies. Slaves on Santo Domingo had revolted, had killed or expelled their white masters, and had in effect destroyed the French power structure. The Premier Consul perceived Santo Domingo as the keystone of an arch that would bind his whole colonial system together. Because of this view, because he did not have enough troops to reconquer Santo Domingo and occupy Louisiana at the same time, and because he did not yet have possession of Louisiana, he chose to assert his power first on Santo Domingo. The urgings of refugee Creole planters in his entourage and of his wife, Josephine, who was of Martinique Creole lineage and who owned a plantation in Santo Domingo, also influenced his decision.

At the time Toussaint L'Ouverture, an audacious, talented, and ruthless former slave, ruled the island's half million or more blacks, along with thousands of mulattoes and whites

* This is the Spanish name for the island, and the one commonly used. The French called it Saint Domingue.

who had not fled. Toussaint, who gloried in being called the "First of the Blacks" and the "Bonaparte of the Antilles," retained a nominal allegiance to France but in fact governed Santo Domingo as though it were independent. He was not the kind of man who would surrender power easily, especially to whites who had long enslaved his people.

During the Quasi-War, in order to survive and to maintain Santo Domingo's commercial viability, Toussaint had made secret agreements with Britain and the United States granting them a trading monopoly in return for goods and other assistance. As part of the price of peace with France after it had concluded the Treaty of Môrtefontaine, the United States ended its aid arrangement with the black rebels. Thomas Jefferson, who became president in 1801, had little regard for Toussaint and sympathized with France's desire to regain control of the island. Yet the president was also concerned about rumors of France's repossession of Louisiana, so he kept open channels of trade with Toussaint.

When Louis André Pichon, a French diplomat knowledgeable in the ways of the American political system, arrived in Washington as *chargé d'affaires* in 1801, he quickly sought assurances from Secretary of State James Madison that the American government would continue to recognize France as the legitimate sovereign of Santo Domingo even if Toussaint declared the island independent. Madison said that the American government would do nothing to jeopardize French interests on the island but that it also wished to avoid making an enemy of Toussaint.

Dissatisfied with Madison's ambiguous response, Pichon in July approached the president. The *chargé* explained that his government did not seek to have the United States terminate all commerce with the island, for that would drive Toussaint into the arms of the British. What the First Consul desired was American cooperation in the restoration of French rule. Jefferson

99

was reported as answering, first make peace with Britain, "then nothing would be easier than to furnish your army and fleet with everything, and to starve Toussaint." [8] He reminded Pichon that America's ruling establishment had no love for the black leader. His example menaced white rule in every slaveholding state.

This conversation, relayed to Talleyrand, apparently played a part in Bonaparte's decision to go ahead with his plans, which had long been in preparation, for conquering Santo Domingo. Three weeks after concluding the preliminaries for a peace settlement with England and also receiving the implicit consent of the British government to sending a large force to Santo Domingo, the Premier Consul placed his brother-in-law and one of his ablest generals, Charles Victor Emmanuel Leclerc, in command of the expedition. Leclerc's instructions, dated October 31, 1801, assumed American collaboration in the destruction of Toussaint's regime. "Jefferson has promised," they said, "that from the moment that the French army arrives, every measure shall be taken to starve Toussaint and to aid the army." [9]

Leclerc's main squadron sailed from Brest on December 14 with some twenty thousand soldiers crowded into the ships, followed later by another squadron. The first ships from the fleet reached Santo Domingo at the end of January 1802. After Toussaint showed defiance of French authority, Leclerc's army attacked. The blacks lost battle after battle but retreated into the hills, destroying settlements as they went, and kept fighting. French losses were heavy.

Leclerc did not receive the American help he had anticipated and even complained about lack of cooperation from the United States and about the munitions Americans supplied the rebels. When he occupied the charred ruins of Le Cap François early in February, he found about twenty American ships in the harbor loaded with provisions he badly needed. When he failed to obtain the cargoes at his price, Leclerc seized them and imprisoned the crews. This arbitrary conduct aroused indignation in the United States, but Jefferson played down the differences. Madison explained that the president wanted to give the French "no just ground or specious pretext" for "complaint or suspicion" against the United States because it did not accord their authority "due respect." It would, he said, "be better to leave the Island altogether, than to remain under circumstances which might hazard the confidence or good will of the French Republic[an] Governmt." [10]

At about this time Jefferson learned something of the size of Leclerc's army, of Bonaparte's intention to use Santo Domingo as a base for taking over Louisiana, and of rumors, relayed to him by Rufus King in London, that part of Leclerc's force was destined for the occupation of Louisiana. He asked Pichon to explain the purpose behind Leclerc's large expedition. Why did the French government not tell the United States about it beforehand? Would Leclerc's soldiers occupy Louisiana?

Receiving no satisfactory answers to his concerns, Jefferson changed his attitude toward helping the French on Santo Domingo. When Leclerc proclaimed a blockade of the ports under rebel control, the American government refused to cooperate. When Pichon pressed claims for money and supplies for Leclerc, he found the president "reserved and cold." Although American shippers had been supplying guns and provisions to both sides, Jefferson now took anti-French action by stepping up aid to the rebels.

Developments in Europe also contributed to the growing strain in France's relations with the United States. On March 27, 1802, the First Consul's older brother, Joseph, signed the Treaty of Amiens, which confirmed the preliminaries of the peace with England. Although the negotiators at Amiens did not discuss Louisiana, its fate was linked to this peace settlement. The Bonapartes in part concluded this peace so that they could proceed to build France's North American empire with a feeling of assurance that England would not strangle it in its infancy.

In an effort to speed up this empire building, the Premier Consul instructed Leclerc to offer the blacks on Santo Domingo freedom under French rule if Toussaint would surrender. Leclerc promised such freedom and offered to make Toussaint a general in the French army again. The black leader believed him. So on May 1, when the fighting had stopped for a while, Toussaint rode into Leclerc's camp and gave himself up. The French at first received him well but a month later arrested him and shipped him to France. Less than a year later he died in a French prison of maltreatment and pneumonia.

Meanwhile during the early fighting on Santo Domingo an article appeared in Paris in the semiofficial *Gazette de France* charging the United States with furnishing contraband guns, cannon, and powder found at Le Cap François to the blacks. It tied such aid to American expansionism and criticized both, saying that by its rapid increase of population, industry, trade, and wealth the United States appeared destined "to rule over the new world, and to place under its yoke all the West-India colonies." It called on Europe to oppose that imperialism and asserted that French Louisiana, as "a counterpoise to the domination of the United States," would block it.[11] These comments, reprinted in the United States in June 1802, appeared to many Americans to represent the true attitude of the French government and intensified the distrust toward Bonaparte's activities in the Caribbean.

In Santo Domingo a new message from the Premier Consul arrived a few days after Toussaint's arrest. It ordered reenslavement of the blacks. When Leclerc tried to carry out the order, the rebels fought with renewed fury. Leclerc and his aides allowed stories to spread of a plan to exile rebellious blacks to Louisiana. As though to substantiate the rumors, they sent shiploads of them to American ports. "The infernal French," a

South Carolinian complained, "at this moment are vomiting all their wretched blacks upon our coast." [12]

The slaughter on Santo Domingo continued. By September 1802 Leclerc had lost seventeen thousand men. Then yellow fever, which had been taking a steady toll of French troops, reached epidemic proportions. By the end of the month soldiers dead from the disease numbered four thousand. Accustomed to the climate and having built up some immunities to local diseases, the blacks did not suffer comparable losses. Leclerc wrote at this time that nearly twenty-four thousand Frenchmen had died in Santo Domingo since his arrival there.

While difficulties were mounting in the Caribbean, Bonaparte gave careful thought to a permanent French occupation in Louisiana. Several times he put aside advanced plans for an expedition to take possession of that province. Finally in April 1802, after considering two other candidates, he appointed Claude P. Victor, duc de Bellune, captain general of Louisiana and commander of an occupying expedition. In June the Premier Consul ordered Admiral Denis Decrès, his minister of navy and colonies, to organize the necessary military forces and administrators. "My intention, Citizen Minister," he said, "is that we take possession of Louisiana with the least possible delay, that this expedition be made in the greatest secrecy, and that it have the appearance of being directed to St. Domingo." [13] The First Consul also ordered the admiral to prepare maps and data on Louisiana's geography, population, and resources.

Decrès brought together the troops, munitions, and supplies for the expedition, while Victor, as Louisiana's governor and chief military officer, and Pierre Clément de Laussat, a loyal thirty-six-year-old politician, as colonial prefect, looked after other matters. They gathered presents to be distributed to the Indians, whom they hoped to use as allies in case of conflict with the United States. The French planned to give each Indian chief a special medal engraved with the likeness of the First

Consul. Like his predecessors, Bonaparte assumed he could pop-
ulate the colony with unemployed French people and with crim-
inals.

These preparations cost almost two million francs, an in-
dication of the high value Bonaparte placed on his Louisiana
dream. Despite the scale of this expedition, he persisted in try-
ing to keep it secret. Even most Frenchmen believed he was
gathering reinforcements for Santo Domingo rather than for the
occupation of Louisiana. Secrecy was difficult to maintain.
Officers on Santo Domingo knew of the expedition and boasted
that it "would bring the United States to its senses." Moreover,
even if Decrès completed the outfitting of the Louisiana fleet
swiftly, the Premier Consul still had to wait until Spain deliv-
ered the official papers of transfer before he could occupy the
colony, and such delay endangered the desired secrecy.

Bonaparte burned with anger because Godoy, again power-
ful within the intricacies of Spain's royal establishment, held
back the desired documents. He and Cevallos, Spain's minister
of foreign affairs, reminded him that since France had not car-
ried out her own obligations under the Convention of Aranjuez,
Carlos IV had no reason to go ahead with the formal transfer of
Louisiana. While Bonaparte had placed the prince of Parma on
the throne of Etruria, French troops occupied the kingdom and
French generals administered the government. Moreover, nei-
ther England nor Austria had recognized Etruria as the agree-
ment at Aranjuez had stipulated.

The First Consul did not attempt to crush Godoy or Spain
because such action would cause more delay in implementing
his imperial design. But he did use threats. "Tell the Queen
and the Prince of the Peace," he wrote his ambassador in Ma-
drid, "that if they continue this system [of delay], it will end
with a thunderbolt." [14]

In May 1802, after more delay, the Spanish leaders ap-
peared to bend under such pressure, but in fact they merely res-

tated the substance of their old terms. Cevallos said that Spain would formally hand over Louisiana to France if she met two important conditions. First, Bonaparte had to carry out his promise to obtain international recognition of Etruria and agree to restore Louisiana to Spain if the prince of Parma should lose his new throne.

The second restated condition reflected the persisting Spanish suspicion that England or the United States, known to covet Louisiana and willing to fight for it, might prevent the transfer. So Cevallos insisted that France "guarantee not to sell or alienate in any manner the property and usufruct of this Province." [15] To placate the Spaniards, France's ambassador in Madrid, Laurent, marquis de Gouvion Saint-Cyr, in July repeated in writing Bonaparte's earlier promise, saying, "I am authorized to declare to you in the name of the First Consul that France will never alienate it." [16] Three days later Cevallos notified the French government that King Carlos would deliver Louisiana without insisting upon Bonaparte's complete fulfillment of the obligation toward the house of Parma.

Finally at Barcelona on October 15, 1802, more than two years after agreeing to retrocede, Carlos IV signed the documents formally ordering his colonial officials to transfer Louisiana to French authorities. For Spain this delay in carrying out the retrocession ultimately proved as costly as a military defeat. It intensified Napoleon's * contempt for Godoy and for Spain's government in general.

---

* In August 1802 Bonaparte had himself proclaimed consul for life. After that he chose to be called by his given name, as did kings.

Chapter VII

✦

Mississippi Crisis

We are the first Power in our own hemisphere, and . . . are disinclined to perform the part of the second.

Rufus King, 1802 [1]

*I*n the United States, as has been seen, rumors of Louisiana's retrocession to France had been rife since 1796. Yet almost as soon as Thomas Jefferson, a man who had long held a clear vision of the imperial destiny of the United States and who also wished for a close relationship with France, became president, such rumors not only increased but also seemed to carry a ring of authenticity. Under such circumstances Jefferson could not cling to both his expansionist creed and his desire for a special friendship with France. At some point those ideological commitments were bound to clash.

Although American newspapers carried earlier reports, Jefferson first heard with some certainty of Spain's secret cession of Louisiana to France in May 1801 from Rufus King, the Federalist minister in London, who explained that what had been meditated "has, in all probability, since been executed." [2] This news elicited an immediate negative reaction. The president considered the reported transfer as unwise, ominous, and as undoing the peace settlement of Môrtefontaine. It would be, he told his son-in-law, "an inauspicious circumstance to us." [3]

Secretary of State James Madison quickly queried Louis André Pichon, the newly arrived French *chargé*. Was the report true? If France had been trying to reacquire Louisiana as part of her strategy in fighting the Quasi-War, the secretary said, he hoped she would abandon the project now that she had made peace with the United States. He wondered when France had begun to give earnest attention to regaining the Louisiana empire.

Pichon, who did not sympathize with the objectives of Bonaparte's regime, replied that he had no idea of whether the stories were true or false. He himself considered the transfer "unlikely," but he pointed out that in the past decade France had tried several times to regain Louisiana. "I assured him [Madison]," Pichon reported, "that since the Revolution we had seriously dreamed many times of an acquisition which offered a means of enhancing our commerce, providing a home for immigrants." [4]

Why was the American government concerned? Did the United States, the *chargé* asked, intend to expand beyond the Mississippi? Perhaps with a twinge of conscience, Madison dismissed this idea as fanciful. Surely, Pichon continued, Jefferson's government could not consider it a crime for France to recover lost territory? The secretary of state responded with a threat. If the transfer took place, he said, France would collide with the United States.

The *chargé* passed on the warning to Talleyrand. In regaining Louisiana, Pichon added, France would have to move circumspectly and overcome American hostility. Since Bonaparte and other French leaders anticipated an angry American reaction, the harsh news came as no surprise to Talleyrand.

Bonaparte also had to act carefully to surmount British opposition to a change in status for Louisiana. The British worried about the possibility of French power extending up the Mississippi, through the Great Lakes, and into Canada. Lord Hawkesbury, the foreign secretary in London, told Rufus King that England had no wish to see the results of the Seven Years' War reversed, with Canada and the British West Indies menaced by French power entrenched in Louisiana and the Floridas. To prevent such a development, Hawkesbury said, England would be willing to seize New Orleans and then, when peace came, cede it to the United States. King replied that the United States was content to have the Floridas and Louisiana "remain in the hands of Spain, but should not be willing to see them transferred except to ourselves." Condescendingly the two men agreed with Montesquieu's witticism that "it is happy for trading Powers that God has permitted Turks and Spaniards to be in the world, since of all nations they are the most proper to possess a great empire with insignificance." [5]

Jefferson liked the British offer of help but saw some danger in it. Earlier he and other American leaders had heard of the Directory's scheme to acquire Louisiana, conquer Canada, and then unite the two empires into one. The Jeffersonians thought that Napoleon now had adopted that plan.

Madison advised Rufus King that Jefferson's government would do what it could, mainly through peace and persuasion, to prevent Louisiana's transfer to France. But, he added, the shift in power in North America would be worse for the United States if the British, in trying to frustrate the French, seized Louisiana and the Floridas for themselves. Britain already "flanks us on the North," the secretary said. With Louisiana she would have settlements "in our rear, as well as flank us on the

South also. . . . she is the last of Neighbors that would be agreeable to the United States." [6] The president, with his eye on Louisiana as an area for American expansion, preferred the Spaniards as neighbors.

Earlier Jefferson had appointed Robert R. Livingston, who had been the first secretary for foreign affairs under the Confederation and was now a prominent New York politician and a francophile, minister to France. Now, in September 1801, less than a month before Livingston's departure for his new post, the secretary of state instructed him to find out if Spain had actually retroceded Louisiana to France. If the transaction had not been completed, Livingston was to express America's opposition to any change in the status of Louisiana and the Floridas. He should point out that a French move into Louisiana could drive the United States into the arms of Britain. Then France's possessions "would be exposed to the joint operation of a naval and territorial power." [7]

If the cession had taken place, the president wanted Livingston to persuade the French to sell the Floridas and New Orleans, or at least West Florida, to the United States. If the Floridas were not included in the transfer, he might induce the French to help the United States in obtaining them from Spain.

Possession of those territories fitted the vision of an expanding empire held by Jefferson, Madison, other policy makers, and Federalist leaders before them. The more aggressive among these men desired all of Louisiana and the Floridas soon, if not immediately, and urged their conquest before the French could take possession.

Such sentiments reached Pichon. He reported to Paris, "I am afraid they may strike at Louisiana before we can take it over." [8] He stressed the growth of American population and its pressure on the west and south. Spain should take care not to provoke the westerners and thereby lose Louisiana to them.

A month later Jefferson learned that France and England

had agreed on the peace preliminaries, and his anxiety over Louisiana mounted. "However our present interests may restrain us within our own limits," he said in explanation of his concern and of his imperialist attitude, "it is impossible not to look forward to distant times, when our rapid multiplication will expand itself beyond those limits, and cover the whole northern, if not the southern continent, with a people speaking the same language, governed in similar forms, and by similar laws; nor can we contemplate with satisfaction either blot or mixture on that surface." [9]

From London, Rufus King sent a copy of the Treaty of Aranjuez, confirming the earlier stories of Louisiana's retrocession to France. He explained the American position to Lord Hawkesbury, saying that the United States desired Louisiana but for the present wanted it "to remain in the quiet hands of Spain." [10] He asked if England would cooperate with his government by using her influence in the peace talks at Amiens to keep Louisiana in Spain's possession. Hawkesbury refused to make a commitment.

Shortly before, on November 10, Livingston landed in France, and on December 3, while the Consulate was moving ahead with the Santo Domingo expedition and with peace plans, he arrived in Paris. Livingston had difficulty in launching negotiations because he was deaf and could not speak French. Nonetheless, he quickly inquired about Louisiana and tried to reach the Premier Consul with an offer to buy it and the Floridas in exchange for debts France owed the United States. "None but spendthrifts satisfy their debts by selling their lands," Talleyrand responded, and after a pause added, "but it is not ours to give." [11]

Neither French nor Spanish officialdom would admit that Louisiana was changing hands. Yet Paris buzzed with excitement over the western empire the Premier Consul was trying to resurrect. Publishers brought out several books extolling the province, and in the salons people talked about it as a promised land. The reacquisition of Louisiana, Livingston said, "is a very favorite measure here." [12]

Now faced with the real possibility of having Europe's greatest military power as a neighbor, a worried Jefferson again resorted to menace. When Pichon protested a pamphlet that appeared in Alexandria, Virginia, urging seizure of Louisiana, however, the president called it nonsense. The United States, he explained, "would eventually have Louisiana through the force of things." [13] Then he repeated an old threat, that if Bonaparte actually took possession, the United States would ally itself with England and fight France. The French would remain in Louisiana, the president prophesied, no longer than it pleased the United States. Only by ceding New Orleans, the Floridas, and all the territory she obtained from Spain, he said, could France retain American friendship.

Many Americans apparently felt as did the president. Edward Thornton, the British *chargé* in Washington, reported that virtually every American politician he met disliked the idea of having the French as neighbors. They assumed that France would anchor a "military colony" in Louisiana. Southerners, still frightened of revolutionary doctrines, feared that French neighbors would contaminate their slaves with a "spirit of insurrection." Regardless of the various reasons for antipathy toward France, the Consulate's vigorous colonial policy was in itself sufficient cause to drive the United States closer to Britain.

The British attitude toward cooperation with the United States, however, had shifted. Rufus King reported that the English government, anxious not to upset Europe's new balance of power, would now do nothing about Louisiana's changing status.

Livingston reported Talleyrand as "decidedly unfriendly" toward the United States and explained that since the Consulate anticipated American hostility anyway, it intended to occupy Louisiana without notice. Such information as well as the launching of Leclerc's expedition without forewarning prompted Jefferson, who had often thought of France as a "natural friend," to speak of her as a potential enemy.

Rufus King thought that Americans would prefer to buy rather than fight. So he suggested a policy of "Iron and Gold" wherein the government should "attempt to acquire the legitimate title to Louisiana and the Floridas" by "a direct purchase." It is "actual money and a great deal of it," he said, "which can serve our purpose." [14] At the same time American newspapers, such as the *Kentucky Palladium,* carried rumors that Bonaparte was considering the sale of Louisiana to the United States.

News of Britain's reluctance to act on Louisiana's change of status, meanwhile, upset American leaders. They reproached the British ministers "in the most bitter terms" for standing aside and permitting "that vast country to fall into the hands of France." Americans were particularly infuriated by Lord Hawkesbury's declaration in the House of Commons "that it was sound policy to place the French in such a manner with respect to America as would keep the latter in a perpetual state of jealousy with respect to the former, and of consequence unite them in closer bonds of amity with Great Britain." [15] Several days later, on April 18, 1802, in a private letter to Livingston, Jefferson ironically stressed precisely this theme.

"There is on the globe one single spot, the possessor of which is our natural and habitual enemy," the president explained. "It is New Orleans, through which the produce of three eighths of our territory must pass to market." After this assertion of power over land that belonged to another country came words that reiterated an old threat and were to become among the most famous in American history. "The day that France takes possession of New Orleans fixes the sentence which is to restrain her forever within her low water mark," he warned. "From that moment we must marry ourselves to the British fleet and nation."

France could hold on to Louisiana only for a short time, Jefferson warned, while peace prevailed in Europe. Like an awaited signal, the first shot of cannon there would rouse Americans to arms. With their British allies they would evict the French from New Orleans, even from all of Louisiana. France could avoid such trouble by "ceding to us the island of New Orleans, and the Floridas," he said. "Every eye in the U.S. is now fixed on this affair of Louisiana. Perhaps nothing since the revolutionary war has produced more uneasy sensations through the body of the nation," the president said in stressing the importance of the probable confrontation.[16] The likely results of France's occupation, in his view, must be jealousy, irritation, and finally hostilities.

The man to whom Jefferson entrusted the carrying of this message was Pierre Samuel Du Pont de Nemours, a distinguished Physiocrat and old friend who was about to return to France to raise capital for his business and to seek a post in the government there. Du Pont, who had heard rumors that the United States wished to buy Louisiana, thought that this idea, worked out in negotiation, might resolve the friction between his native land and his adopted country. So he offered his services to stimulate discussion. Considering him a friend of both France and the United States, Jefferson took up his offer. Du Pont might be able to impress upon Bonaparte the gravity of the situation.

In a personal note to Du Pont the president stressed the "inevitable consequences" of France occupying Louisiana. "The cession of N. Orleans & the Floridas to us would be a palliation, yet I believe it would be no more." France's reacquisition would cost "a war which will annihilate her on the ocean," he warned. "This speck which now appears as an almost invisible point in the horizon, is the embryo of a tornado which will burst on the countries on both sides of the Atlantic, and involve in its effects their highest destinies." To eliminate the possibility of war, not just the crisis, Jefferson suggested, as he had to others, that France should cede all of her new North American empire to the United States.[17] His government would consider any attempt to land troops a cause for war.

Du Pont agreed that the United States should have a guarantee on free use of the lower Mississippi, but he minimized any danger to Americans from French control of Louisiana. France could assure freedom of navigation as effectively as could Spain. Touching on the Americans' expansionist appetite, he said that Jefferson betrayed "an ambition of conquest" and "that your nation in general, Mr. President, and above all the ambitious of your nation, think of conquering Mexico, is not questionable." Committed to the idea of purchase through negotiation, Du Pont disliked Jefferson's use of threat, suggesting that it would offend Bonaparte rather than persuade. "To say: 'Give us this country; if you do not we will take it,' " Du Pont pointed out, "is not at all persuasive." If Jefferson desired land rather than a guarantee of navigation rights, he should try to buy New Orleans and the Floridas. But he must offer enough money, Du Pont advised, to tempt the First Consul before France took possession and also must renounce the desire for territory west of the Mississippi.[18]

Du Pont had misunderstood him, Jefferson replied. He had not intended to menace France. He also denied any present desire for conquest or the expansion of American territory beyond the Mississippi. Actually, as has been seen, Jefferson believed that the pressure of an increasing westward-moving population had destined all of Louisiana for the United States.

The secretary of state immediately pressed the purchase idea. He ordered Livingston to spare no effort in persuading the Consulate to abandon its imperial design. It could avoid a clash either by leaving Spain in possession of Louisiana or by selling New Orleans and the Floridas to the United States. In case France in fact had not regained Louisiana, he instructed the American minister in Madrid to try to obtain New Orleans and the Floridas from Spain. Events in the Caribbean gave the secretary hope that France might lose her desire for Louisiana. "The prospect of a protracted and expensive war in St. Domingo," he told the president, "must form a very powerful obstacle to the execution of the project." [19]

Americans who followed national and international political developments shared the government's apprehension. Public sentiment, especially as expressed through newspaper articles, indicated that fear of France as a neighbor who would stand as a barrier to expansion was still rising. "We have a right to the possession [of Louisiana]," an expansionist asserted. "The interests of the human race demand from us the exertion of this right." Others advanced the old argument that "the United States will either take possession of New Orleans" or the western territory would separate from the Union. Some, particularly Federalists, urged the president to ask Congress for a declaration of war. The bitterness of the American reaction apparently exceeded French expectations. "It will be difficult," Charles Leclerc said of the Americans in May 1802, "to make them relish the occupation of Louisiana." [20]

Edward Thornton observed that the Jeffersonian leaders were cured of their "bitterness against Britain" and that their "predilection for France scarcely exists even in name." The president "regards the cession of Louisiana and New Orleans as a certain cause of future war" with France.[21]

Biographers and sympathetic historians have played down evidence of Jefferson's repeated truculence. They stress instead his alleged pacifism, saying that the essence of his genius and statesmanship "lay in peace." Despite his menacing words, they insist, he would not have taken his people into war even if the

French had occupied New Orleans. He was willing to make an English alliance and to fight only to protect the nation against French armies. Yet to many contemporaries his belligerence and willingness to go beyond mere defense in the cause of expansionism seemed genuine. The bellicosity of extreme Federalists has made Jeffersonian aggressiveness appear more moderate than it was.

In discussing Louisiana's retrocession with Pichon at this point, Madison, for example, again used threat. He accused the French of trying to split the American nation. This tactic would not work; custom, language, geography, and the West's need for security drew Americans together. So, he concluded, "it should be admitted that France cannot long preserve Louisiana against the United States, and nothing would do more to unite the whole continent than having France in the neighborhood."

Jefferson also again warned Pichon that French policy was "making a union with Great Britain universally popular." If Britain consented to France's possession of Louisiana, he explained, it would be because she thought it would result in a Franco-American war. The *chargé* relayed these various arguments to Paris, urging a conciliatory policy toward the United States to prevent an Anglo-American rapprochement.[22]

In Paris, before Pichon's warnings arrived, Livingston tried to pump Talleyrand for firm information on Louisiana's status. "The Minister will give no answer to any inquiries I make on the subject," he complained. "He will not say what their boundaries are, what are their intentions, and when they are to take possession." Even though news of the retrocession was well known in Europe's capitals and had appeared in newspapers, Talleyrand continued officially to deny it. Opinion in France, Livingston reported, favored the reacquisition of Louisiana.

Early in August 1802 Livingston prepared a lengthy memoir and sent it to leading figures of the Consulate. In it he attempted to prove that France would gain nothing but disappointment by taking possession of Louisiana. The attraction must be strong, he observed, for France to "convert a natural and warm ally into a jealous and suspicious neighbor, and perhaps, in the progress of events, into an open enemy." [23] He asked Talleyrand, who promised to read the memoir, for assurance that France would respect American rights on the Mississippi.

In less than two weeks Livingston's patience gave out. He reported that Bonaparte had decided to occupy Louisiana. "There never was a government in which less could be done by negotiation than here," Livingston exploded. "There is no people, no legislature, no counsellors. One man is everything. He seldom asks advice, and never hears it unasked. His ministers are mere clerks. . . . Though the sense of every reflecting man about him is against this wild expedition, no one dares to tell him so." Yet the American minister retained some optimism about Louisiana. He added prophetically, "I am persuaded that the whole will end in a relinquishment of the country and the transfer of the capital to the United States." [24]

Through independent, on-the-spot observation Pichon corroborated Livingston's warning that France was losing American friendship. The *chargé* explained that Jefferson's administration desired better relations with France, while the Federalist party, seeking to regain power, "sounds the tocsin against our supposed ambition, our tendency to universal empire, and our principles." The effect of France's colonial policy "is to alienate one party from us irrevocably without the slightest chance of winning the one which hopes to profit from it." The Federalists were systematically hostile to France and friendly to England. If they rode back into power, Pichon maintained, they would not hesitate to use the general feeling of danger to push the United States into an alliance with England.[25]

Livingston, feeling ignored by Talleyrand, turned to Joseph Bonaparte later in October. The American suggested that their two countries could easily wipe away their differences. All that France had to do was to return most of Louisiana to Spain, retain New Orleans and the Floridas, and deliver them to the United States in payment for war claims American citizens held against her.

Avoiding a direct answer, Joseph asked if the United States preferred the Floridas to Louisiana. Livingston replied with the official policy of the moment, "that we had no wish to extend our boundary across the Mississippi. . . . all we sought was security and not an extension of territory." [26] Joseph at least raised the possibility that France might cede Louisiana, an idea that under the influence of British gold he would later reject.

Late in the following month, November 1802, when disturbing news from New Orleans reached Washington, American relations with France over Louisiana encountered a new and more pressing crisis. On October 18 Juan Ventura Morales, the acting intendant in Louisiana, had suddenly ended the American right of deposit in New Orleans. Technically the privilege had expired in 1798, but as a war measure Spanish authorities had allowed westerners to continue to leave their goods on wharves or in warehouses in New Orleans for transshipment. Spain had an unquestionable legal right to terminate the deposit at New Orleans, but not, according to the Treaty of San Lorenzo, without shifting it to an "equivalent establishment" elsewhere.

Morales justified his action as merely the recognition of an expired privilege. He maintained that privileges given to Americans as neutrals in time of war need not continue now that England and Spain were at peace. Moreover, Americans were abusing the deposit. In addition to bringing in legal merchandise, they smuggled contraband into the city. Spaniards and Frenchmen considered the entrepôt "a large door, constantly, publicly, inviolably, and inevitably opened in favor of the Anglo-

Americans to a smuggling trade without bounds and privileged in all Louisiana." [27] Morales also claimed that New Orleans was losing money by allowing Americans to use its port without paying duties.

Westerners argued that Spanish duties were so high that they could not afford to pay them. They complained that their flour, bacon, ham, tobacco, and other produce would often rot on barges or at wharves because Spaniards would not handle it. They also claimed that New Orleans profited from the payments that they, as Americans, made for storage on the docks.

For more than a century historians assumed that Morales had acted on his own. What made this interpretation convincing was the fact that the suspension astonished Don Manuel Juan de Salcedo, the senile and indecisive governor of Louisiana, as well as other Spanish officials in North America. Salcedo, like Morales, had no love for Americans, but he seemed incapable of independently initiating rash measures that might provoke them to war.

A document uncovered in Spanish archives for historian Edward Channing shows that Morales acted directly on secret instructions from Carlos IV. The intendant kept the secret well, telling no one, not even Spanish officials who outranked him. Two considerations apparently motivated the order to Morales—American smuggling, especially of gold and silver, and the desire of the Spanish government to embarrass the French.

Contrary to some contemporary opinion, suspension of the deposit did not deny Americans the right of free navigation on the lower Mississippi or kill their export trade. It terminated a convenience. Flatboats could still float the length of the river without interruption and American shippers could transfer their cargoes directly to vessels lying in New Orleans's harbor. Moreover, in January 1803 Morales allowed the importation of flour and provisions from the United States, subject to a duty of 6 percent, as had been the case before the establishment of the deposit.

Since Americans were able to use other channels of trade and could evade the Spanish restrictions, the suspension did not cause much economic harm. Even the depression in the West at this time did not stem from the closure of the deposit but from loss of overseas markets. Americans could and did operate through Spanish nationals residing in New Orleans. Under various guises American ships continued to enter the port in greater numbers than did those of other nationals. But the psychological effect was bad. So agitated were many westerners that they refused to send goods down the river, even when ships were waiting in New Orleans to load them immediately. For a few months, therefore, it seemed that the suspension had brought Spain and the United States to the brink of war. "The act justified war, to which ever government it might be imputed," James Monroe explained, "and many were prepared to risk it by removing the obstruction by force." [28]

The fiercest reaction came from the western country. Governor William C. C. Claiborne of the Mississippi Territory reported "considerable agitation at Natchez and its vicinity." The withdrawal of the deposit, he said, "has inflicted a severe wound on the agricultural and commercial interest of this territory." Legislature after legislature in the western states passed resolutions denouncing the suspension. In the South some maintained that "we would be justified to ourselves and to the world *in taking possession of the port in question and reclaiming, by force of arms, the advantages of which we have been unjustly deprived.*" [29]

By now especially sensitive to western grievances, Madison quickly wrote to Charles Pinckney, the American minister in Madrid, that the termination of the deposit so directly violated the Treaty of San Lorenzo that he could not believe the Spanish government had authorized it. He directed Pinckney to ask the crown to revoke the suspension immediately. To the westerners, the secretary of state explained, the Mississippi was everything. "It is the Hudson, the Delaware, the Potomac, and all the navigable rivers of the Atlantic states formed into one stream." [30]

Although Morales's order affected the West most of all, its repercussions also touched the eastern seaboard, where merchants were more and more profiting from the Louisiana trade. The widespread reaction to the Mississippi crisis reminded the president that in the affair of Louisiana he had a national, not just a sectional, problem on his hands. "Scarcely any Thing has happened since the Revolution . . . . which has so much agitated the minds of all Descriptions of People in the United States," a British observer reported, "as this decree." [31]

What prompted such reactions was the mistaken belief of many Americans that Napoleon, anxious to possess Louisiana without the encumbrance of the deposit, had inspired Morales's action. Even if the order of suspension had come from Madrid, they reasoned, Paris had directed it. So in the public mind retrocession became connected to the fate of the deposit. France, not Spain, became the target of the worst indignation. Federalists stepped up their demands for war—on France, Spain, or both. They talked about avenging national honor, conquering Louisiana, and keeping the Mississippi open to American commerce forever.

The war hawks insisted that Jefferson must act before France moved a large army into Louisiana. "What force from Europe can stand in competition with *our* force," one of them wrote, "exerted on our own ground?" No wise man would think war "too great a price to give for the expulsion of foreigners from this land; for securing, to our posterity, the possession of this continent." These agitators, and many others, too, believed that the French intended to keep New Orleans closed to American commerce. Actually at this time, late in 1802, Napoleon promised to observe American treaty rights in Louisiana. Although skeptical, Livingston promptly forwarded this news to Washington.

American policy makers who were absorbed in the immediate handling of the crisis did not, of course, know of this assurance. But they had before them constantly the threat of disunion being voiced by Federalists, belligerent rivermen, and settlers in the Southwest, many of whom had long been eager to invade New Orleans on their own. The war hawks argued that for Americans "to forbid the transfer, and to prevent its execution, by forcible means, if need be, is indisputably just. . . . Louisiana is ours, even if to make it so, we should be obliged to treat its present inhabitants as vassals." They demanded that the government exclude "from our vitals the most dangerous enemy that ever before threatened us."

Neither the president nor his advisers could ignore this *"war whoop* . . . from the open enemies of the government and administration and its insidious friends." [32] The sections were only loosely attached to one another. If one quarreled with another and civil war erupted, the Union could easily break apart. The cement holding the states together had not yet had time to harden.

The suspension of the deposit placed Jefferson in a dilemma that had sectional, national, and international implications. First of all, he had somehow to keep the western territories from taking secession seriously. Secondly, he had to defuse the Federalist political bomb backing the demand for instant war. Even though he had to placate westerners to prevent them from joining with Federalists to wreck his administration, this problem was not as urgent as it seemed on the surface. Many of the westerners still retained a "peculiar confidence" in Jefferson, believing he would help them. So they were less difficult to restrain than were the Federalists. Thirdly, the president had to work out some kind of an agreement with Spain and France that would calm the political furor, particularly within his own party. If these efforts failed, then he had to face the possibility of immediate war and step up necessary preparations.

The president followed a broad policy, if it can be called that, of threat and procrastination. He also took positive measures. In addition to preparing for hostilities, he tried to get the deposit restored through diplomacy. He himself sought out Spain's representative.

Carlos Martínez de Irujo, the young, aggressive Spanish minister in Washington, was an old friend. He had served in the United States a number of years, had married a daughter of the Republican governor of Pennsylvania, spoke English well, and had developed a fondness for the country. When Jefferson inquired about the deposit, Irujo explained that the Spanish king had not ordered its suspension. Impressed by the gravity of the situation, the minister feared that this crisis could be the excuse for an invasion of Louisiana. So he sent a special packet to New Orleans with the American protest and with his own request to Morales to restore the deposit. Governor Salcedo of Louisiana also urged the restoration, but to no avail.

Irujo's concern was valid. Madison told the British that the United States must obtain absolute sovereignty over some position near the mouth of the Mississippi that would assure it unimpeded navigation. Otherwise westerners would, in time, seize New Orleans. He warned the French that justice "to the Western citizens of the United States is the only tenure of peace with this country. There are now or in less than two years will be not less than 200,000 militia on the waters of the Mississippi, every man of whom would march at a moment's warning to remove obstructions from that outlet to the sea, every man of whom regards the free use of that river as a natural and indefeasible right and is conscious of the physical force that can at any time give effect to it." This reminder of American power, he assumed, should cure the French of their "frenzy which covets Louisiana." [33]

France's recovery of Louisiana and the abrupt withdrawal of the deposit were at first unrelated. Talleyrand did not learn of the suppression until two months after it happened. Neither he nor Napoleon knew why the Spaniards had done it, but they were not upset. They even offered congratulations. "The First Consul . . . orders me to make known to your Court how much he is pleased with the firmness it has shown in this circumstance," Talleyrand told the Spanish ambassador in Paris. Talleyrand also thought that "the difficulty of maintaining it [the suspension], will be less for us than would have been our establishing it." [34]

So when Livingston solicited Talleyrand's help in regaining the deposit, the Frenchman stalled. When the New Yorker asked what Napoleon would do when France took possession, the foreign minister replied that France would consider the problem after she had occupied the city. Then, as they learned more of the emotional American reaction, the French leaders came to realize that the problem could not wait. They were reminded that the men of the West, if not restrained or if they lost confidence in Jefferson, could go berserk and still smash the French dream of empire. The Consulate therefore tried to placate the United States. The depth of American resentment, the threats of war, and the whole issue of the Mississippi gave France a taste of the kind of problem the possession of Louisiana could generate.

Chapter VIII

✤

The President's Dilemma

It belongs of *right* to the United States to regulate the future
destiny of *North America.* The country is *ours;* ours is the right to
its rivers and to all the sources of future opulence, power and
happiness.

New York Evening Post, 1803 [1]

W hen the Seventh Congress began assembling in Wash-
ington early in December 1802, Americans of all kinds realized
that the country faced a foreign crisis of considerable dimension.
This knowledge imparted to the lawmakers a sense of excite-
ment and of destiny. Many of them assumed that the president's
second annual message, as though an expression of God's will,
would chart the course for the nation's expansion, whether by
war or peace.

The message, delivered on December 15, did not live up
to these expectations. Thomas Jefferson dealt with various mat-
ters before alluding to the fate of New Orleans and of all Loui-
siana. Only at the end did he refer to the most important ques-
tion perturbing the nation, the one the legislators most eagerly
wished to have discussed. If France occupied Louisiana, he said,

it would produce "a change in the aspect of our foreign rela-
tions." He implied that war might be necessary but did not
even mention the crisis over the deposit. Those who were cla-
moring for a more decisive policy, even instant war, were most
openly disappointed.

Alexander Hamilton, still a power in his party and impa-
tiently demanding action as did other Federalists, dismissed the
message as a lullaby. "I have always held that the *unity of our
Empire,* and the best interests of our nation, require that we
shall annex to the United States all the territory east of the Mis-
sissippi, New Orleans included," he wrote. "Of course, I infer
that, in an emergency like the present, energy is wisdom." He
considered this an opportune time for an expansionist war.[2]

Within the Congress also, numerous voices called for ac-
tion. To forestall the stronger Federalist demands, John Ran-
dolph, the majority leader in the House of Representatives, a
fellow Virginian and friend of the president, on December 17
introduced a resolution asking for whatever documents the exec-
utive branch had in its possession relating to the removal of the
deposit. The House voted immediately and unanimously for
this resolution. This lopsided vote showed the deep concern of
congressmen of both parties with Jefferson's public policy of re-
straint.

Louis André Pichon shrewdly observed that Jefferson now
faced a new dilemma. If he persisted in his course of apparent
procrastination, he might alienate his staunchest political sup-
porters. If he took vigorous, open measures against the Span-
iards or the French, he might trigger a premature or unneces-
sary war.

The president tried to escape his dilemma by first defend-
ing his position. When he sent the requested papers to the
House, he asserted that he had lost no time in taking every step
required by the situation. As for the suspension of the deposit,
he said that Intendant Juan Ventura Morales had acted on his

own. About a week later Jefferson backed up this interpretation with a letter from the governor of Louisiana. Juan Manuel de Salcedo denied responsibility for the intendant's action, saying that no one in his government had authorized it. Jefferson thus supported his assumption concerning the deposit issue with the best information available to him. In his view it warranted the hope that the Spanish government would heed the protest James Madison had quickly sent to Madrid.

Even though the westerners were as impatient for action as any others, they continued to go along with the president's tactics. Those close to him knew that although he preached restraint, he approved of the westerners' eagerness for empire. He continued to see in Spain no real obstacle. Until the United States became strong enough and ready to snatch Louisiana and the Floridas, Spain was in his judgment filling quite well the role of trustee.

In response to the charge of being a procrastinator, Jefferson explained that he said little publicly on the explosive subject of the Mississippi and the deposit because at the time of his message he had not yet worked out a firm policy for handling the crisis. He counted on Anglo-French antagonisms, on the probability of war breaking out in Europe, and on the fighting in Santo Domingo to allow him time to resolve his dilemma. He guessed correctly that Napoleon would not attempt to occupy Louisiana until he had conquered Santo Domingo. Since Jefferson thought the fighting on the island would continue a long time, he assumed he need not move in haste.

The president nevertheless did take additional measures to meet the clamor for action. He prepared frontier forces for war and intensified efforts to get negotiations in Paris moving, essentially to purchase New Orleans and the Floridas. Confidants privately urged such tactics.

On Christmas Day, for example, Thomas Paine sent Jefferson "a thought on Louisiana." In this Mississippi crisis, Paine said, the question was "What is the best step to be taken first?" Among alternatives, he urged accommodation, not belligerent confrontation. "Suppose then the Government begins by making a proposal to France to re-purchase the cession made to her by Spain of Louisiana" with the consent of the people there? he asked. Thus "by beginning on this ground anything can be said without carrying the appearance of a threat. The growing power of the Western Territory can be stated as a matter of information, and also the impossibility . . . of France to prevent it." Paine maintained that the French would at least listen because their treasury was empty and the government was in debt.[3]

Six days later the president received another letter, this one from Pierre Samuel Du Pont de Nemours, advising delay in any action against Louisiana, especially war. Du Pont suggested once more, as he had months earlier, that the United States should try to buy all the territory France controlled east of the Mississippi. He believed that Napoleon was acquiring the Floridas as well as Louisiana. Du Pont again proposed that in return the United States acquiesce in France's control of all territory west of the river. He named a specific sum, an offer of six million dollars for the eastern lands, and he even included the draft of a treaty designed to resolve the crisis as he suggested.

On the basis of Du Pont's advice, Jefferson and James Madison assumed that the French government would be willing at least to discuss such a proposal. Their hunch was shrewd. Du Pont had talked to high French officials such as Talleyrand and Charles François Lebrun, the third consul. They encouraged him to go ahead with his purchase plan and unofficial diplomacy.

Robert R. Livingston, who had been trying for some time to buy New Orleans and the Floridas, as Jefferson had instructed, meanwhile had gotten nowhere. Earlier in December Livingston had sent a complicated, broad proposal for purchase to Napoleon, but through Joseph Bonaparte rather than through

Talleyrand. As in the past, Livingston asked for West Florida and New Orleans. Now he also expressed a desire for that part of Louisiana lying north of the Arkansas River. He thus became the first American diplomat to suggest officially to the French that the United States was interested in expanding west of the Mississippi.

In this arrangement France would retain East Florida and, Livingston explained, would also have command of the Gulf of Mexico. Otherwise, in time of war Louisiana and the Floridas would fall into England's hands. The English could attack by sea and also by land from Canada and could dominate the West Indies. His own plan, he said, would place a French buffer between the United States and Mexico and an American buffer between Canada and Louisiana. It would assure France of American friendship and would prevent the United States from joining with Britain. It would therefore be good policy for France to cede these territories, but if she would not, the United States would be willing to "purchase them at a price suited to their value, and to their own circumstances." [4]

With the proposal, advanced in a series of notes that reached Napoleon in January 1803, Livingston condemned the closure of the deposit at New Orleans. His protest menaced the French by pointing out that America's rapid growth, unruly ambition, and compulsive expansionism would not permit their tampering with American use of the port. He again raised the threat of an Anglo-American alliance, a possibility that disturbed Napoleon. But at this point the First Consul ignored the offer of purchase.

Earlier in the month Madison had expressed similar threats to Pichon. The French government's refusal to answer queries on the status of American rights on the Mississippi, he said, could be regarded "as a sort of declaration of war." [5] Elsewhere in the United States, too, talk of war continued to seem commonplace. The British *chargé,* Edward Thornton, reported that forcible seizure of New Orleans "would be the most popular step the President could take." [6]

Jefferson and his secretary of war, Henry Dearborn, had been preparing for just such an assault. Dearborn strengthened troop concentrations on the frontier and placed Fort Adams, located on the Mississippi thirty-eight miles south of Natchez and just above the Spanish border, in a state of readiness. There he concentrated seven companies, three of artillery and four of infantry. Governor William C. C. Claiborne of the Mississippi Territory, who commanded the forces in the area, wrote from Natchez that he had two thousand well-organized militia. In his opinion, six hundred of them could take New Orleans, "provided there should be only Spanish troops to defend the place." [7]

The government did not concentrate all military preparations in the Southwest. It deployed some forces to protect the northern frontier. Jeffersonian leaders thought that the British, as well as the French, had designs on the Mississippi Valley. The government also prepared fortifications on the Atlantic coast to repel either a French or a British attack.

Jefferson tailored his land and Indian policies, as well as his military preparations, to advance his expansionist program. In his annual message he had recommended that Congress break up the monopoly of land speculators in territory obtained from the Choctaw Indians and assist whites in settling there. A few weeks later he explained to his secretary of war that "an object, becoming one of great importance, is the establishment of a strong front on our Western boundary" through the rapid purchase of Indian lands along the Mississippi. Federal agents immediately began buying all the lands, at a liberal price, that the Indians would sell. Jefferson sought in particular to acquire a wide strip along the eastern bank of the Mississippi from the Yazoo River on the south to the Illinois River on the north. Into this and other areas on the Louisiana frontier he wished to move a white population. As he put it, "We shall have that country filled rapidly with a hardy yeomanry capable of defending it." [8]

A month later the president expressed fear that the arrival of a French army in Louisiana would stiffen the resistance of Indians to offers for their lands. "Should any tribe be foolhardy enough to take up the hatchet at any time," then he would seize "the whole country of that tribe" and drive it across the Mississippi in "furtherance to our federal consolidation." To William Henry Harrison, governor of the Indiana Territory, he confided that "the crisis is pressing" and directed him to buy what he could at once. "We bend our whole views to the purchase and settlement of the country on the Mississippi, from its mouth to its northern regions. . . . The occupation of New Orleans, hourly expected, by the French, is already felt like a light breeze by the Indians." [9]

Since Federalists were exploiting the Mississippi crisis for political advantage and for expansionist purposes, these measures had internal as well as external significance. Jefferson believed that Federalist leaders were trying to force the country into a premature war that would win over westerners and bring their party back into power. In the House of Representatives the Republican majority blocked the belligerent measures Federalists introduced. As long as Jefferson's party leaders were satisfied that he was doing something, they were willing to allow him time to carry out his Louisiana policy in his way. "Uncandid must be the mind, and depraved the heart," a party journal commented, "that could raise the standard of revolt against a government which has not lost a moment to redress the grievances of which we so justly complain." [10]

Federalists in the House rallied behind a resolution introduced by Roger Griswold of Connecticut on January 4. It called on the president for a report and documents "explaining the stipulations, circumstances, and conditions" relating to the cession of Louisiana. This strategy allowed Federalists to publicize their solicitude over the problems of the West and to portray themselves as defenders of the national interest. Since it had now become obvious that the fate of Louisiana was a national concern, a number of Republicans supported the resolution. It carried on the following day by a vote of thirty-five to thirty-two.[11]

After debates behind closed doors, the House on January 7, 1803, by majorities of two to one, approved several other resolutions on New Orleans. While affirming an "unalterable determination" to maintain American boundaries and rights of navigation on the Mississippi as established by treaties, the House accepted Jefferson's interpretation of the suspended deposit. It also expressed confidence in him and in his policy.

Jefferson then decided to meet Federalist tactics with a grand gesture of his own that made use of Du Pont's latest advice as well as that of other confidants. On January 10 he hurriedly sent a note to James Monroe, a lifelong friend popular in Washington and in the West who had served as minister to France and recently as governor of Virginia, asking him to go to Paris and Madrid as a special emissary. Circumstances were such, the president said, "as to render it impossible" for Monroe to decline, "because the whole public hope will be rested on you." [12] So Jefferson presented the nomination to the Senate on January 11, before he possibly could have received an acceptance from Monroe in Virginia.

On the next day, with Federalist senators in firm opposition, Monroe won confirmation by the scant margin of fifteen to twelve. Some opponents felt that Bonaparte might not receive Monroe well because he had been friendly with deposed French republicans. Acting on the assumption that New Orleans must either be fought for or bought, Congress on the same day implemented the mission by appropriating two million dollars for use in the possible purchase of New Orleans and the Floridas.

By openly expressing its desire to acquire crucial territory and by publicizing the special mission as an alternative to war, the administration deflated many of its critics.

"The agitation of the public mind on the occasion of the late suspension of our right of deposit at N. Orleans is extreme," the president told Monroe. "In the western country it is natural and grounded on honest motives." But people in the seaports and Federalists, he said, were trying to force the nation into war. "The measures we have been pursuing, being invisible, do not satisfy their minds." So "our object of purchasing N. Orleans and the Floridas" made it essential to send to France at once a minister extraordinary "with discretionary powers. . . . All eyes, all hopes, are now fixed on you." [13]

Jefferson felt that Livingston could probably do as much with Napoleon as could Monroe. He also knew that the people of the West considered Monroe, who owned property there, a special friend. Merely by sending him to Europe, Jefferson would placate western constituents and show the people that the president was not taking the crisis lightly. "Their confidence in Monroe will tranquilize them," the president told his son-in-law.[14] Being an astute politician, he realized that diplomacy in a country aspiring to democracy needed popular acquiescence, if not active support.

To maintain a popular backing if negotiations with France should not work out satisfactorily, Jefferson proceeded with preparations for war and with plans for an alliance with England. British leaders encouraged such a rapprochement. Some had an aversion to seeing France again entrenched in North America and were willing to act "in a common Cause" with the United States to keep her out. Jefferson told Edward Thornton "that some day these possessions [New Orleans and the Floridas] would become of indispensable necessity to the United States." [15] On his own the British *chargé* urged Jefferson to send Monroe to England as well as to France.

Monroe, who agreed with the president's Louisiana strategy, accepted the Paris appointment and traveled to Washington for instructions. While preparing those instructions, the president's advisers debated their content. They assumed that France had acquired the Floridas as well as Louisiana and that she wished to avoid war with the United States. So the instructions directed Monroe and Livingston to procure "a cession to the United States of New Orleans and of West and East Florida, or as much thereof as the actual proprietor can be prevailed on to part with." The diplomats could pay up to fifty million *livres* * ($9,375,000) and could fix the boundary between the United States and French possessions. If the French refused to sell, then the envoys were to seek an expanded right of deposit at New Orleans and similar rights at the mouths of other rivers emptying into the Gulf of Mexico.

The envoys had implicit authority to use the threat of forcible expansion. They were reminded that "the Western people believe, as do their Atlantic brethren, that they have a natural and indefeasible right to trade freely through the Mississippi. They are conscious of their power to enforce this right against any nation whatever." [16]

While these instructions were being written, Jefferson went ahead with other preparations for possible expansion. Shortly before Congress had assembled, he had asked Irujo if Spain would object if he sent a scientific expedition to explore the course of the Missouri River and then to proceed to the Pacific coast. The Spanish minister replied that such a venture would offend his government. He viewed the contemplated expedition as an effort by Jefferson "to perpetuate the fame of his administration" by "attempting at least to discover the way by which Americans may some day extend their population and their influence up to the coasts of the South Sea." [17] Jefferson had considered such a project several times in the past. Now his

* The livre and new franc were worth about 18.75 cents.

apprehension over having the French in Louisiana caused him to gloss over the Spanish opposition and to take action.

On January 18, only five days after gaining approval for the Monroe mission, the president sent a special message to Congress requesting support for an exploring expedition into upper Louisiana to establish trade with the Indians there and to gain knowledge of the area and its people. More immediately important than the scientific purposes, in light of the political crisis, were its expansionist objectives—to conduct military reconnaissance, to ascertain whether the Missouri country was suitable for white settlement, and to investigate a route from the Mississippi to the Pacific. He said he wanted "to provide an extension of territory which the rapid increase of our numbers will call for." [18]

After discussing the proposal behind closed doors, Congress authorized the expedition. The president then chose his twenty-nine-year-old private secretary who had served on the western frontier, Captain Meriwether Lewis, to lead it. Lewis selected another army officer who had also seen service in the West, William Clark, the younger brother of George Rogers Clark, to assist him. Critics quickly pointed out that the public purposes masked the real one of empire. One of them said that Jefferson himself admitted that "we might through those agents purchase land of the Indians or think of conquest." [19]

Another of Jefferson's reasons for preparing for possible conquest was his desire to prevent the British from seizing northern Louisiana if they again went to war against France. For execution of this plan he needed information on the Spanish forces in the area and advice on what posts to occupy if necessary. Secretary of the Treasury Albert Gallatin explained this strategy clearly, saying that events may "ere long, render it necessary that we should, by taking immediate possession, prevent G.B. from doing the same." The future of upper Louisiana was of vast importance to the United States, he insisted, "it being perhaps the only large tract of land, and certainly the *first* which lying out of the boundaries of the Union, will be settled by the people of the U. States." [20]

Later, in voicing the expansionist view of the Jeffersonians, Lewis said they had "very sanguine expectations . . . that the whole of that immense country watered by the Mississippi and its tributary streams, Missourie inclusive, will be the property of the U. States" in less than a year. So his expedition had to become acquainted with Indian "tribes that inhabit that country" and to impress them with the "rising importance of the U. States." [21] Thus, while moving to buy New Orleans or more, Jefferson also put into operation his imperial plans for the rest of Louisiana.

Federalists meanwhile had been attacking the administration because it had not shown itself to be sufficiently expansionist. Jefferson's outward reliance on diplomacy rather than on the immediate use of force infuriated the extremists. They wanted to keep popular resentment against France at fever heat so they could win support for an early assault on Louisiana.

"It belongs of *right* to the United States to regulate the future destiny of *North America*," a leading Federalist journal stated. "The country is *ours;* ours is the right to its rivers and to all the sources of future opulence, power and happiness . . . ; we shall be the scorn and derision of the world if we suffer them to be wrested from us by the intrigues of France." [22]

Federalist leaders argued that France was reaching for the entire Mississippi Valley. As proof they pointed to the statement in the second Treaty of San Ildefonso that gave Louisiana to France with the boundaries of 1763. This could mean that the colony extended eastward to the Appalachians. They repeatedly urged a prompt alliance with England and a war of conquest for Louisiana. These sentiments were similar to Jefferson's, only more extreme. He wished through diplomacy to delay a showdown until France and England again became embroiled in war.

Writing under the pseudonym Pericles, Alexander Hamilton said the government had two courses open to it. "First, to negotiate, and endeavor to purchase; and if this fails, to go to war. Secondly, to seize at once on the Floridas and New Orleans, and then negotiate." In contrast to the Jeffersonian leadership, he favored the second alternative.[23]

In line with such reasoning, Federalist expansionists argued "that the acquisition of the Spanish province is, at once, easy, desirable, necessary and just, is the unanimous opinion." They denounced the Monroe mission as a "monster," a futile political sop, and "the weakest measure that ever disgraced the administration of any country." They even exulted in the suspended deposit, saying that "the infraction of the treaty [of San Lorenzo], by affording us an adequate excuse for invading the province . . . was the most auspicious event that could have happened." [24]

Even though Federalists ridiculed the idea "of purchasing the river" as "chimerical," Jefferson's use of a special mission followed Federalist precedent. Both George Washington and John Adams in earlier crises with England and France had employed special peace emissaries before accepting the alternative of war. So the announcement of the Monroe mission soothed moderate Federalists. "This is certainly the best thing that can be done," one of them commented. "It will save us from the expenses, hazards, and evils of a war." Jefferson himself said of his less extreme Federalist opponents, "If we can settle happily the difficulties of the Mississippi, I think we may promise ourselves smooth seas during our time." [25]

Before there could be smooth sailing, the issue of immediate force versus diplomacy had to be resolved in Congress. Federalists fought for their stand that Louisiana's retrocession and the suspended deposit justified an appeal to arms. In an especially fierce speech on February 16 Senator James Ross of Pennsylvania demanded immediate action. The Federalist leadership chose him to attack the administration for weakness because he lived in Pittsburgh and hence could speak as a westerner. Ross introduced resolutions authorizing the president to call out as many as fifty thousand militia from the Mississippi Territory and neighboring states for prompt seizure of New Orleans and for an appropriation of five million dollars to finance this expansion. "Why not seize what is so essential to us as a nation?" he asked. "When in possession, you will negotiate with more advantage." The French might be persuaded to sell "if they found us armed—in possession, and resolved to maintain it." [26]

Madison said the Ross resolutions "drove at war through a delegation of unconstitutional power to the Executive." Other Republicans called them expansionist war measures pure and simple. One remarked, "Presently we shall be told we must have Louisiana; then the gold mines of Mexico—these would be good things, if come by honestly—then Potosi—then St. Domingo, with their sugar, coffee, and all the rest. . . . But what have we to do with the territories of other people? Have we not enough of our own?" [27]

Another Republican counseled patience. "God and nature have destined New Orleans and the Floridas to belong to this great and rising empire. . . . and the world at some future day cannot hold them from us." [28] So why the rush?

After lengthy debate lasting three days, the Senate on February 25 defeated the Ross resolutions, one by one, by a margin of fifteen to eleven. On the same day the Senate pressed a substitute bill introduced by John Breckinridge, a Republican from Kentucky, authorizing the president to call into service eighty thousand militiamen whenever he deemed it expedient. A week later, on March 4, Congress adjourned. The issues of the Mississippi River and Louisiana had consumed most of the ten-week session. Despite the heated rhetoric, Federalists and Republicans seemed to agree on the basic objective of western empire. They differed only on the immediate means of achieving it.

The president made astute use of Federalist bellicosity. He and his advisers let the French and Spaniards know that his government needed concessions to keep extremists from dragging the country into war. The "occlusion of the Mississippi is a state of things in which we cannot exist," he said. Since the westerners "will keep up a state of irritation which cannot long be kept inactive, we should be criminally improvident not to take at once eventual measures for strengthening ourselves for the contest," he warned. "Whatever power, other than ourselves, holds the country east of the Mississippi, becomes our natural enemy." [29]

Pichon, who reported that Louisiana's survival depended upon America's goodwill, noted that the Federalist party was moving heaven and earth for war. He assumed that if France rejected Jefferson's overtures and denied free navigation of the Mississippi, hostilities would follow. One of the toasts at a public dinner for Monroe, whose departure had been delayed by sickness, suggests that Pichon understood the current mood of Americans. It went: "Peace, if peace is honorable; war if war is necessary." [30] Such sentiments fitted Monroe's own attitude as he and his family, on March 8, 1803, sailed from New York.

In Paris Livingston meanwhile had made no real progress. Believing Talleyrand to be personally hostile to the United States, he had written late in February directly to the First Consul about American concerns over Louisiana. Talleyrand rebuked him. "With respect to a negotiation for Louisiana," the American minister then reported, "I think nothing will be effected here." [31] He believed that Napoleon would negotiate only after a new French minister arrived in Washington. After that minister and the prefect of Louisiana had investigated the American claims concerning the deposit and sent their reports to Paris, then the Consulate would make appropriate decisions. Even so, Talleyrand ruled out the question of purchase. Knowing that Monroe was on his way, Livingston deplored the French plan to shift negotiations to Washington. He told the French, who also were aware of the purpose of Monroe's coming, that the shift would merely delay any agreement.

Unknown to Livingston, Du Pont was telling Jefferson that the Consulate would negotiate in Paris. Du Pont said the French government had decided to give the United States every possible consideration in its concern over Louisiana and the deposit. Reports even reached London newspapers that Napoleon now considered the suspension of the deposit a mistake and deplored it.

In Madrid Jefferson's policy of pressure and patience was bringing dividends not discernible in Paris. Pedro de Cevallos, the foreign minister, received Irujo's dispatches telling of the mounting hostility of Americans toward Spain because of the suspended deposit in February and of repeated demands in Federalist gazettes for seizure of Florida and Louisiana. "I am convinced," Irujo wrote, "that if the proclamation of the Intendant is not revoked in three months the clamor of the Federalists, the impulse of public opinion, and party policy will force the President and Republicans to declare War against their wish." [32]

Cevallos and Manuel de Godoy immediately backed away from a possible confrontation with the United States. On February 28, 1803, Godoy promised Charles Pinckney, the American minister in Madrid, that his government would restore the deposit. On March 1 the Spanish crown ordered Morales to make the restoration. It sent the order on a special fast mail ship to reach Irujo in Washington so that he could inform the American government promptly and avert a clash and then forward it to New Orleans. About a week later, as though in confirmation of rumors, Pichon published a letter to Louisiana's governor announcing the Consulate's disapproval of the suspended deposit.

The Spaniards gave in to American pressure mainly because they expected war in Europe soon and wanted no hostilities over a colony they were relinquishing anyway. Distrusting the French, Godoy willingly approved a renewal of the deposit because he did not wish them to derive any benefit from its suspension. Restoration of the deposit before Monroe reached Europe eliminated the most obvious reason for his mission and the most pressing part of the president's dilemma. Psychological factors buried in personal antagonisms between Spanish and French leaders, as well as Jeffersonian policy and the situation in Europe, made possible this victory.

European developments aided Jeffersonian policy in other ways, too. At this time Napoleon's imperial design appeared headed for new trouble. Reports reaching Washington from London stressed British preparations for renewal of war against France. In case of hostilities, Prime Minister Henry Addington told Rufus King, one of Britain's first acts would be to send a fleet up the mouth of the Mississippi to New Orleans.

While Jefferson was willing to use England to threaten France, he still distrusted the British and felt that in command of Louisiana they would be as dangerous as the French. Either France or England would, in his view, use New Orleans to dominate Louisiana and to stifle American expansion.

King conveyed the president's attitude to Addington. "We had no objection to Spain continuing to possess it [Louisiana]," he said; "they were quiet neighbors, and we looked without impatience to events which, in the ordinary course of things, must, at no distant day, annex this country to the United States." [33]

Addington explained that England did not desire Louisiana. If she seized New Orleans, it would be only as a war measure designed to keep France out. He encouraged American conquest, suggesting that the United States could capture the area more readily than could England. "If you can obtain it [Louisiana], well," he said, "but if not, we ought to prevent its going into the hands of France." [34]

Unaware of the actions of either the Spanish or the English government, Jefferson now more seriously than ever considered resort to war. From New Orleans came a report that when General Claude P. Victor occupied Louisiana he would exclude Americans from the deposit and bar their shipping from use of the Mississippi. On April 8 the president asked his cabinet what Monroe should do if France refused to sell. Jefferson suggested an alliance with England. The cabinet voted not to permit England to take Louisiana for herself but also agreed that Monroe and Livingston should "enter into conferences with the British Government" and "fix principles of alliance" with England if they failed in Paris. [35]

The secretary of state instructed Monroe and Livingston on the cabinet's decisions. "Your consultations with Great Britain," he advised, "may be held on the ground that war is inevitable." In case of war, the two countries should consider a joint invasion of Louisiana and pledge themselves to no "peace or truce without the consent of the other." [36]

On April 19, just after the Jeffersonian leadership had made its decision on alliance and war, the order for restoration of the deposit reached Irujo in Washington. He quickly informed Jefferson and forwarded the directive to the intendant at New Orleans. The president also received assurances that Spain's treaty commitments, now reaffirmed, would be binding on the French when they took possession of Louisiana.

Delighted with his triumph, Jefferson claimed that through peaceful diplomacy he had gained in four months what would otherwise have required seven years of war and great cost in blood and money. "To have seized New Orleans as our federal maniacs wished, would only have changed the character & extent of the blockade of our Western commerce," he explained. "It would have produced a blockade by superior naval force of the navigation of the river as well as of the entrance into N. Orleans, instead of a paper blockade from N. Orleans alone while the river remained open." [37]

Republicans and Westerners generally agreed with this kind of assessment. They praised Jefferson's "energetic and virtuous government" for this accomplishment. "People of America!" one of their journals announced, "forever remember that it was the republican administration of the government that preserved peace; and it was their federal opponents who were for hurrying you into war." [38]

Now the only thing that still cast a shadow over the country was the status of the mission in Paris. The president admitted some pessimism on its success, saying he could not "count with confidence on obtaining New Orleans from France for money." But news from Europe even helped dispel some of this concern.

Early in May Jefferson received convincing reports that war would soon break out again in Europe. This being what he had long counted upon to further his expansionist policy, he called the cabinet into session. It decided that when hostilities began the United States would use its strategic position to bargain for New Orleans and the Floridas. "In this conflict," the president said, "our neutrality will be cheaply purchased by a cession . . . because taking part in the war, we could certainly seize and securely hold them and more." [39] Even if the mission in Paris failed, an alliance with Britain would not now be necessary. The Jeffersonians could win Louisiana or part of it with the forces they had been building up.

On May 17 Intendant Morales restored the deposit. On the following day, seven months after he had revoked the privilege, American flatboats began floating down the Mississippi by the dozen. Boatmen and traders poured into New Orleans. Earlier Pierre Clément de Laussat, who had come to New Orleans as prefect to prepare for the French occupation, had complained when he saw fifty-five American ships, compared to only ten Spanish and French vessels, tied up at the wharves. The new American influx now astonished him. "I can scarcely persuade myself that the court of Madrid," he said of the renewed deposit, "has taken such a step with the concurrence of the French government." [40]

The Americans swaggered ashore, it seemed, as though they owned the town. They sang, caroused, acted contemptuously of Spanish customs and regulations, and boasted that soon New Orleans would belong to the United States. If it could be obtained in no other way, they said, then they and their frontier brethren would take it by force. Such threats, though a repetition of what Americans had long been saying, alarmed Laussat and other officials in New Orleans. For them the dilemma of war or peace over Louisiana still seemed pressing.

Chapter IX

❧

Shattered Dream

The conviction at present of the weakness of every ultramarine power to maintain itself in Louisiana against the will of the United States has determined the French cabinet to cede to this power that colony.

Georges Henri Victor Collot, 1826 [1]

N either the Spanish nor the French officials in New Orleans nor the Americans who confronted them there nor the government in Washington realized that events in Europe and in the Caribbean were now moving swiftly to help resolve the larger crisis of Louisiana as well as that of the Mississippi. For Americans these developments would, as population expanded westward, remove the risk of war with the French. For the French leaders the new situation, taken in conjunction with their growing apprehensiveness over American opposition, would shatter their dream of western empire.

Since the destiny of France appeared to rest in the hands of one man, so too did the fate of the dream. For that man, Napoleon Bonaparte, the new developments fitted a pattern of disillusionment that had begun to take form in October 1802 when Carlos IV of Spain had finally ordered the actual transfer of Louisiana to France. At that time the First Consul again tried to persuade Carlos to give up the Floridas as well as Louisiana.

Talleyrand, a more ardent advocate of western empire than even his master, advised against pressing for East Florida, believing that the United States would be particularly hostile to that cession. West Florida, which included the Apalachicola River and the port of Pensacola, he explained, would enhance France's empire without arousing deep American antagonism. Why, he suggested, should France add unnecessarily to American antipathy?

Ignoring this advice, Napoleon offered Carlos additional territory in Italy, namely the duchy of Parma, in exchange for both Floridas. Fernando, who had ruled the duchy, had died, and the French had taken it over. Eager to add this family territory to her son-in-law's kingdom of Etruria, Queen María Luisa urged her husband to consent to the exchange. In this instance the queen did not have her way. Supported by Manuel de Godoy and by the British who had become apprehensive over French objectives in North America, Carlos refused to part with the Floridas at any price. Godoy said that neither England nor the United States would allow France to possess them.

The First Consul, who had written to Carlos about the Floridas, took the refusal as a personal affront. He also viewed it as a critical blow to his plans for western empire. Without the Floridas and their extensive coastlines, France could expect difficulty in trying to defend Louisiana against either England or the United States. So in Napoleon's eyes Louisiana now began losing value as the anchor of his New World empire.

Difficulties in the preparations for the expedition to occupy Louisiana also upset the Premier Consul's imperial plans. After having received assurances in the summer of 1802 that Carlos of Spain would deliver the colony to him according to agreement, Bonaparte ordered the Louisiana expedition to sail from Dunkirk in the first week of October. Carlos's delay in actually transferring Louisiana and in providing him with critical information on the military situation there forced the Premier Consul to depart from this schedule.

Carlos's documents ordering delivery of Louisiana to the French finally arrived in Paris on October 25. Even then the expedition of occupation could not sail. Admiral Denis Decrès, the minister of the navy and colonies in charge of the preparations, had been unable to bring together enough ships to transport the large army to New Orleans. Short of money and equipment, he had been diverting what ships, troops, and supplies he could gather to Santo Domingo to reinforce General Charles Leclerc's army.

The campaign in Santo Domingo had gotten so bogged down in guerrilla fighting that it also upset Napoleon's timing in securing his western empire. It demanded more attention, men, and money than he had anticipated. Then on November 2, 1802, an "irresistible malady," yellow fever, killed Leclerc.

Unaware of his brother-in-law's death, the First Consul now jettisoned the Dunkirk project and concentrated on massing troops, ships, and supplies for the Louisiana expedition in Helvoët Sluys, a small Dutch port about thirty kilometers southeast of Rotterdam. He expected the transports to depart sometime between November 22 and 27. The time proved too short.

Nonetheless, Decrès ordered General Claude Victor to leave Paris and to take command at Helvoët Sluys. "The First Consul had ordered me to warn you that he desires you to depart without delay," the minister said.[2] He also gave Victor secret instructions. Not only was the general to take possession of Louisiana broadly defined; he was also to fortify it against possible American or British attack and to make alliances with Indians east of the Mississippi, in American territory. He was warned to watch closely the reaction of the United States, "whose numerous, warlike, and frugal population may offer an enemy to be feared." Although the French government desired peace, the instructions said, Victor should realize "that if war should come, Louisiana would certainly become the theater of hostilities." Napoleon wanted, Decrès wrote, "to give Louisiana a degree of strength which will permit him to abandon it without fear in time of war, so that its enemies may be forced to the greatest sacrifices merely in attempting an attack on it." [3] Victor was expected to do all this without jeopardizing American friendship.

When the general arrived at Helvoët Sluys, he found the expedition still not prepared to sail. Pierre Clément de Laussat, designated colonial prefect for Louisiana, had been scheduled to sail with the expedition. Napoleon now ordered him to go to New Orleans in advance of Victor to prepare for the arrival of the army of occupation.

Eleven days later Decrès again urged Victor to depart. If the Louisiana expedition did not move promptly, the minister feared "that the ice will surprise the convoy and indefinitely delay its sailing." [4] Victor shared this apprehension of sudden cold weather. Nonetheless, he replied on December 22 that he needed two or three more weeks to bring supplies from Dunkirk and to complete essential repairs on the transports.

During this waiting period Napoleon went ahead with another part of his imperial design. On December 31 he appointed General Jean Baptiste Jules Bernadotte, considered by many to be the second most powerful man in France, to the empty post of minister to the United States. The appointment may have represented nothing more than exile in disguise for the First Consul's rival for power. But Bernadotte, who had earlier in effect turned down the governorship of Louisiana, accepted the diplomatic post, apparently with reluctance. The general, who was to have arrived in Washington at about the time Victor's expedition reached New Orleans, received no authority to adjust France's differences with the United States through negotiation. He was, however, to avoid anything that "might even remotely lead to a rupture." [5] Napoleon wanted to use Bernadotte's considerable prestige and his reputation of friendliness toward the United States to persuade the American government to accept peacefully the imminent French occupation of Louisiana.

A week later, or by January 7, 1803, the Premier Consul received the news of Leclerc's death. He also learned of the heavy losses suffered by Leclerc's army and by the reinforcements he had sent to the Caribbean. Without the Floridas and now perhaps without Santo Domingo, the Corsican's plan of empire lost much of its attractiveness. "Damn sugar, damn coffee, damn colonies," he reportedly muttered in anger several days later in an after-dinner conversation, when reflecting on his setbacks. [6]

Despite these reverses, the French preparations for occupying Louisiana continued. Laussat, his wife, three daughters, and a small staff managed to sail from La Rochelle early in January. His ship made several stops on the way and was held up by winter weather and strong winds. He did not reach New Orleans until March 26. There he found the people concerned over the future, particularly as affected by the debacle on Santo Domingo. Refugees from the island had brought with them horror stories of indiscriminate carnage and white defeat.

These reports spread a sense of foreboding through the city. The blacks of New Orleans, haunted by thoughts of white vengeance against them for what was happening on the island, were terrified by the prospect of the French taking over Louisiana. The Creoles, on the other hand, trembled because they believed that the French occupation would or might set off a slave uprising as bloody as that on Santo Domingo. Despite this ambience of foreboding, Laussat went ahead with preparations for Victor's arrival and for the formal delivery of the colony to

France at that time. The prefect surveyed Louisiana's military needs, stockpiled supplies, and prepared barracks.

Before Bonaparte's troops could use those accommodations, they had to cross either the Atlantic or the Gulf of Mexico from Santo Domingo, where the French offensive against the blacks continued. Napoleon felt he had to subdue the blacks before he could shift troops from the island to Louisiana. After Leclerc's death General Donatien de Rochambeau, the second-in-command and an officer who had served on Santo Domingo, took over the leadership of the French forces there. He immediately asked for thirty-five thousand more troops. Napoleon brooded, but he promised to send fifteen thousand soldiers at once and 'other fifteen thousand later. Meanwhile black resistance and yellow fever took more French lives.

Appraisals of Rochambeau's leadership vary widely. Some say he showed fewer results than had Leclerc. Others describe him as quite successful, maintaining that he steadily defeated the blacks and drove them into the hills. In the United States, according to reports circulated at the time, there were serious doubts about the stability of his regime. Critics said he levied forced loans on American merchants and jailed those who resisted. American ships did continue to supply rebel ports with provisions and even fought off blockading French corsairs. In any case, American relations with Rochambeau were about as bad as they had been with Leclerc.

Across the sea in these months of January and February 1803 severe freezes kept General Victor's expedition, which included troops scheduled for Santo Domingo, icebound in Helvoët Sluys. Apparently ignorant of the weather in Holland, Napoleon in February ordered "the entire Louisiana expedition to sail directly to its destination" without diverting any soldiers to Santo Domingo. [7] Admiral Decrès told Victor that the First Consul wanted him to hasten his departure, indicating that Louisiana still held relatively high priority in French policy.

Two weeks later Talleyrand made this point clear to Livingston. The thought of selling Louisiana, the foreign minister said, was out of the question; it would be beneath the dignity of France.

As spring approached, the ice in the North Sea ports melted. The Louisiana expedition was now free to sail. But nature's delay, in combination with the politics of war, brought another setback to the First Consul's imperial plan.

When Napoleon had been most active in the assembling of the Louisiana expedition, the Peace of Amiens had seemed stable enough to permit him to consolidate his North American empire even in the face of mounting American opposition. That peace now was breaking apart. Inwardly the British had always been suspicious of the Louisiana venture and the Santo Domingo campaign. They had observed the French military buildup in the channel ports with considerable concern. They also became alarmed by a report made by an observant officer, Colonel François Horace Bastien Sébastiani, and published in the French government's paper, *Le Moniteur,* on January 30. It indicated that Napoleon might try to reconquer Egypt. Now the British acted openly suspicious and took precautionary measures.

In a speech from the throne on March 2, 1803, George III of England told Parliament that "very considerable military preparations are carrying on in the ports of France and Holland," and although the alleged objective of the troops there was the French colonies, "he had judged it expedient to adopt additional measures of precaution for the security of his dominions." [8] English leaders anticipated that Bonaparte might use his Louisiana fleet, once war commenced, to mount an invasion of England. British warships therefore hovered off the coasts of France and Holland as if ready to destroy the Victor expedition the moment it reached the open sea.

George III's speech, with its overtones of war, arrived in Paris on March 11. Two days later, on a Sunday at a diplomatic

reception, Napoleon spoke to Lord Whitworth, the British am-
bassador in Paris. "So you are determined to go to war," the
Premier Consul said. He denied that France was preparing for
offensive action. "There is not a single vessel of the line in
France's ports." [9] All the ships capable of service had been sent
to Santo Domingo, he explained; the armament in the harbors
of Holland, as was well known, was destined for Louisiana.

A short time later Rufus King attended a meeting of the
British cabinet. He learned that as a consequence of the British
concern over French troops in Holland and of the British deci-
sion not to evacuate Malta as agreed upon at Amiens, war with
France seemed certain. The English ministers told him that
Britain was willing to seize Louisiana at once and turn it over to
the United States. Without committing himself on this matter,
King responded that his government was trying to purchase
New Orleans.

Napoleon's knowledge of this British determination to
fight quickly influenced his plans for Louisiana. He informed
the British government in the middle of March that as a conse-
quence of its naval menaces he had ordered his ships in the
Dutch harbors, though designated for duty in America, not to
proceed. "The Americans, whose fears never suffered them to
doubt the preferred destination of the armaments in the Dutch
ports," Lord Whitworth commented, "are now delivered from
their apprehension." [10]

Although Napoleon permitted Decrès to continue prepara-
tions for the eventual departure of the Victor expedition and
gave no outward signs of abandoning his western colonial ambi-
tions, sometime in these days of March he apparently decided to
give up Louisiana. Napoleon never directly revealed the timing
for this decision or his reasons for it, and so his precise motives
were a source of conjecture among contemporaries and have
remained so among scholars ever since. In their analyses histo-
rians usually split into two broad categories, those who place

the causes for the decision mainly in Europe and those who see the developments in North America as being more important. Of course, events in Europe and America were not independent of each other, and usually there was some kind of connection between them.

The European interpretation says simply that Napoleon's hatred of England and the imminence of war with her, essentially "European necessities," moved him to decide to offer Louisiana to the United States. This thesis, expressed in a number of ways, also states that sometime after Leclerc's death Napoleon began losing interest in Louisiana and seemed to have decided that his destiny lay in Europe and the Middle East rather than in North America. He became interested in reconquering Egypt. He realized that to do so he needed Malta and to get it he must fight England. Another variation holds that the Premier Consul wished to placate the United States and perhaps regain its goodwill before war broke out, and so he decided to sell.

This latter variation dovetails with the American interpretation, which points out that for two years Pichon, Du Pont, Livingston, and others had been reporting on the unrelenting hostility of Americans to France's possession of Louisiana. Intelligence from the United States warned again and again that Americans would seize Louisiana at the first favorable opportunity and that the public as well as the Jeffersonian leadership agreed on this strategy.

Late in January, for example, James Madison had told Pichon that even if France actually took possession of Louisiana and the Floridas a clash between their two countries could still be prevented. All that France had to do was to cede territory east of the Mississippi to the United States. The Floridas, he said, would be useless to France but would become increasingly important to the United States as cotton growing expanded on the upper reaches of the Mobile and other rivers. "The free navigation of these rivers," Madison explained, "was inseparable from the very existence of the United States."

In passing on this information to Talleyrand and Napoleon, Pichon spoke of a crisis in Franco-American relations. French colonies in North America, he pointed out, could not exist for long at any time without American friendship. Echoing ideas expressed by Jefferson, he wrote that "we are dependent on them [Americans] in time of peace: at their mercy in the first war with England." This dispatch arrived in Paris in March while the Premier Consul was apparently weighing the fate of Louisiana.[11]

James Monroe's mission also stepped up the pressure on the First Consul for a decision. From the end of February Napoleon knew through Pichon's dispatches that the special emissary was coming to Paris to try to obtain at least part of Louisiana. He could wonder if this mission represented the warlike or the peaceful side of American opinion. Monroe himself believed that the mere knowledge of his mission influenced the Corsican's decision because it showed that the American government was determined to do something about New Orleans and not let chance run its course. The First Consul also apparently knew that if Monroe could not obtain satisfaction in Paris he would go on to London and there cement an Anglo-American alliance. Obviously, if Napoleon sold Louisiana to the United States, he would kill the need for such an arrangement.

Monroe and others also believed that the American furor over the deposit question, which took Napoleon and his advisers by surprise, "gave the first and decided impulse to his mind to make the cession." The American threat to regain the deposit by force—which, according to Monroe, the First Consul knew the United States could accomplish—when followed by Jefferson's offer to purchase New Orleans, clinched the decision. If this affair of Louisiana had turned on the relation between France and England only, Monroe added, "we do not think that any proposition of cession to our government, or even the idea of it [would] have occurred." [12]

Some supporters of the American thesis stress the failure in Santo Domingo as being crucial in Napoleon's decision. By the middle of March fifty thousand French soldiers had died on that island. As Bonaparte read dispatches from Rochambeau, he apparently realized that he did not have enough money, men, or ships to conquer, occupy, and hold both Santo Domingo and Louisiana. He could not risk another overseas war against a foe as powerful as the United States in its own backyard, a foe that would probably have British help. Realism dictated that he recognize his failure and cut his losses.

News of the belligerent anti-French moves in Congress that provided for a military buildup if needed, according to a variation of the American interpretation, "put the final touch to a decision which had been taking shape for some time." [13] The First Consul learned about the Ross resolutions from the *Times* of London of April 7, 1803, which had come to Paris on the following day in a diplomatic pouch. Regardless of who possessed Louisiana—Spain or France—the article said, the deliberations in Congress represented the feelings of the American people. "The government and people seem to be aware that a decisive blow must be struck before the arrival of the expedition now awaiting in the ports of Holland." [14]

Shortly after reading this story, Napoleon is said to have summoned one of his ministers, apparently Talleyrand. "I will not keep," he explained, "a possession which will not be safe in our hands, that may perhaps embroil me with the Americans, or may place me in a state of coolness with them. I shall make it serve me, on the contrary, to attach them to me, to get them into differences with the English, and I shall create for them enemies who will one day avenge us, if we do not succeed in avenging ourselves. My resolution is fixed; I will give Louisiana to the United States. But as they have no territory to cede to me in exchange, I shall demand of them a sum of money to pay the expenses of the extraordinary armament I am projecting against Great Britain." [15]

If Napoleon wanted only money, he did not even have to consider selling Louisiana to the United States. Spain would have paid—probably more than the United States would have—to keep it out of American hands. Instead he ignored his promise to return Louisiana to Spain if he should have to get rid of it. Napoleon felt that Godoy's delaying tactics and refusal to part with the Floridas had been crucial in preventing his own plans for occupation from being carried out promptly. Now Spain had to suffer the consequences.

Emotion and pique also probably influenced the First Consul's decision. He detested Godoy and Pedro de Cevallos, the two Spanish ministers he held most responsible for thwarting him. Moreover, he could gain no advantage by returning Louisiana to Spain, who might lose it to the English. He was convinced that the Americans, who were ready to wrench the province from Spain and to block French possession, would never let it pass to England without a fight. Also he may have thought that if the Spaniards reacted violently and quarreled with the Americans over Louisiana both would be weakened and would be unable to join England in fighting France.

If Napoleon had wanted American goodwill as well as some money, he did not have to consider parting wth all of Louisiana to get them. As Jefferson and Madison had made clear, for a while at least they would have been satisfied with New Orleans alone. But in the course of the coming war Napoleon was bound to lose the province to England. If he won the war, that loss would be just a temporary inconvenience. He would regain the colony at the peace table. But if the United States seized it, either alone or as England's ally, its return without another war was unlikely. Such a seizure by Americans seemed probable. "The Spaniards and Americans almost to a man," a typical expression of opinion from New Orleans went, "are wishing with unceasing fervour, that the People of the United States would at this important crisis come down and take possession of this province." [16]

For over a decade Americans had been dominating the economic life of Louisiana and were getting stronger there day by day. So it seemed logical to surrender all of Louisiana to them for a price and some goodwill rather than lose it to them anyway without compensation and after bitter strife. In a sense, the decision to sell to the United States would merely add political legitimacy to economic reality.

As Georges Henri Victor Collot, a man who knew the North American empire and its politics quite well, explained, French leaders finally realized that no overseas power at the time was strong enough "to maintain itself in Louisiana against the will of the United States." [17] So in the final analysis Napoleon recognized the reality of this situation. His dream and that of France, of empire in the New World, was shattered beyond repair. He could not, any more than could the decaying Spanish monarchy, stop the westward tide of American expansion.

Chapter X

❖

Paris

Now the Americans have Just cause, now a favourable opportunity, to take possession of this Country [Louisiana], and then would be the time to open a negotiation for it, with an imperious Nation.

James Smith
New Orleans, 1803 [1]

*I*n Paris Robert R. Livingston, having worked alone for months to promote negotiations over New Orleans's status, felt neglected and unappreciated. He particularly disliked being bypassed, as when the president dealt with the French government through Pierre Samuel Du Pont de Nemours. Even though the Consulate's officials gave Livingston no real encouragement, he had persisted in pushing the idea of France selling Louisiana to the United States. Neither Napoleon nor his advisers responded openly to this suggestion, but obviously they did not ignore it.

Livingston's sense of alienation from the administration in Washington increased when he learned from the secretary of state that James Monroe would join him clothed with extraordinary power. "Mr. Monroe will be the bearer of the instructions under which you are jointly to negotiate," James Madison informed him.[2]

Although Madison assured Livingston that Monroe did not outrank him, Livingston resented the Virginian's coming. The New York patrician considered it an affront to his own competence and an embarrassment in his operations. In the light of his own difficulties in gaining any real hearing, he also wondered how the new emissary could induce the First Consul even to listen to Jefferson's proposal. When Monroe was on his way to France, apparently only one of Napoleon's intimate advisers, Talleyrand, knew that he was thinking of giving up Louisiana, and that minister disliked the idea. So the First Consul kept his intention to himself because he assumed that others, too, would oppose him.

When Monroe arrived at Le Havre on April 8, 1803, Napoleon still had not revealed his plan to others, and Livingston still felt a sense of despair over dealing with the French. On Easter Sunday, April 10, Livingston sent a greeting to Monroe reflecting his lack of hope. "War may do something for us," he wrote; "nothing else would. I have paved the way for you, and if you could add to my means an assurance that we were now in possession of New Orleans, we should do well." [3]

On that same Sunday the First Consul, who learned of Monroe's arrival by semaphore telegraph from Le Havre, decided to reveal more of his thinking on Louisiana by sounding out two of his counselors. After attending Mass, he summoned Marquis François de Barbé-Marbois, his minister of the treasury, and Admiral Denis Decrès to his palace at Saint-Cloud. He related his recent discussion with Talleyrand concerning the colony and asked for their advice. He explained that England would seize Louisiana as soon as war began. "The conquest of Louisiana would be easy, if they only took the trouble to make a descent there. I have not a moment to lose in putting it out of their reach," he said.

"I think of ceding it to the United States," Napoleon went on. "I can scarcely say that I cede it to them, for it is not yet in our possession. If, however, I leave the least time to our enemies, I shall only transmit an empty title to those republicans whose friendship I seek. They only ask of me one town in Louisiana, but I already consider the colony as entirely lost, and it appears to me that in the hands of this growing power, it will be more useful to the policy and even to the commerce of France, than if I should attempt to keep it."

"We should not hesitate," Barbé-Marbois responded in agreement, "to make a sacrifice of that which is about slipping from us. War with England is inevitable; shall we be able with very inferior naval forces to defend Louisiana against that power?" [4]

Decrès, a warm advocate of western empire, disagreed. "We are still at peace with England," he said; "the colony has just been ceded to us, it depends on the first consul to preserve it. It would not be wise in him to abandon it, for fear of a doubtful danger. . . . it would be as well, if not better, that it should be taken from us by force of arms. . . . It does not become you to fear the kings of England." Napoleon terminated the discussion without revealing that he had made a firm decision.

Early the following morning, April 11, the Premier Consul again summoned Barbé-Marbois. "Irresolution and deliberation are no longer in season," he explained. "I renounce Louisiana. It is not only New Orleans that I will cede, it is the whole colony without any reservation. . . . I renounce it with the greatest regret. . . . I direct you to negotiate this affair with the envoys of the United States. Do not even await the arrival of Mr. Monroe: have an interview this very day with Mr. Livingston; but I require a great deal of money for this war, ... I want fifty millions [francs], and for less than that sum I will not treat." [5]

At this juncture, as far as is known, the First Consul confided only in Barbé-Marbois, Decrès, and Talleyrand. He entrusted Barbé-Marbois with the negotiations rather than Talleyrand because the treasury minister favored the cession, knew the American leaders, such as Thomas Jefferson, quite well, and also had a reputation for honesty, which the foreign minister did not possess. Barbé-Marbois had lived in the United States for six years as secretary to the French legation there, had served as an intendant in Santo Domingo, and had married an American woman.

Assuming war imminent and that England intended to capture Louisiana, Napoleon wanted swift secret negotiations so that he could complete the transaction before English forces could strike. Speed and secrecy would also keep Spain off balance and prevent her from interfering with the negotiations.

Later that day Talleyrand invited Livingston to meet with him. Would you wish "to have the whole of Louisiana"? the French minister asked with seeming casualness while in the process of reversing his previously haughty position on this important imperial problem. Even though he desired the entire province and Joseph Bonaparte had already touched on the possibility of its purchase to him, the question apparently startled Livingston. So he responded with the official American line. No, Livingston said, "our wishes extended only to New Orleans and the Floridas."

If France gave up "New Orleans the rest [of Louisiana] would be of little value," Talleyrand countered. He asked what the American government "would give for the whole."

That was a subject "I had not thought of," Livingston answered, as though he spoke the truth and might be believed. "But . . . I supposed [that] we should not object to twenty millions [francs], provided our citizens were paid."

That was "too low an offer," Talleyrand commented. He

suggested that Livingston reflect upon it and tell him more the next day. Livingston closed the conversation by stating that since Monroe would arrive in two days, he would delay further offers until that time.[6] He was, however, elated by the idea of acquiring all of Louisiana. If he could make a deal immediately, even though he had no authority to do so, he alone would reap the glory of acquiring an empire. So on the next day he called on Talleyrand to press the matter further. The foreign minister asked for an offer for Louisiana but otherwise was evasive.

Napoleon meanwhile discussed the sale of Louisiana with his older brother, Joseph, who relayed the information to their younger brother, Lucien. The brothers, whose true motivation is not clear in this episode, decided apparently for reasons of their own to plead with the First Consul not to dispose of the colony. According to the only available account of their reaction, on the next morning they rushed to the Tuileries, the royal palace in Paris. They were ushered into Napoleon's presence as he was taking a bath. In a good humor, he settled back into the tub and they talked.

After a while the General, as the brothers called him, turned to Joseph. "Well, brother, so you have not spoken to Lucien?" "About what?" Joseph asked. "About our plan in regard to Louisiana, you know?" Napoleon answered. "About yours, my dear brother, you mean," Joseph countered. The two brothers argued for a moment; then the First Consul addressed Lucien, saying, "I have decided to sell Louisiana to the Americans."

For a few moments Lucien, who considered France's reacquisition of Louisiana the jewel in his own diplomatic career, hesitated; then indicating agreement with Joseph, he replied, "I flatter myself that the Chambers will not give their consent to it." Napoleon responded that he would do without the approval of these legislative bodies. He said in a loud voice, "Give this affair up as lost, both of you; you, Lucien, on account of the sale in itself; you, Joseph, because I shall get along without the consent of anyone whomsoever, do you understand?"

Infuriated by this disclosure, Joseph shouted that he himself would head the movement to block the sale of Louisiana. Napoleon laughed derisively. Half rising from the tub, he told Joseph there would be no legislative discussion of the sale. "It is my idea. I conceived it, and I shall go through with it, the negotiation, ratification, and execution, by myself," he said. "Do you understand? By me who scoffs at your opposition."[7]

After further exchanges the First Consul rose suddenly and then fell back into his tub with a slash, drenching Joseph. When his rage ended, Joseph permitted his brother's body servant to dry him off. The family quarrel thus ended with Napoleon unmoved in his determination to sell.

Relying on the memoirs of Lucien Bonaparte, the historian Henry Adams believed that a patriotic concern motivated Joseph and Lucien in their opposition to the sale of Louisiana. Other evidence suggests that a desire for personal gain was an equal or stronger motive. Joseph, Talleyrand, and some other high officials were apparently involved in secret negotiations with the British ambassador in Paris to head off war between France and Britain. In return for a large sum of money Napoleon's relatives and advisers were to persuade him to withdraw his demand on the British government to evacuate Malta. The British were ready to bribe for peace but to fight rather than give up the island.

Louisiana was involved in this European political maneuvering because the First Consul implied that he wished to sell the colony because he soon expected hostilities with England. If his brothers and Talleyrand could persuade him to keep Louisiana, he might drop his demand for Malta. Then he most likely would concentrate his energies on consolidating his New World empire and probably would not wish to renew the war in

Europe. They argued that the best way of keeping the British, and the Americans, too, out of Louisiana would be to hold on to it and to the peace.

At about this juncture, on April 12, Monroe arrived in Paris unaware of these and the other developments concerning Louisiana. Livingston, who had just recently communicated Senator James Ross's sentiments to the First Consul, immediately asked Monroe "what had been the fate of Mr. Ross's resolutions." [8] When Livingston learned of their failure, he expressed regret, commenting that only force and the actual occupation of territory could bring success to their mission. He said nothing about Talleyrand's overtures of the previous evening or of the conversation with him earlier that day.

On the following morning a "confidential friend" called and informed Monroe of Napoleon's discussions on Sunday concerning Louisiana. That evening, after the two American diplomats discussed the latest developments in the Louisiana situation, Livingston gave a small dinner party to honor Monroe's arrival. During the meal Barbé-Marbois called. After a brief conversation while coffee was being served, the French minister asked the American host to visit him at his home that night at any time before eleven o'clock. Monroe wanted to go along, but Livingston put him off. He used the excuse that Monroe had yet to be presented to the foreign office and hence had no official status as a negotiator.

Later at his home Barbé-Marbois, who spoke English well, revealed to Livingston that the First Consul had decided to sell Louisiana to the United States and had entrusted the negotiations to him. Barbé-Marbois asked for an offer "as to the purchase of Louisiana." Although instructed to request fifty million francs, he said Napoleon wanted one hundred million and liquidation of the claims against France by Americans who had suffered property losses through illegal seizures at sea. Livingston expressed astonishment at the amount. The Frenchman agreed that it was exorbitant but added that the United States could borrow the money. Diplomatic sparring followed.

Livingston reiterated interest only in New Orleans and the Floridas but said "we would be ready to purchase provided the sum was reduced to reasonable limits." Barbé-Marbois finally suggested a price of sixty million francs as well as the American government's assumption of the claims in exchange for Louisiana. The New Yorker responded that he could make no decision except in conjunction with Monroe. Inwardly Livingston knew that his country was being offered a bargain and he was elated with the progress of negotiation. He believed that his earlier offers to purchase territory east of the Mississippi, which had seemingly fallen on barren ground, had at last come to fruition. He returned home after midnight and immediately wrote an account of the conversation for Madison. "We shall do all we can to cheapen the purchase," he explained, "but my present sentiment is that we shall buy." [9]

The formality of presenting Monroe to Talleyrand occupied the negotiators on April 14, but on the following day their maneuvering began in earnest. So eager were the Americans to consummate the deal that "they were unwilling to lose a day." [10] Livingston and Monroe opened the bargaining with an offer of forty million francs. Pretending indifference, Barbé-Marbois said that such a small tender displeased Napoleon. A day later he reported that the First Consul had cooled considerably toward the idea of ceding Louisiana. Nevertheless, that evening at the home of the third consul, Charles François Lebrun, who was himself actively interested in the problem of Louisiana and with whom Livingston was dining, the minister of the treasury again brought up the subject of the offer. The American raised his bid to fifty million francs, "the greatest length to which the United States would go."

This offer placed the negotiations on firm ground. Seeing success within reach, Livingston apparently forgot his former despair, but not his resentment against Monroe. This hostility came through to Monroe soon after he had arrived in Paris. He told Madison privately that Livingston regretted "my arrival, since it took from him the credit of having brought everything to a proper conclusion without my aid." [11] To friends Livingston complained openly. "I had prepared everything," he wrote, "first by creating a personal interest, next by showing the inutility of Louisiana to France. . . . I had advanced so far as to have been upon the point of concluding when the appointment of Mr. Monroe stopped my operations." [12]

Despite their jealousies, the two Americans did not waver in their cooperation to acquire an empire with the most extensive boundaries possible. What they knew of the actual content of the secret second treaty of San Ildefonso was substantial, but their information still represented guesswork. So Livingston and Monroe tried to obtain a definition of Louisiana's boundaries. Failing in that, they assumed that Louisiana included at least West Florida. It did not.

When England possessed the Florida territory, she had divided it at the Apalachicola River into two provinces, East and West Florida. Spain reacquired both provinces twenty years after obtaining Louisiana. Although she ruled them as well as Louisiana, she did not incorporate them into Louisiana. Moreover, as has been seen, Bonaparte could not persuade Spain to part with the Floridas. So in the negotiations with Livingston and Monroe, Barbé-Marbois did not specifically include West Florida because it did not belong to France. To facilitate the sale and to embarrass Spain, he purposely clothed the matter of Louisiana's boundaries in a fog.

This attitude came up clearly in discussion over a treaty draft Barbé-Marbois submitted to the American envoys. Assuming they would have no real objections to it, he informed Talleyrand on April 21 that the Louisiana project was now "on the right track." On the following day Livingston and Monroe told

Barbé-Marbois that his draft was too indefinite. Monroe argued for wording that sanctioned France's claim to West Florida, "which without it we should not have." Barbé-Marbois advised against such a precise statement, warning the Americans that "the mere name of Florida" would produce difficulties with Spain.

Monroe and Livingston yielded reluctantly on this issue but insisted on vague language that would somehow permit the United States to assert a claim to West Florida as part of Louisiana. The draft therefore mentioned no precise boundaries. It said that Spain had retroceded to France and that France now transferred to the United States "the Colony or Province of Louisiana, with the Same extent that it now has in the hands of Spain, & that it had when France possessed it; and Such as it Should be after the Treaties subsequently entered into between Spain and other States." [13]

When the French had owned Louisiana, in theory it had stretched eastward to the Appalachians. Since they had not been able to force such an extensive territorial claim, Louisiana as France had previously possessed it defied definition. So the confusing phraseology in the treaty led nationalistic historians to maintain that the United States came to claim West Florida almost unconsciously as a fortuitous by-product of the wording in the treaty. Actually the American negotiators represented well the expansionist desires of the Jeffersonian administration. The American claim to West Florida was no accident or afterthought. Monroe and Livingston had the Floridas on their minds throughout the negotiations. Both sides agreed that the sale did not include the Floridas. Apparently anticipating future expansion, the American diplomats then asked Napoleon to support "our claim to the Floridas with Spain." He promised to do so but would not insert the pledge into the treaty draft. Later, when the Americans again raised the question, Barbé-

Marbois insisted that the United States "had nothing to fear from Spain" and said that France would use "her good offices with Spain in support of . . . [the United States] negotiation for the Floridas." [14]

On April 27 the three negotiators met at Monroe's lodgings to debate treaty drafts, one of them drawn up by Napoleon himself. Livingston did most of the bargaining. Suffering from a back injury, Monroe remained on a couch throughout this conference. Three more days of haggling followed, most of it over price. Then the Americans, who still felt most strongly that "we must not lose time," accepted Barbé-Marbois's revised terms. They initialed the treaty of cession and two conventions attached to it on April 30. Everyone was in a hurry because they all wanted to complete the whole arrangement before war broke out or before England or Spain intervened.

The three agreements, all of them drawn in haste, formed one transaction and were interdependent. In the treaty the United States agreed to a price of sixty million francs ($11,250,000) for Louisiana. Since the Americans did not have the necessary cash, they arranged to pay in bonds carrying an interest rate of 6 percent and not redeemable for fifteen years. The American government also assumed the claims of its citizens against France up to twenty million francs ($3,750,000), thus making the total price fifteen million dollars. Other terms stated that for twelve years French and Spanish ships and merchandise would not pay higher duties in Louisiana's ports than did American commerce. The people of Louisiana were to be incorporated within the United States and to be given the rights of citizenship as soon as possible under the Constitution. Meanwhile they were to be secure in their personal privileges.

One of the conventions provided for the payment of the sixty million francs and the other for settlement of the claims. The claims convention was so carelessly drawn that it later led to considerable difficulties. "I considered the [claims] convention as a trifle compared with the other great object," Livingston later explained.[15]

If Napoleon had followed the letter of France's new constitution, he would have submitted the treaties to his legislature. Instead he approved the agreements on May 1 entirely on his own. That evening, after an official reception at the Louvre, he dined with Livingston and Monroe. He said little about legalities or about the whole transaction, except that he wanted it settled quickly. He desired the money, but now he was also eager to complete the restoration of good feelings between France and the United States that he had begun less than three years earlier with the Treaty of Môrtefontaine. The Louisiana treaty, in this sense, complemented the earlier agreement.

Talleyrand, whose true thoughts were seldom revealed to anyone, at this point at least explained the Consulate's attitude toward the United States quite simply. "We can only base a durable peace on the cession of this colony," he said.[16] This attitude, if sincere, marked a considerable change from his earlier thinking that the Louisiana empire as a barrier to American expansionism was worth the price of American antagonism.

Two of the agreements were signed on May 2, 1803, after they had been translated from the original French into English, and the third was signed a week later. French banks would not buy or market the American bonds. In order to obtain his money quickly, Napoleon through his treasury minister made arrangements with two banking firms, Baring Brothers and Company of London and Hope and Company of Amsterdam, the largest handlers of American securities in Europe, to convert the bonds he would receive into cash. Since the Corsican offered these foreign bankers an opportunity to turn a handsome profit, about three million dollars, they were delighted to be of service.

Even though the British government had an expedition ready to sail for Louisiana when war with France would begin, it did not interfere with the purchase arrangements. At this point England had no designs on Louisiana, except to keep France out. The English government not only accepted the transfer to American ownership but also assisted in its consummation. The British treasury granted Alexander Baring, one of the bankers, permission to transfer specie from London to Paris.

The American negotiators, who had also been active in the heady events of revolution and independence, were proud of their work and boasted of peaceful expansion harmful to no one. "We have lived long, but this is the noblest work of our whole lives," Livingston said. "The treaty which we have just signed has not been obtained by art or dictated by force; equally advantageous to the two contracting parties, it will change vast solitudes into flourishing districts. From this day the United States take their place among the powers of first rank." He also claimed that he himself had always desired Louisiana and had believed "that the possession of New Orleans alone would not render us secure." [17]

French *Idéologues,* a group of republican thinkers who disapproved of western empire and had worked to induce the Consulate, especially Talleyrand, to agree to the American acquisition of Louisiana, praised the transaction as wise and also, for Americans, as a splendid example of peaceful expansion. Du Pont, who worked with the *Idéologues* and shared their views, congratulated Jefferson on the wisdom of avoiding war and obtaining "without shedding blood a territory ten times as important in surface and fertility as the one you desired." [18]

Napoleon, too, supposedly commented on the nature of the American expansion. "This accession of territory," he said, "strengthens for ever the power of the United States; and I have just given to England a maritime rival, that will sooner or later humble her pride." [19] As though he had the ability to foresee the future, he persisted in thinking that he could use Louisiana to make life difficult for the British.

According to traditional interpretations Napoleon, rather than the Americans, deliberately kept Louisiana's frontiers undefined in order to embroil Britain in border conflicts with the United States. When Livingston and Monroe again brought up the question of boundaries, the conventional story goes, the French were purposely evasive. Talleyrand said he did not know what the boundaries were. So Livingston asked, do you mean "we shall construe it [the treaty] in our own way?" "I can give you no direction," Talleyrand answered; "you have made a noble bargain for yourselves, and I suppose you will make the most of it." Similarly, the First Consul, according to Barbé-Marbois, had said "that if an obscurity did not already exist, it would perhaps be good policy to put one there." [20]

Another thesis claims that Napoleon desired vague boundaries so that the United States and Spain would clash in trying to define them. Only he would hold the key to the proper interpretation. In this way both countries would need to seek French support for their claims. He could side with one country or the other, depending on the requirements of his foreign policy, or he could remain neutral and allow the two to work out their own solution.

Regardless of Napoleon's true motivation, the matter of Louisiana's boundaries did not occupy his close attention for long. On May 18, slightly more than two weeks after the sale of Louisiana, England shattered the Peace of Amiens by declaring war on France because of Napoleon's refusal to pull his troops out of Holland. Hostilities began five days later, on the very day that the Premier Consul ratified the treaty ceding Louisiana. He did not wait for the American ratification because he did not want "to leave any ground for considering the colony as still French." [21]

This prompt renewal of Anglo-French hostilities simplified the problems facing the Jeffersonians in their taking possession of Louisiana. Only one serious obstacle now remained, a trou-

bled and enfeebled Spain. Theoretically the Spanish troops hold-
ing the province could fight until Madrid rushed in reinforce-
ments. Thus Spain could make the transfer to American
sovereignty a bloody affair.

Spain realized, however, that if she resisted she had to do
so on her own. She had no ally who could help her. Neither
France, who had sold her out, nor England, who distrusted her,
was available. So fortune and timing not only helped make pos-
sible the quick realization of America's imperial design but also
made the task of taking possession of the mid-continent empire
seem easier than it might have been if the Peace of Amiens had
lasted longer.

Chapter XI

✦

The Constitutional Sanction

I knew as well then [1787] as I do now, that all North America must at length be annexed to us—happy, indeed, if the lust for dominion stop there.

Gouverneur Morris, 1803 [1]

Even though they were optimistic expansionists who expected to make the most of every opportunity for national aggrandizement, neither Thomas Jefferson nor his advisers were prepared for the news they received from Paris in June 1803. Nor were they surprised. Robert Livingston and James Monroe reported that Napoleon had offered the United States the entire province of Louisiana and to obtain this empire they had only to agree on price.

"The dawn of your negotiations," James Madison replied, "has given much pleasure and much expectation." The diplomatists had not been empowered to purchase Louisiana "because it was not deemed at this time within the frame of probability," but they were instructed to continue "your negotiations on the enlarged scale." They were to assure the French that despite their lack of powers, the United States would confirm the agreement. As for the Floridas, the secretary of state continued, the president felt "that it will be best to take time for deciding this question. The Floridas can easily be acquired, especially in case of a war, and perhaps by arrangements involving little or no money." [2]

On July 3 the president learned from Rufus King, who had recently arrived in New York from London, that the envoys in Paris had consummated the bargain. The *Boston Independent Chronicle* first broke the news of Louisiana's acquisition to the public on June 30. Five days later the announcement reached Washington, where the *National Intelligencer* printed it. A few days after that this journal discussed the purchase according to a theme that would become standard in the nation's history. "We have secured our rights by pacific means," it said; "truth and reason have been more powerful than the sword." [3]

The envoys explained their departure from instructions as the proper reaction to an unprecedented opportunity, a justification the president readily accepted. They described the result as a diplomatic triumph that would bring enduring benefit to the nation. Most Americans who were to express themselves on the subject also saw the acquisition in that way and approved of it regardless of how it was done. Some of the Federalists who had been clamoring for a war of conquest against French Louisiana now abruptly changed their tune to one of harsh criticism of the purchase.

"The cession of Louisiana is an excellent thing for France. It is like selling us a Ship after she is surrounded by a British fleet," George Cabot, a pillar of New England Federalism, commented. "It puts into safekeeping what she could not keep herself." A Boston paper called Louisiana "a great waste, a wilderness unpeopled with any beings except wolves and wandering Indians. . . . We are to give money of which we have too little for land of which we already have too much," it said. [4] Others tried to create the impression that the administration was about to impose an intolerable burden on the people. They claimed it was risking national bankruptcy to buy a desert. In 1803 fifteen million dollars seemed enormous. Critics pointed out that it equaled 433 tons of pure silver and that in the form of silver dollars piled in a column this sum would extend upward a distance of three miles.

While Alexander Hamilton favored acquisition of the new empire, his attitude represented the dilemma of many Federalist expansionists who could not express approval without criticizing either the negotiation or the conditions. "Every man possessed of the least candour and reflection will readily acknowledge that the acquisition has been solely owing to a fortuitous concurrence of unforeseen and unexpected circumstances," Hamilton announced, "and not to any wise or vigorous measures on the part of the American government." It resulted from "the kind interpositions of an over-ruling Providence." [5]

Administration defenders promptly rejected such criticism and took delight in denouncing Federalist inconsistencies. Before the purchase, one Republican pointed out, Federalist leaders had demanded immediate acquisition, but now that the negotiation had succeeded, "from a Paradise *Louisiana* has degenerated to a desert." [6] Federalist opposition, however, was limited in scope, and even in its area of greatest strength, New England, it waned quickly. Elsewhere many Federalists hailed the news of the purchase with delight.

On July 14 the official documents, comprising the treaty of cession, the two conventions, and the First Consul's ratifications, arrived by courier in Washington. In order to speed up formalities and to get its money quickly, the French government had decided to exchange ratifications in Washington rather than in Paris.

If the frigate assigned to transport him to the United States had not been delayed by the performance of other duties,

Jean Baptiste Jules Bernadotte would have handled the exchange for Napoleon. Because of a delay, General Bernadotte was still in France awaiting transportation when the Louisiana agreements were signed. As he waited, he became convinced that the rumors of a renewal of war with England had the ring of truth. He decided therefore that he could do more important work in France than in Washington and that he should not sail for America.

As a result, France still had no minister in Washington when the Louisiana treaties arrived. So the Consulate entrusted the negotiations over the exchange of ratifications to its *chargé d'affaires* in Washington, Louis André Pichon. He received authority to transmit the orders to Pierre Clément de Laussat to take possession of Louisiana from Spain and then deliver it to the United States.

Newspapers quickly published more of the available details on the Louisiana transaction. The additional information confirmed that virtually overnight the United States had acquired an empire "the size of four or five European kingdoms" and had doubled its territory. In some places, such as Natchez, the news produced demonstrations of delighted approval. Elsewhere in the West, leading politicians such as Andrew Jackson congratulated the president on the purchase, saying this was "the golden moment . . . when all the Western Hemisphere rejoices at the Joyfull news of the cession of Louisiana, an event which places the peace and happiness of our country on a lasting basis." Madison was delighted with the "universal approbation," saying that the uses to which Louisiana "may be turned, render it a truly noble acquisition." [7]

Jefferson, too, was pleased. He considered the purchase a victory for his policy of mixing caution, threat, and military preparedness and a confirmation of the nation's territorial destiny that would ensure "the tranquility, security and prosperity of all the Western country." He made this view known to his

French friends. "Your government has wisely removed what certainly endangered collision between us," he told one of them. "I now see nothing which need ever interrupt the friendship between France and this country." [8]

On July 16 the president placed the agreements before his cabinet. He indicated that Congress should have all the information possible about Louisiana. "They will be obliged to ask from the people an amendment to the Constitution," he explained, "authorizing their receiving the province into the Union, and providing for its government, and the limitations of power which shall be given by that amendment." [9]

The department heads responded coldly to this idea of an amendment; they tried to dissuade the president from pursuing it. Then, since the Louisiana treaty called for the exchange of ratifications within six months of signing, or by October 30, and Congress was not scheduled to convene until November, they voted for a special session beginning October 17. The purpose of the session was to gain Senate approval for the treaties and House authorization for payment of the purchase. This decision also gave the Jeffersonians the remainder of the summer to find out more than was presently known about the actual status of Louisiana, time to deal with the political opposition, and time for their leader to resolve his own doubts concerning the constitutional issue.

Despite his constitutional concerns, on July 17, three days after the treaties had arrived from France, the president took steps for occupying the new empire. He ordered William C. C. Claiborne, governor of the adjoining Mississippi Territory, to make preparations for taking over Louisiana as soon as possible after the exchange of ratifications and to hold it until Congress decided what to do with it. At the same time Jefferson began reading everything he could find that could tell him something more than he already knew about Louisiana. To friends and others who might be able to supply sound information he sent

181

lists of questions covering such topics as the geography, population, economic conditions, military position, and laws of the province.

All along, the legality of the acquisition kept nagging the president. He had long believed that the Constitution offered no obstacle to the enlargement of the Union with new territory. This belief fitted his attitude that American expansion was inevitable, but it also clashed with his principles as a strict constitutional constructionist. As such, he had to assume logically that since the Constitution did not specifically grant the government authority to obtain new land, it prohibited the acquisition of territory regardless of size.

More than six months earlier, or just before nominating Monroe for the Paris mission, Jefferson had anticipated expansion, essentially the acquisition of New Orleans, and had asked Congress for an appropriation to support it. He had also turned to his closest advisers for their views on the constitutional sanction. Out of these cabinet discussions came the theoretical justification for expansion across the continent and beyond.

Attorney General Levi Lincoln suggested an "indirect mode," that is, a bypassing of the Constitution, to sanction expansion through the purchase of territory. He advised an agreement with the French that would make any acquisition appear as though it could be added to an existing territory or state merely by an adjustment of boundaries. This approach, he thought, would conform to the spirit of strict construction and calm expected Federalist alarm over the enlargement of "executive power." [10]

When the president showed this proposal to Albert Gallatin, the secretary of the treasury, this adviser attacked it as too limited. Gallatin then prepared a memorandum of his own wherein he constructed the constitutional doctrine for building a democratic empire. "The existence of the United States as a nation presupposes the power enjoyed by every nation of extending their territory by treaties," he said, "and the general power given to the President and Senate of making treaties designates the organs through which the acquisition may be made." [11] According to this doctrine, the nation had an inherent right to expand. When it did so by treaty, those who held the treaty-making power could provide the constitutional sanction.

"You are right, in my opinion, as to Mr. L's proposition," the president told Gallatin five days later. But he also hedged his approval of the secretary's doctrine. "I think it will be safer," he added, "not to permit the enlargement of the Union but by amendment of the Constitution." [12] Jefferson then left the issue of constitutional expansion unresolved until his envoys consummated the Louisiana treaties. He never questioned the idea of accepting the whole province, whatever its boundaries, but the great size of the cession magnified the constitutional issue for all involved in it.

For this reason in July and August 1803 the president again seemingly retreated from the Gallatin position. He stressed the need for a constitutional amendment to legalize the acquisition and prepared a draft of one. "Our confederation is certainly confined to the limits established by the revolution," he said. "The general government has no powers but such as the constitution has given it; and it has not given it a power of holding foreign territory, and still less of incorporating it into the Union." At the same time he insisted that "we must ratify & pay our money . . . for a thing beyond the constitution" and hope for the nation's approval of "an act done for its great good." [13]

Three days later Jefferson expressed similar thoughts to another friend. "The Executive, in seizing the fugitive occurrence which so much advances the good of their country," he said, "have done an act beyond the Constitution." But he also wrote that Congress in "casting behind them metaphysical subtleties" on constitutional theory must accept the Louisiana treaties and do for the people what "they would have done for themselves had they been in a situation to do it." [14]

According to Dumas Malone, Jefferson's most scholarly biographer, the president never questioned the wisdom of expansion and was willing without much regret to yield his doubts on constitutionality. He seemed to consider the affair of Louisiana at this point a national emergency that justified stretching the Constitution beyond its original shape. He assumed that Congress would approve the purchase and that then both friends and foes would have to recognize it as a *fait accompli.*

News soon arrived from Paris indicating that regardless of legal scruples there would not be time for thorough exploration of the constitutional issue. On August 17 the president received a letter from Livingston saying that the First Consul now regretted his own ratification of the Louisiana agreements and threatened to cancel them if the American government did not ratify within the time prescribed. Livingston urged the government to act quickly, "without altering a syllable of the terms. . . . Be persuaded that France is sick of the bargain, that Spain is much dissatisfied, and that the slightest pretense will lose you the treaty." [15]

Alarmed by this possibility, Jefferson revised his tactics so as not to permit the French even a pretext for backing out of the agreements. Necessity demanded "that we execute it with punctuality and without delay," he said of the Louisiana treaty. "It will be well to say as little as possible on the constitutional difficulty, and that Congress should act on it without talking." [16]

The president nonetheless clung to his idea that the best way of solidifying the new empire would be through a constitutional amendment. So in view of the French doubts he thought he would ratify first and later seek an amendment. He put aside one draft of an amendment, worked on another, and asked his advisers for comment. They insisted that an amendment was unnecessary and warned that if he suggested that the treaty ex-

ceeded constitutional authority, the Senate would reject it. Such
a declaration would also permit opponents to charge that he
knew he was violating the Constitution.

Thomas Paine, for example, said that the framers of the
Constitution probably did not think much about "the acquisi-
tion of new territory, and even if they did it was prudent to say
nothing about it, as it might have suggested to foreign nations
the idea that we contemplated foreign conquest. . . . The ces-
sion makes no alteration in the Constitution," he advised; "it
only extends the principles of it over a larger territory, and this
certainly is within the morality of the Constitution." Since the
time of the Revolutionary War, "the idea of extending the terri-
tory of the United States was always contemplated." [17]

Jefferson decided finally that legalistic concerns should not
stand in the way of practical achievement. He dropped his idea
of adding an amendment to the Constitution to legalize the
acquisition. Acquiescing "with satisfaction" to the views of his
friends, he maintained that the "good sense of our country"
would correct the evils of broad constitutional construction
"when it shall produce evil effects." The nation's best interests
demanded the extension of the empire for liberty, he main-
tained. "The world will here see such an extent of country
under a free and moderate government as it has never yet
seen." [18] He also assumed that the people approved of such ex-
pansionism and that therefore Louisiana's acquisition would
strengthen his party and administration.

Even though the American people were at the moment
entangled in their first national debate over expansion, this was
a shrewd observation. They argued not over the right of acquir-
ing territory, which most of them took for granted, but over
the means of doing so. Most justified the acquisition of Loui-
siana and the spread of dominion over allegedly "inferior" peo-
ples, such as Indians and Spaniards, as morally right.

In the face of such popular support Federalist opposition to the administration's Louisiana policy appeared strong mainly in its rhetoric. Federalist leaders were aware of their weak position. One of them lamented, for instance, that "such is the force of prejudice and popular delusion that the measure cannot yet be even brought to the bar of argument." [19]

Accepting the anti-Louisiana rhetoric as representing the Federalist party's stance, scholars usually depict Federalists as political opportunists who quickly cast aside their commitment to broad constitutional construction just to embarrass the Jeffersonians. By reversing their positions on constitutional interpretation, Federalists and Republicans both appear to have placed the practicalities of politics ahead of consistency in principles. Actually Federalist opponents of the purchase, however vocal, comprised a minority, mainly from New England, within their own party. Most Federalists appear to have remained faithful to their party's earlier expansionist credo. Like most other Americans, they wanted Louisiana.

Some outspoken Federalist critics were undoubtedly genuine antiexpansionists and even advanced arguments that were to be echoed later in the century by a new breed of antiimperialists. Such opponents denounced the president's assumption of broad powers to justify the acquisition and apparently saw no inconsistency in their stand. A few Federalists deplored the haste of embarking on an unknown, momentous imperial course. As one of them commented, with Louisiana "we rush like a comet into infinite space." [20] Aside from individual commitments to conscience and principle, the most important cause for New England Federalist opposition lay in the view that the acquisition favored the agricultural interests of the frontier regions over the commercial welfare of the eastern states and that it would solidify western support for the Republican party.

Some opponents of Louisiana spread rumors, which the Jeffersonians denied, that England would prevent the cession. When Napoleon heard those reports, he immediately suspected

Anglo-American collusion. As a result, he insisted on a reservation to the Louisiana agreements wherein he threatened to declare France's approval void if he did not receive the funds for payment precisely within the time set by treaty.

When the Eighth Congress convened on October 17, therefore, Jefferson measured the words of his third annual message, devoted mostly to foreign affairs, to fit the realities of both national and international politics. He praised the purchase of Louisiana but said nothing about its constitutionality. Taking approval for granted, he submitted the treaty of cession, the two conventions, and related official correspondence to the Senate. After that body acted, he would ask Congress to enact measures "for the immediate occupation and temporary government of the country" and for its ultimate "incorporation into our Union." [21]

In this first legislative test of expansion Republicans dominated both houses of Congress and imperialists held the trumps. Only nine senators were Federalists. Despite their rhetoric, they could organize no effective opposition. After only two days' debate and without allowing time for careful examination of the documents, the president's "friends" rammed the treaties through the Senate by a vote of twenty-four to seven. No one raised doubts about the constitutionality of such expansion. "The Senate," one frustrated Federalist commented, "have taken less time to deliberate on this important treaty, than they allowed themselves on the most trivial Indian contract." [22]

In this manner the Senate cooperated eagerly with the president in setting the legal precedent for expansion. Both the executive and legislative branches assumed that the Constitution, as Gallatin had suggested, sanctioned through implied powers an inherent right in the government to acquire additional territories or peoples. This doctrine strengthened federal power, especially that of the executive. Without meeting significant opposition, it also made way for another important theory—that in time of "national necessity" the president or the Congress could ignore or perhaps violate the Constitution in order to protect the national interest.

On the following day Madison and Pichon discussed the Premier Consul's reservation. The secretary of state said that if France did not deliver Louisiana as stipulated the United States would also be free to nullify the treaties. This counter reservation carried with it the threat that if for any reason, such as Spanish resistance, France delayed delivery, Americans could move into the province on their own and withhold payment. It was designed mainly to force the French to omit their own reservation.

Actions by the American negotiators in Paris that again exceeded their instructions made possible such an omission without further threat or bitter repercussion. Earlier, as a guarantee of American good faith, the envoys had given the French an advance of two million dollars on the purchase price of Louisiana. This down payment, obtained from the banking houses handling the financial aspects of the transaction, placated the Premier Consul and made it unlikely that he would at the last minute reject the treaties because of his own reservation. Alexander Baring, the British banker who crossed the Atlantic to ensure that no slipup would endanger the delivery of Louisiana and his firm's money, handed this information to Madison late in September.

Given this knowledge and the threatening American counter reservation, Pichon in his discussions with Madison on his own dropped the First Consul's reservation and consented to a simple exchange of ratifications. Any uncertainty or unusual delay, such as Spain's opposition, he explained in justifying his act, would otherwise have endangered the transaction and the payment to France.

Immediately after the exchange of ratifications on October 20 the president proclaimed the Louisiana treaty the law of the land. An admirer from Tennessee repeated a common Republican theme and expressed a gratitude to the president that many probably felt. "You have secured to us the free navigation of the Mississippi. You have procured an immense and fertile country: and all these great blessings are obtained without war and bloodshed." [23] This gave an accurate enough appraisal of the Jeffersonian accomplishment, but Louisiana's acquisition did more. It transformed the character of the Union. Few outside New England, however, doubted that the change would bring great benefits to the nation. This attitude quickly found expression in the first congressional debates over the status of the new empire and the laws for governing it.

On October 21 Jefferson sent a special message on Louisiana to both houses of Congress announcing the exchange of ratifications and asking for laws to carry out provisions in the treaty and conventions. Even though American leaders had been dreaming of a trans-Mississippi empire since the time of independence, now, with no precedent within the national experience to guide them, they had to grapple with the consequences of expansion. So even though the debates on the legislation necessary for occupying and governing Louisiana were brief, they are noteworthy.

In the House of Representatives on the next day the Republican leader, John Randolph, submitted a resolution for carrying the treaties into effect. Two days later Gaylord Griswold, a Federalist from New York, called upon the president for a copy of the second Treaty of San Ildefonso, the deed of cession of Louisiana from Spain to France, and other documents pertaining to the purchase. Federalists argued that Napoleon had concocted a fraudulent sale to squeeze money out of the United States and so they wished to ascertain for themselves if he had a legal title to Louisiana. It would be foolish, they said, to pay fifteen million dollars for a clouded property. Since the president could not produce a clear title, administration supporters

denounced the request "as useless, dangerous, & an encroach-
ment on the prerogatives of the Executive." They barely suc-
ceeded in voting down the resolution, fifty-nine to fifty-seven.
This tactic permitted critics to argue with truth that the French
had "given away that which belonged to their neighbor." [24]

Griswold next questioned the power of the president to in-
corporate territory and people into the Union as provided in the
third article of the Louisiana treaty. In general, even adminis-
tration opponents such as Griswold and John Quincy Adams in
the Senate supported expansion. They conceded that the govern-
ment could acquire territory by purchase or conquest, but only
to hold as a colony. They argued that neither the president nor
Congress had clear authority to incorporate new territory into
the Union without the consent of the states or without an
amendment to the Constitution. In the Senate Timothy Picker-
ing stated the extreme Federalist view. He argued that the gov-
ernment could acquire territory by conquest or purchase but
could not bring it into the Union without "the assent of each
individual state." A few New Englanders mumbled threats of
secession if their objections were ignored.

Republicans maintained that the nation, represented by
the president, had not only the power to acquire territory but
also the authority to stipulate terms necessary for the acquisi-
tion, such as admission of states into the Union. Considerable
majorities in both houses of Congress supported the administra-
tion's case. They authorized the president to take possession of
Louisiana with whatever forces were necessary and to govern it
immediately, though temporarily, as he deemed proper. This
legislation, passed into law at the end of October, empowered
him to use as many as eighty thousand men to occupy the prov-
ince and appropriated one and a half million dollars to pay for
mobilizing army, navy, and militia units.

During the congressional debates over the constitutionality
of expansion and incorporation, some critics argued, as had the
French philosopher Montesquieu, that a republic should remain

small or it would destroy itself. So someone asked Gouverneur
Morris, who had been prominent in the writing of the Constitu-
tion, what the intentions of the framers had been on these is-
sues. He was unable to recollect if they had or had not desired
to limit the size of the nation in order to preserve republican
government. He had himself opposed such a restriction and in-
stead favored a constitution that sanctioned expansion, he said,
because "I knew as well then as I do now, that all North
America must at length be annexed to us—happy, indeed, if
the lust for dominion stop there." [25]

When the House and Senate considered legislation calling
for the appropriation of funds to pay for the Louisiana bonds,
the arguments in both houses were similar and, like the earlier
debates, touched on the nature of American government as an
instrument for expansion. New England Federalists feared
most that incorporation of Louisiana would alter the original
balance between the states by permitting the South and West to
dominate the Union.

John Breckinridge of Kentucky, speaking in the Senate,
summarized the administration position and the usual argu-
ments as well as anyone. He ridiculed die-hard Federalists for
their inconsistencies and defended the power to expand as an in-
defeasible right inherent in the government. "To acquire an em-
pire . . . from the most powerful and warlike nation on earth,
without the oppressing of a single individual, without in'the
least embarrassing the ordinary operations of your finances, and
all this through the peaceful forms of negotiation," he said, was
an unparalleled achievement.

Breckinridge also attacked as an "old hackneyed doctrine"
the idea that a republic in order to survive had to be small. "I
believe, on the contrary, that the more extensive its domin-
ions," the senator said, "the more safe and durable it will
be." [26] Few in Congress would question this Jeffersonian doc-
trine that a republic should of necessity be large, expansive, and
imperialistic. The legislation implementing the purchase passed

through both houses of Congress by large majorities early in November. "It seems," an uncompromising Federalist commented, "the powers that be concern themselves little about the Constitution. The *fact* that the treaty is carried into effect is enough for them." [27]

During the course of these congressional debates, late in October 1803 Pichon tried to speed up the transfer of Louisiana in order to solidify American good will and to get the purchase money to Napoleon as soon as possible. The *chargé* still thought that Spanish threats to resist an American occupation might be serious enough to jeopardize delivery of the money, particularly since by treaty the United States did not have to make payment until three months after it took possession of Louisiana. Under France's contract with the firms of Baring and Hope the bankers were to receive one-third of the Louisiana bonds directly from the American government. Contrary to Pichon's anxieties, neither Spain's threats nor protests cast sufficient doubt on the French title to cause either the Americans or the bankers to delay payment. Americans were still so eager to wrap up the transaction that they did not take advantage of the three-month period before beginning payment. Right after Congress passed the legislation creating the Louisiana bonds, Madison told Pichon that the American government would deliver them to the bankers as soon as France placed New Orleans in American hands.

All along, the pace of the Louisiana diplomacy had been swift, and so the Jeffersonians saw no reason for slackening now, especially since their impressive constitutional victory had enhanced their self-confidence. They had harnessed into a kind of troika the traditions of Anglo-American expansion, the popular lust for empire, and constitutional principles. Now that the representatives of the people had clearly established that the Constitution in fact sanctioned expansion, all that stood in the way of consummating this affair of Louisiana was a weak and friendless Spain.

1. Aaron Burr, by John Vanderlyn. *Courtesy of The New-York Historical Society, New York City*

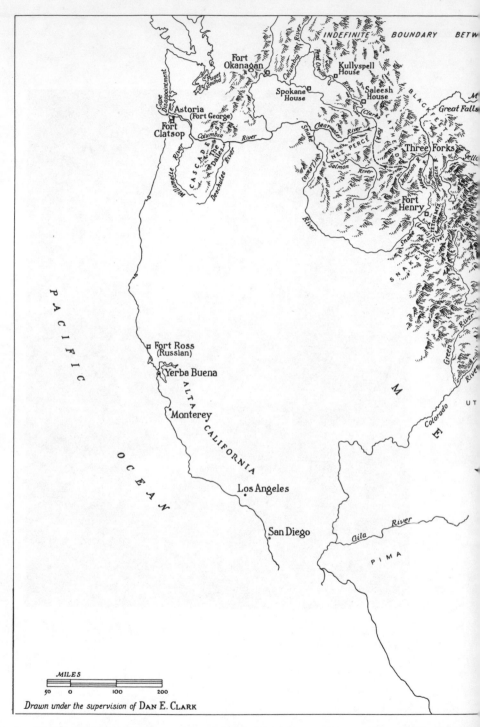

2. The Louisiana Purchase. *From James T. Adams,* Atlas of American History *Copyright 1943 by Charles Scribner's Sons. Reprinted with permission.*

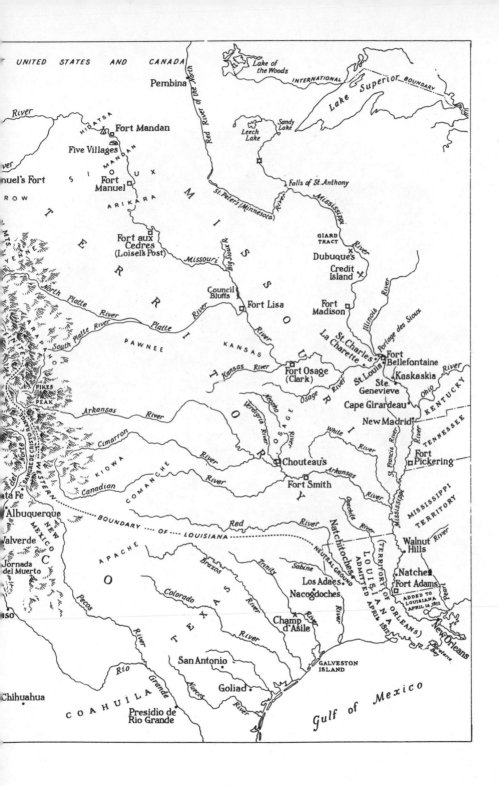

UNITED STATES AND CANADA

Pembina

Lake of the Woods

Lake Superior

INTERNATIONAL BOUNDARY

River

HIDATSA

Fort Mandan

Five Villages

nuel's Fort

Fort Manuel

SIOUX

MANDAN

ARIKARA

CROW

Leech Lake

Sandy Lake

St. Peters (Minnesota)

Falls of St. Anthony

Mississippi

T E R R I T O R Y

GIARD TRACT

Dubuque's

Credit Island

CHEYENNE

Fort aux Cedres (Loisel's Post)

Missouri

Big Sioux R.

Council Bluffs

Fort Lisa

Fort Madison

Illinois River

St. Charles

La Charette

Portage des Sioux

Fort Bellefontaine

River

North Platte River

South Platte River

ARAPAHO

PLATTE

PIKES PEAK

PAWNEE

Platte

KANSAS

River

River

St. Louis

Kaskaskia

St. Charles

Fort Osage (Clark)

Ste. Genevieve

KENTUCKY

Osage River

Missouri

Kansas River

Cape Girardeau

New Madrid

TENNESSEE

Ohio River

S A N G R E   D E   C R I S T O

Arkansas

River

Cimarron

KIOWA

River

Neosho River

Verdigris River

O S A G E

White River

St. Francis River

Fort Pickering

Santa Fe

WESTERN

Canadian

COMANCHE

River

Chouteau's

Arkansas

Fort Smith

T E R R I T O R Y

MISSISSIPPI

River

Ouachita River

TERRITORY

Albuquerque

NEW MEXICO

BOUNDARY ---- OF ---- LOUISIANA

Red

River

Natchitoches

Walnut Hills

River

Valverde

C

APACHE

O

NEUTRAL GROUND

LOUISIANA (TERRITORY OF ORLEANS)

ADMITTED APRIL 30, 1812

Jornada del Muerto

Brazos

Trinity

Sabine

Los Adaes

Nacogdoches

Natchez

Fort Adams

RIO Grande

Pecos

Colorado

River

T E X A S

River

Champ d'Asile

River

ADDED TO LOUISIANA APRIL 14, 1812

aso

Rio

del Norte

Rio

San Antonio

River

New Orleans

Grande

Nueces

Goliad

GALVESTON ISLAND

Chihuahua

C O A H U I L A

Presidio de Rio Grande

River

Gulf of Mexico

3. William C. C. Claiborne. *Library of Congress*

4. Prince Charles-Maurice de Talleyrand. *Picture Collection, The New York Public Library*

5. Thomas Jefferson, by Rembrandt Peale. *White House Collection*

6. Emperor Napoleon, by Ingres. *Bulloz-Art Reference Bureau*

7. James Monroe, by Gilbert Stuart. *The Metropolitan Museum of Art, Bequest of Seth Low, 1929*

8. Robert R. Livingston, by John Vanderlyn. *Courtesy of The New-York Historical Society, New York City*

9.   A View of New Orleans taken from the Plantation of Marigny. Aquatint
engraving by Bouqueta de Woiseri, 1803. *Historic New Orleans Collection*

10. The Transfer of Louisiana to the United States. From the painting by T. de Thulstrup. *Louisiana Historical Society*

Chapter XII

✦

Ineffectual Protest

The government of Spain has protested against the right of
France to transfer [Louisiana]; and it is possible she may refuse
possession, and that this may bring on acts of force.

Thomas Jefferson, 1803 [1]

Despite Jeffersonian optimism, for a while the debate
over Louisiana's future had about it a cloistered, academic qual-
ity, mainly because Spain appeared determined to block the ces-
sion. For Spanish North America the transfer loomed as a disas-
ter. It would bring aggressive and difficult neighbors to the
doorstep of Texas and within striking distance of Mexico. So
Spanish protests began while James Monroe was still on his way
to Paris and before Napoleon had even alluded to selling the
whole of Louisiana.

Early in April 1803 Carlos Martínez de Irujo carefully
explained his government's attitude on the possible sale of New
Orleans to James Madison. France had no right to give up any
part of Louisiana, the Spanish minister pointed out, because it
still belonged to Spain. Neither Carlos IV nor Napoleon had

carried out the terms of their contract on the cession to France. Even if French ownership became valid, Irujo insisted, the agreement on retrocession forbade Napoleon to hand over even a portion of the colony to any other country.

Thomas Jefferson did not ignore this or later protests, but neither did he permit them to deflect him from his expansionist policy. Yet the Spaniards spoke the truth. Napoleon knew it and Jefferson knew it. This knowledge did not stop their cooperation in despoiling Spain's New World empire, but it did prevent the American government from assuming the role of an innocent purchaser.

Manuel de Godoy and Pedro de Cevallos heard of the larger negotiation indirectly and only after the deed was done. The Spanish ambassador in Paris informed them on May 19 that France "has just sold Louisiana to the Americans, and the treaty has been signed and sent to America for ratification." [2] If Godoy could have persuaded the king and queen to go along, he would have turned Spain against France and brought her into the war on England's side.

Cevallos denounced the sale as illegal because French troops still occupied Etruria and Napoleon therefore did not have clear title. He also labeled it a betrayal of France's promise not to cede Louisiana to a third power and a personal affront to Carlos IV. The foreign minister argued that the cession endangered Spain's entire empire. To keep the Americans out of Louisiana, he said, Spain would have paid Napoleon's price for it and would also have settled France's debts to the United States. He asked the French government to revoke the Louisiana treaties.

Godoy assumed that the cession would stimulate further American expansion at the expense of Spain, the very danger his government had sought to avoid by turning over Louisiana to France. "If for the simple denial of the right of having warehouses at New Orleans," he said, the American government had voted to mobilize troops and threatened war, even when France supported Spain, what danger would Spain encounter later "when the door to Mexico will be open to our natural enemies [Americans] and we shall have only our own unaided forces to oppose them with?" [3]

In responding to the protests, Talleyrand said that Spain's own policy toward the United States had been an important factor in forcing the sale. He claimed that Carlos's government itself had violated its agreement on Louisiana by arbitrarily terminating the deposit at New Orleans (an action the French minister had applauded only four months earlier). He said it provoked the United States into threatening war against France when she faced a renewal of hostilities with England. Then, again without consulting France, the Spanish government did what it had later promised not to do—it suddenly restored the deposit privilege. Whereas this concession had previously been temporary, it now became definite, Talleyrand argued, and thereby reduced all of Louisiana's value to France. The restoration of the deposit ensured that New Orleans would be a source of continuing friction between France and the United States. The renewal of the privilege also effectively prevented the French government from moving the deposit to some other port to stop its abuse. Spain's thoughtless policy, he insisted, left France with no alternative; she had to give up Louisiana.

Given Talleyrand's previous commitment to western empire, his initial opposition to the sale of Louisiana, and his acceptance of a bribe to influence Napoleon's foreign policy, it is difficult to know if these views represented his own feelings, the position of the Consulate, or merely a rationalization to counter the Spanish protests. If Talleyrand's words reflected the Consulate's attitude, then the American threats over the deposit and Spain's capitulation had been crucial in the First Consul's decision to retreat from Louisiana. They also reinforce the theory, held by Monroe and others, that the pressure of American expansionism, more than the politics of Europe, had forced his hand.

Even so, if Spain had been more than a shadow of her former self, Napoleon would not have been able to act so peremptorily. A strong, determined Spain could have wrecked the cession to the United States. Even a relatively weak Spain could refuse to evacuate Louisiana and bring together an army of some ten thousand militia and thirty-five hundred regular troops scattered through her colonies in the vicinity to block or make costly any American efforts to take possession. She could also hold back on treaty obligations requiring her to pay a heavy annual subsidy to France and in her participation in the war against England.

These possibilities did not bother Napoleon much. He considered Spain a client state that could do no more than protest or argue for violated rights. Now that he had agreed to part with Louisiana, any quarrel between Spain and the United States did not directly concern him. Yet he could not truly remain aloof. He wanted the American money promptly, and he knew that if Spain provoked the Americans they would seize Louisiana with or without his assistance and they might not pay him. So the First Consul tried to conciliate the Spaniards while sticking to his position on the transfer so that they would soften their protests. He also took measures to overcome whatever objections the Creoles might have.

The Creoles and others who lived in Louisiana, essentially those people whose lives were most directly affected by the sale, were among the last to hear of it. Rumors of the American purchase reached New Orleans in late spring 1803. They startled Pierre Clément de Laussat, who had received no official word from Paris for months but who nonetheless continued his preparations for the French occupation. At first he labeled reports of the sale an "incredible and impudent falsehood," seeing them as part of the Jeffersonians' electioneering tactics designed to keep them in power. He became more concerned when Westerners spoke openly of Louisiana as "this Anglo-American land" and said of the rumored cession, *"If it is not true, it must become so."* [4]

Late in July news arrived in New Orleans that the French troops of occupation were not coming. On August 18 a ship from Bordeaux brought Laussat a letter from Napoleon that struck "like thunder out of a clear sky," officially notifying him of Louisiana's cession. The First Consul, who had for a while considered advancing Laussat to the governorship of the province, now designated him France's commissioner empowered to receive Louisiana from the Spaniards and then to deliver it to the Americans.

Reaction in New Orleans to the news of Louisiana's sale was mixed. "The Anglo-Americans," Laussat wrote, were "extravagant in their joy," while the Spaniards were happy to escape French domination. "The French, that is to say nine-tenths of the population, are stupefied and disconsolate; they speak only of selling out and fleeing far from this country." [5] He attributed the cession to the persistence and power of American westward expansion, to American skill in exploiting the deposit crisis, and to the ability of Americans to dominate Louisiana's economic life.

The politics of the cession apparently caused no deep concern among the ordinary people of Louisiana. Although most of them, especially in the populace of New Orleans, were now reasonably satisfied with Spanish administration and hostile to the idea of American ownership, they had no desire to resist. Distasteful though the change might be, they wanted a peaceful transfer. Some even anticipated that the connection to the United States would bring greater commercial prosperity and enhance their well-being.

Regardless of the various reactions to the transfer and Laussat's own views on the causes for the fate of Louisiana, Madrid's policy for a time seemed to dim his chances of carrying out his new instructions or merely of taking possession of the colony. Moreover, as soon as Spain's representatives in America learned of the sale, a number of them assumed that war would follow and prepared for it as best they could. Irujo, for instance, asked officials in New Orleans to stand fast in defense of Louisiana. Thinking that the United States intended to occupy the Floridas as well, he also sent warnings to the governors of those provinces. Instructions went to officials in Havana to prepare a naval squadron to blockade the mouths of the Potomac, the Delaware, and the Mississippi rivers and various American ports.

In West Florida Governor Vicente Folch y Juan took measures to strengthen the military deployment on his frontier. Along the Texas frontier the Spaniards sent more troops to Nacogdoches, a new fort on the Sabine River already manned by fifteen hundred men, and positioned soldiers in other strategic locations. Irujo also urged his superiors to expend thousands of dollars for weapons to be distributed among the discontented tribes the Jeffersonians were driving across the Mississippi; he hoped these Indians would fight back and help check the westward thrust of Americans. He advised the use of troops from Chihuahua and Sante Fe to intercept Lewis and Clark and also to block the advance of Daniel Boone and other American settlers into central Missouri.

Such tactics became part of a fourfold plan that Spanish officialdom in North America followed in preparing defenses on the borderlands. The officials forbade all foreigners to cross Spanish frontiers; they garrisoned Texas and tried to colonize it; they sent out agents to gain control of the Indians; and they tried to intercept American exploring expeditions.

Stories of these preparations and other rumors persuaded some Americans that Spain would rather fight than see Louisiana fall into their hands. This impression stimulated talk of war and triggered a crisis. Henry Clay of Kentucky felt that the war fever had reached a temperature so high that the "government will find it necessary to restrain the public ardor." In August 1803 Andrew Jackson, then in command of the Kentucky militia, ordered his troops "to be in complete order and at a moment's warning ready to march." [6]

Taking into consideration continuing Spanish protests as well as the military threats, some American leaders interpreted the views of the colonial administrators as reflecting policy emanating from Madrid. Irujo's tactics at first lent credence to this assessment. In September and October he notified the American government that Spain regarded the sale of Louisiana as void. He repeated Cevallos's arguments that Napoleon had no legal right to alienate the colony without Spain's consent and that the United States was trafficking in stolen property. Also when Pichon asked him to certify documents needed by Laussat in the formal delivery of Louisiana to France, Irujo refused.

Irujo did not expect these objections to have any effect on the cession. He lodged his protests merely to carry out instructions. Personally, he wished somehow to obtain American goodwill and to reconcile his own government to the loss of Louisiana. "I do not look upon the alienation of Louisiana as a loss to Spain," he reported in one instance. "That colony cost us heavily and produced very little for us." [7]

Irujo's private assessment was sound. His rhetoric and his government's protests in general did not easily sway Jeffersonian policy makers. Without the support of another great power, the secretary of state told the president, Spain, regardless of her objections, posed no obstacle to the possession of Louisiana. Madison interpreted the protests as fitting a diplomatic strategy whereby Spain hoped to obtain a price, such as a narrow definition of boundaries, for consenting to a peaceful cession.

Albert Gallatin, too, saw no real reason for alarm in Spain's attitude, but he thought "it wise to be as perfectly prepared as if it had a real ground." The government should lose no time in building a supply of arms at Natchez and in instructing Claiborne "to prepare the way with the inhabitants [of Louisiana] so as to meet no opposition from them." [8]

Although willing on his own to resort to force, Jefferson asked his cabinet officers on October 4, "Will it be advisable for forcible possession of Louisiana to be taken if [ownership is] refused?" They answered unanimously, "It will." [9] All agreed that he should step up military preparations immediately so that troops would be ready to move when Congress authorized such action, which it did within a month's time.

Madison meanwhile refuted the protests Irujo had passed on to him. Referring to the contention that France's title to Louisiana was invalid, the secretary of state said that the orders signed by the king of Spain for delivery of the colony to France "are an answer which admits of no reply." The American government, he added, would proceed with arrangements to take possession. In this exchange of notes Irujo characterized Madison's replies as elusive, destitute of logic, and lacking good faith. Nonetheless, Irujo realized that Spain's position, regardless of its legality and justness, would not deter Jeffersonian expansionism. He saw that "the acquisition of a so vast province flatters the national vanity greatly and is so powerful an instrument in the hands of the dominant party" that the Jeffersonians would go ahead with it even if it brought "evil" to the country. [10]

On November 5, 1803, two days after Congress had passed the legislation enabling payment for and occupation of Louisiana and the president had signed the law, Jefferson, Madison, and Pichon all moved swiftly to carry out the actual transfer of territory. They knew on the basis of reports from the American consul, Daniel Clark, Jr., and others within New Orleans that the Spanish officials there recognized their weakness and would not oppose the American occupation unless directly and firmly commanded to do so. The Jeffersonian policy makers, however, were bothered by the thought of just such a contingency or by the possibility that Carlos IV might merely revoke the orders he had given for delivery of Louisiana to France.

Pichon immediately sent Laussat the documents necessary for the transfer of Louisiana to the United States. That same evening in Washington Madison entrusted a post rider with presidential papers for the change of ownership, including commissions for William C. C. Claiborne and General James Wilkinson, now the ranking officer in the army in direct command of the southern frontier, to receive delivery of the province. The secretary of war instructed these commissioners to gather boats and provisions for the occupying forces and advised them on the tactics to use in taking Louisiana if they encountered resistance.

Jefferson and his advisers still viewed the situation as delicate, especially if the Louisiana administrators received last-minute orders to resist and obtained reinforcements from Havana. So the president ordered regular troops from Fort Adams and from various river ports in the Mississippi Territory, who numbered about a thousand, and six thousand volunteers from Kentucky, Tennessee, and Ohio to mobilize for movement southward. He wanted to assemble an army large enough to overwhelm quickly any possible Spanish resistance, if such should materialize. He also asked Daniel Clark, Jr. to raise an "insurrectionary force" of Creoles to cooperate with the American troops if military action were needed. Jefferson tried to convey the impression to the Spaniards and to his fellow Americans, too, that the French desired such a buildup and large-scale military occupation.

Despite a common knowledge of Spanish weakness, newspapers carried stories of possible hostilities. One important Federalist journal described the situation as dangerous. If war should ensue, it said, the fault would be Spain's and "the blood would be on the hands of those who have resorted to arms to enforce injustice." [11]

While still haunted by thoughts of unhampered American expansionism, Spanish policy makers recognized that they could do little to shake the determination of the Jeffersonians to take possession of Louisiana. Manuel de Godoy thought not only that resistance was useless but also that it would deepen Spain's humiliation and bring more loss. Even token self-defense would trigger war with the United States and produce an unnecessary rupture with France.

Some Spanish leaders, nonetheless, were so concerned over the defenses of Mexico that they were willing to take a considerable risk to keep Americans east of the Mississippi. They thought the gamble might succeed if they offered the Jeffersonians uncontested title to the Floridas and New Orleans in exchange for a guarantee to Spain of the rest of Louisiana. Knowing that earlier guarantee proposals had failed, Godoy disagreed. He preferred a policy of concentrating on the defense of the Floridas and Texas, areas accessible to Spanish sea power, and of acquiescence to American possession of Louisiana.

James Madison explained the Spanish dilemma succinctly. "What is it that Spain dreads?" he wrote to Charles Pinckney, the American minister in Madrid. "She dreads, it is presumed, the growing power of this country, and the direction of it against her possessions within its reach. Can she annihilate this power? No. Can she sensibly retard its growth? No." So "common prudence" suggested that she yield to the inevitable! [12]

As though in recognition of inevitability, Spanish policy before the end of October took another turn. The government in Madrid decided to stop protesting, as Madison thought it should, and to go ahead with the delivery of Louisiana to France for transfer to the United States. Jefferson's threat to use force, conveyed by Pinckney, as well as French pressure, also influenced Spain to abandon her strategically weak but legally strong position on the Louisiana cession.

American policy also played a part in a last-minute gamble by the French to cling to power on Santo Domingo. In August General Donatien de Rochambeau had asked the American government for a loan of one hundred thousand dollars to save the island for France, but the Jeffersonians refused him. In November he signed an armistice with the rebels and then surrendered his army to the British navy. All that remained in the liquidation of France's imperial design was delivery of Louisiana to the United States.

While aware of the ebbing of French and Spanish power in North America, Irujo did not know of his government's changed policy toward Louisiana. On November 1 he heard a rumor that Madrid had ordered the transfer to France suspended. So he again warned the administrators in Louisiana and the Floridas, in case they had not themselves received the order, to prepare for possible American attacks, pointing out that American public opinion would support such an offensive against them. "This is a favorite object not only of the government, . . . but also of the whole nation." [13]

A few days later Jefferson himself made clear his government's position toward the Spanish protests, saying that the matters of Louisiana's title and Napoleon's broken promise on alienation "were private questions between France and Spain which they must solve together; that we derived our title from the First Consul, and did not doubt his guarantee of it." [14] The president also explained to Irujo that if Spain did not deliver Louisiana according to his schedule, "there would be no time to enter negotiations on the other side of the Atlantic." His people would not only take Louisiana by force but would "also attack the Floridas." [15]

Jefferson's anger impressed the Spaniard. Irujo himself felt that Louisiana "is not worth the expense and trouble of a war, provided that we conserve the Floridas." [16] He believed that with his protests and warnings he had done all that he could to carry out his government's Louisiana policy.

In New Orleans the commissioners appointed to transfer Louisiana to the French, Sebastián Casa Calvo de la Puerta y O'Farrill and Manuel de Salcedo, former governors of the province, did not receive the rumored orders from Madrid that would have required them to suspend delivery. Although they wavered almost to the end, when Laussat demanded a definite date for the official transfer, they saw no choice open to them. They had to comply, for existing orders demanded that they do so and Jefferson's threats that a refusal might "bring on acts of force" made resistance foolhardy. [17]

Neither the French nor the Americans knew that the changes in sovereignty would be peaceful. They anticipated some internal violence. So Laussat, who had no troops at his disposal to maintain order, had instructions to deliver Louisiana to the United States on the same day he took possession from Spain. Claiborne and Wilkinson had orders to proceed peaceably if they could, forcibly if they must. If they were convinced that they could enter New Orleans without resistance, they were to leave Fort Adams with whatever troops they had available. Otherwise they had to decide whether to strike anyway or to await the militia units that were being mobilized.

To ease the way for peaceful change the American government issued an "Address to the People of New Orleans," warning them not to join Spain in any rumored resistance to "our dominion or opposition to its course. . . . Nature designed the inhabitants of Mississippi and those of New Orleans to be one single people. It is your peculiar happiness," it pointed out, to come under the rule "of a philosopher who prefers justice to conquest," but who also would not allow the people to destroy their own happiness by attacking American rights. "Your alternative is clear, for it consists only in making your small district, either a field of war or a garden of peace." [18]

After receiving assurance from the American commissioners that they were ready to take over New Orleans promptly and maintain order, Laussat asked the Spanish commissioners to deliver Louisiana to him on November 30, as agreed. The ceremony took place in a peaceful atmosphere in the Place d'Armes, the public square near the river. Laussat announced that soon all those in Louisiana who were willing would find themselves subjects of the United States. Those who wanted to leave were free to do so. The Spanish commissioners explained that those who stayed would owe no further allegiance to the crown.

Since Claiborne and Wilkinson did not complete their military preparations on time, they were unable to meet Laussat's schedule. So France ruled Louisiana again for twenty days. For two weeks the people of New Orleans celebrated this brief change of regime with fireworks, dinners, parties, and balls. Spanish troops and a volunteer force of about one hundred young Americans and friends who were living in the city policed New Orleans. The few French officers available took charge of Spanish posts along the Mississippi and in lower Louisiana. Napoleon's representatives left the upper part of the colony practically untouched.

When the American commissioners learned of the peaceful change in New Orleans, they decided not to use or wait for additional reserve units. They moved some 350 soldiers down the Mississippi in boats and barges and sent the mounted militia ahead by road. These reduced forces were still powerful enough to overwhelm the Spanish garrison if they were required to do so.

On December 20, 1803, in another ceremony in the Place d'Armes, Laussat, flanked by Claiborne on his right and Wilkinson on his left, officially delivered Louisiana to the United

States. Claiborne assured the Creoles—French and Spanish—that the United States welcomed them as brothers, would protect their enjoyment of liberty, property, and religion, and that this would be their last change in sovereignty. Then, accompanied by the rattle of musketry and the roar of cannon, the tricolor of France slipped slowly down the flagpole and the Stars and Stripes rose to the top. The troops who had entered the city with the American commissioners stood at attention. In a corner of the square a few Americans waved their hats and cheered. Theirs was the only loud display of emotion. Most of the Creoles present, among them "the beautiful women and fashionable men of the city," remained silent. A few sobbed.

At the end of the ceremony Laussat lost his composure. Bursting into tears, he turned away and rushed from the square. That afternoon, after containing his emotions, he gave a huge party to honor Louisiana's new owners. Wine, including two kinds of champagne, flowed in abundance, and the guests danced through the dawn. This gaiety failed to mask Laussat's sorrow and that of others who had believed in the French dream of western empire. He expressed it in a brief lament: "What a magnificent New France we lost!" [19]

To the north a sense of suspense and crisis prevailed until Christmas Day when a courier arrived in Washington with news that Laussat had taken possession of Louisiana without incident. This knowledge removed the last uncertainty over possible resistance, for the Jeffersonians interpreted it and Spain's silence as implying consent for delivery to the United States.*

As soon as Pichon learned that Laussat had taken possession according to treaty terms, he asked the American government for payment. Madison held back, saying that the date of interest on the bonds could not be fixed until he knew when the American commissioners took over. That information arrived in

---

* Amos Stoddard, an army officer, took formal delivery of upper Louisiana for the United States in Saint Louis, but not until March 10, 1804.

Washington by special horseman from New Orleans on January 15, 1804. On the next day the president reported completion of the transfer to Congress, and the French received their bonds in payment. On that day, too, the *National Intelligencer* broke the news to the people. It repeated sentiments that Jeffersonians had expressed so often they were already clichés. "The acquisition is great and glorious in itself; but still greater and more glorious," it said, "are the means by which it is obtained. . . . Never have mankind contemplated so vast and important an accession of empire by means so pacific and just." [20]

Pichon saw in this affair a practical as well as an imperial benefit for the Jeffersonians. "The acquisition of Louisiana and the peaceful manner of possession have raised Jefferson and his friends to a high point of popularity and regard," he observed. "His re-election must be considered as assured." The British *chargé* touched on Jefferson's vanity, saying that the Louisiana business "has elevated the President beyond Imagination in his own Opinion." [21]

The Republican members of Congress planned a great dinner in Washington in honor of the president and his cabinet, as well as other festivities, to celebrate the Jeffersonian achievement. "There is a *Jubilee* proclaimed here by the Democrats. . . . There is to be such a feast, it is said, as was never known in America, on account of taking possession of *Louisiana*," a Federalist congressman explained. "There is to be dinners—suppers—balls—assemblies, dances and I know not what. . . . The *Jubilee* is to begin here—but they expect it will run—like *wildfire,* to every dark and benighted corner of America." [22]

This "Louisiana Jubilee," as the Federalists called it, began with a dinner on January 27, 1804, attended by about a hundred guests who cheered and drank numerous toasts while three cannons, brought from the navy yard to Capitol Hill for the occasion, boomed. Four days later Republicans expressed joy in a larger event, a ball for five hundred people in Georgetown.

Republican newspapers wanted the whole nation to celebrate the newly acquired empire, and so they called for a national festival. Republicans in many parts of the country set aside Saturday, May 12, for a "National Jubilee," which in places like Philadelphia led to days, even weeks, of celebrating.[23] For some it seemed incongruous for a republic aspiring to democracy to glory in an imperial venture, but the event was important enough for rejoicing in grand style. The enthusiasm for the acquisition of Louisiana carried over into the campaign of 1804 and contributed to Jefferson's landslide reelection.

Earlier in January Carlos IV openly acknowledged the change in Spanish policy. He told the French, who had been pressuring him, that he acceded "without any reservations" to their sale of Louisiana. In February he informed Charles Pinckney that he was renouncing his "opposition to the alienation of Louisiana made by France, notwithstanding the solid reasons on which it is founded." [24] In May Irujo conveyed a similar message to Jefferson. Once more Spain had appeased the United States. Since she had little choice, she hoped that a graceful acquiescence might earn enough goodwill to save the Floridas and Texas from the Jeffersonian expansionists.

Chapter XIII

✤

Elastic Boundaries

Spain can not look with indifference on the exorbitant proposi-
tions which are beginning to be revealed on the part of the
United States in regard to the east and west boundaries of Loui-
siana.

Marqués de Casa Calvo, 1804 [1]

As the French had explained during the treaty negotia-
tions, the boundaries of the Louisiana territory that the United
States acquired were vague. The American government knew
only that its new unchartered empire ran south from Canada's
Lake of the Woods to New Orleans and west from the Missis-
sippi River to the Rocky Mountains. Even the statistics on its
population were unreliable. According to rough estimates, the
province now had a population of over sixty thousand but fewer
than one hundred thousand people. Less than half were whites;
the rest were blacks and Indians. The majority of whites and
blacks, most of the latter slaves, were bunched in and around
New Orleans. The white townspeople were of French, Spanish,
German, and American origin. In upper Louisiana, with settle-

ments scattered from Saint Louis to New Madrid, there was far less density and the mixture was different.

Many of the Americans who now rushed into the province were office seekers sponsored by western Republican politicians or speculators looking for fast profit. These people desired a massive immigration to complete the peaceful American conquest. Immigrants would compete for land and goods and thereby assure the speculators the profits they sought.

Like any other empire, Louisiana had to be governed, administered, and defended. At first Jefferson did these things, according to the power given him in the law of late October 1803, in his own way through his own appointees, William C. C. Claiborne and James Wilkinson. These men, neither of whom understood French or Spanish, were the president's proconsuls. Claiborne, for example, exercised all the power that had belonged to both the Spanish governor and intendant. Since the delegation of this immense power was temporary and would expire with the Eighth Congress, the Jeffersonians had to decide with reasonable promptness on how to treat the new empire on a long-range basis.

The Jeffersonians—and the Federalists, too—were divided in their views on the governing of Louisiana. Within the president's own party a minority maintained that theorists on democratic government now had an exceptional opportunity to match rhetoric with deeds and should do so. The people of Louisiana should be permitted self-government immediately, at least to the same extent as allowed Americans in other territories. Elitists in both parties thought differently. They wanted the central government to retain a monopoly of power over the new empire. "I always thought," Federalist expansionist Gouverneur Morris wrote, "that when we should acquire Canada and Louisiana it would be proper to govern them as provinces, and allow them no voice in our councils." [2]

Despite Thomas Jefferson's frequently expressed commitment to democratic principles, he also believed that Louisiana should not enter the Union on the basis of equality with existing units, at least not at once. He presumed that the people of lower Louisiana, having lived under despotic rule, were not ready to govern themselves. He maintained that the Creoles were "as yet as incapable of self-government as children" and would not make good citizens until they learned the meaning of democracy.[3] He viewed Louisiana as a possession not immediately acceptable within the Union.

The Creoles had expected more liberal treatment and were quick to express dissatisfaction with their status. Early in 1804, while Congress was considering legislation to provide Louisiana with a territorial government, they sent a delegation to Washington to seek statehood for the region around New Orleans. Using Claiborne's words, Jefferson assured Congress that liberty would be wasted on the Creoles because "the principles of a popular Government are utterly beyond their comprehension." Not one in fifty "understand the English language."[4] In keeping with the president's attitude, Congress refused the New Orleans request.

The debate over the Louisiana government bill explored the nature of empire and what it should mean in the American political system. On examining this bill, one critic said, "It will appear that it really establishes a complete despotism; that it does not evince a single trait of liberty; that it does not confer one single right to which they [the people of Louisiana] are entitled under the treaty; that it does not extend to them the benefits of the Federal Constitution, or declare when, hereafter, they shall receive them."

Defenders of the bill generally argued, as had Jefferson, that the people of Louisiana did not understand liberty and hence could not use it properly. Some legislators considered them so degraded as not to be worthy of representative government. One politician said, "I consider them as standing in nearly the relation to us as if they were a conquered country." [5] With the votes on its side, the administration stood its ground, but it tried to mollify dissenters with the vision of a better future. "It may fairly be expected," Madison said of the people of Louisiana, "that every blessing of liberty will be extended to them as fast as they shall be prepared and disposed to receive it." [6]

The bill for the government of Louisiana that passed both houses of Congress and that became law in March 1804 divided the province into two parts along a line that later separated Arkansas from the state of Louisiana. It designated the area above the line, sprawling northward to the border with Canada, the District of Louisiana, and the southern part, essentially the future state of Louisiana, the Territory of Orleans. The southern territory, but not the District of Louisiana, which was still largely Indian country, could eventually become a state.

The treaty of cession obligated the United States to incorporate the people of New Orleans into the nation. This did not happen. The territorial act did not allow them the limited rights of self-government enjoyed by other Americans. The Creoles had no right to vote; all authority was vested in appointed officials. The law provided for an autocratic government. Even dedicated Jeffersonians were unhappy with it.

Critics deplored the act as providing "a government about as despotic as that of Turkey in Asia." A Federalist argued, "This is a Colonial system of government—It is the first the United States have established—It is a bad precedent—the U.S. in time will have many colonies—precedents are therefore important." [7]

In April Attorney General Levi Lincoln ruled that the president's power under territorial law was virtually unlimited. Federalists then not only condemned Jefferson but also denounced the inconsistencies between his principles and his policies. "You might as well charge Democrats with inconsistency," one of their journalists commented, "because after complaining of the excessive power of poor old [John] Adams, they made the modest Jefferson despot of Louisiana." [8]

With the territorial law the structure of the new American empire took clear form. The people of the original nation, as represented by the president and Congress, had decided to treat the empire as a colony. Those within it who had been annexed to liberty would have to wait a while before they could enjoy the blessings of that liberty. Meanwhile Jefferson and his advisers had been maneuvering to annex more territory to their empire for liberty, essentially by trying to stretch boundaries as though they were made of rubber.

The Jeffersonians began this stratagem immediately after the acquisition of Louisiana by taking advantage of frontier ambiguities. In particular they desired West Florida, a strip of land along the Gulf Coast. It had economic and strategic importance because it contained the mouths of navigable rivers that ran through the Mississippi Territory, and also Mobile Bay, a site suitable for a naval harbor. On the day he signed the Louisiana treaties Robert R. Livingston explained that he and James Monroe had placed West Florida within the acquired empire's eastern boundary "so that there will be no deception should we claim it in treating with Spain." He urged the president, "in the strongest terms," to use force if necessary, because "the time is peculiarly favorable to enable you to do it without the smallest risk at home. . . . With this in your hand, East Florida will be of little moment, and may be yours whenever you please. At all events, proclaim your right and take possession." [9] Livingston also admitted that he must find a means to justify such a seizure.

It was common knowledge that France had not acquired the Floridas. Moreover, François Barbé-Marbois had explained in the negotiations that the purchase did not include any of the Floridas. Nonetheless, Livingston persisted in advising this im-

213

perial thrust on the basis of a simple but deceptive argument. Old French maps, he said, showed the Perdido River as Louisiana's eastern frontier. If Spain had retroceded Louisiana as she had originally received it from France, then the Perdido formed the eastward limit of the territory sold to the United States.

Whether or not Thomas Jefferson believed in this simplistic logic, he consistently maintained that the security and well-being of the United States required possession of West Florida as well as Louisiana. He also regarded expansion into East Florida and westward through Texas to the Rio Grande as inevitable. He asserted that the Rio Grande formed Louisiana's western frontier. So he and his fellow expansionists seemed willing to go along with any plausible boundary contentions that suited their predispositions.

This attitude also appeared to fit the mood of many Americans who assumed that nature had determined that far-flung frontiers would enhance the greatness of the United States. As a New England Federalist observed, when the Mississippi ceased to be a confining boundary, the imagination of his countrymen soared into space to bound the glory of America only by the stars. A July Fourth orator declared that Louisiana was only "the commencement of our anticipating hopes." He envisaged the day when "our boundaries shall be those which Nature has formed for a great, powerful, and free State." A French diplomat commented that Americans entertained so many territorial ambitions that they were eager "to devour the whole of North America." He added that "since the Americans have acquired Louisiana, they appear unable to bear any barriers round them." [10]

In seeking to extend their empire in the east, the Jeffersonians worked out a simple plan, similar in approach to their old Louisiana strategy. They would claim West Florida as part of Louisiana and threaten to seize it as a legitimate exercise of property rights. Then they would offer to forego the use of force if Spain would sell West and East Florida. They thus would merge their claim to territory as far east as the Perdido with an offer to buy both Floridas. As Jefferson himself explained it a short time later, "These [boundary] claims will be a subject of negotiation with Spain, and if, as soon as she is at war, we push them strongly with one hand, holding out a price in the other, we shall certainly obtain the Floridas and all in good time." [11]

In the summer of 1803 the secretary of state instructed Monroe, who was scheduled to go to Madrid to negotiate the boundary issues after winding up his business in Paris, on the government's Florida policy. "The Spanish Government must understand, in fact," Madison said, "that the United States can never consider the amicable relations between them as definitely and permanently secured, without an arrangement on the Floridas."

The secretary of state pointed out that the Floridas, separated as they were from Spain's other colonies, "must ever be a dead expense in time of peace, indefensible in time of war, and at all times a source of irritation and ill blood with the United States." So Jefferson's government offered two and a half million dollars for them. Since this was less than it had been willing to pay the French earlier, Madison explained that with the Mississippi in American control "we are less disposed . . . to make sacrifices to obtain the Floridas, because their position and the manifest course of events guaranty an early and reasonable acquisition of them." [12]

Monroe agreed with this policy. He thought that the Floridas now "would be of little value to her [Spain], since her government must know that at no distant period we should acquire it, the United States being a rising and Spain a declining power." [13]

Spain refused even to discuss the American claims. She insisted that she had received the Floridas from England in 1783 and that West Florida had not come from France as part of Louisiana. The intensity of her objections to Louisiana's sale, moreover, indicated that she certainly would not bargain over border pretensions when she denied the legality of the American title to any part of Louisiana. The Jeffersonians then held back in their Florida strategy until they had Louisiana proper securely within their grasp.

This tactical retreat fell in with advice from French leaders. When Monroe requested their help in obtaining the Floridas, as Barbé-Marbois had apparently promised verbally, they told him not to press the Florida issue because they needed time to reconcile Spain to the sale of Louisiana. At a dinner party the second consul, Jean Jacques Régis de Cambacérès, cautioned, "You must not go to Spain at present." When Monroe asked for an explicit reason, Cambacérès replied, "It is not the time; you had better defer it." [14] Monroe then gave up his trip to Madrid. Instead in July 1803 he crossed the Channel to replace Rufus King as the American minister in London.

At home the Jeffersonians turned to legislative tactics to support their Florida strategy. In November John Randolph, the majority leader in the House of Representatives, introduced a bill known ultimately as the Mobile Act to extend the nation's revenue laws to Louisiana. Its wording implied that West Florida had already become a part of the United States through the acquisition of Louisiana. The bill placed Spanish territory as far east as the Perdido within the jurisdiction of American customs officials. It invited the president to take possession of the Mobile area "whenever he shall deem it expedient." Although the bill intruded on Spanish sovereignty and could have led to war, it passed without producing any recorded debate.

In the following month, as another part of his Florida strategy, Jefferson asked the Senate to approve a special convention for the settlement of indemnities against Spain for American ships seized in Spanish waters during the Quasi-War. Americans estimated their claims to be more than five million dollars. Earlier the Senate had rejected the claims convention, but in January 1804 it approved. Jefferson ratified the convention and sent it on to Charles Pinckney in Madrid. Pinckney then pressed the Spaniards for a settlement, saying that the American government would itself assume payment of the spoliation claims in exchange for the Floridas. Spain refused the convention because she would not trade debts for territory she intended to keep.

The persistent Jeffersonian pressure apparently persuaded Manuel de Godoy that Spain's best chance of retaining the Floridas lay in conciliating Napoleon. At the same time the Jeffersonians sought the First Consul's help in obtaining them. France must be kept "in our scale against that of Spain," Madison said. She should welcome a transfer of the Floridas to the United States. It would be "nothing more than a sequel and completion of the policy which led France into her own treaty of Cession." [15]

Pierre Clément de Laussat indirectly brought another factor into the Jeffersonian boundary maneuvers. He told William C. C. Claiborne and James Wilkinson that no part of the Floridas fell within Louisiana's eastern boundary but in the west he thought that the United States could make a case for including Texas in the purchase. He explained that in his instructions and in those of General Claude Victor, France had claimed a western frontier at the Rio Bravo, later known as the Rio Grande. This information reinforced Jefferson's determination to use the Texas claim.

In February the cabinet backed the president by approving three alternative territorial offers to Spain. For recognition of the Perdido boundary the United States would give up its claim to Texas. For a line farther east on the Apalachicola River it would close a broad belt of territory on the western frontier to white settlers for a designated number of years. For both the Floridas it would supplement these concessions with "one million dollars." The cabinet also voted to make Fort Stoddert, located on the Mobile River in American territory just a few miles north of the boundary separating Louisiana from West Florida, the port of entry for the customs district to be set up under the Mobile Act.

Several days later Carlos Martínez de Irujo, whose goodwill toward the Jeffersonians had evaporated when he realized their determination to take the Floridas, complained about additional American troops going into lower Louisiana. The secretary of state replied that they were needed to protect the white population against possible slave uprisings. The Spaniard believed that this was true enough, but he also felt that American policy makers wanted these reinforcements kept ready so they could move into West Florida on short notice at the appropriate time. All that restrained the Jeffersonians, he assumed, was continued peace between Spain and England.

Such restraint could be seen in the implementation of the Mobile Act, which Jefferson signed into law in February. Secretary of the Treasury Albert Gallatin informed the collector of the new customs district that the president did not intend to take this part of West Florida by force but to negotiate for it. Therefore, Gallatin said, the collector was "to exercise no act of territorial jurisdiction within the said limits, though part of your district." [16] Yet within a few days Irujo protested the Mobile Act as an "atrocious libel" against Spain. Since "there does not exist any well-founded reason by which the United States can establish any pretensions to West Florida," he insisted, it should repeal the law.[17]

Madison had difficulty explaining the law other than as Irujo saw it. While it was true that the legislation embraced part of West Florida, the secretary said, its discretionary terms showed respect for Spain's claim and thereby left the controversy open to negotiation. Irujo replied that since Spain's ownership of the Floridas was beyond dispute, the United States should prove its right to territory before passing laws for it. The minis-

ter's argument made sense, for the Jeffersonians intended the
Mobile Act to coerce the Spaniards. Even Gallatin admitted
later that "every writer, without a single exception, who has
written on the subject, seems to have understood the Act as
Spain did." [18]

Those who formulated Spanish policy were now particu-
larly sensitive to any borderland encroachment. Having given
up opposition to France's cession of Louisiana, they decided as a
matter of policy to try to contain the United States within that
province's most compressed boundaries. This desperately defen-
sive strategy could not avoid conflict with confident Jeffersonian
expansionism.

This confidence was again displayed in March 1804 when a
member of the House Committee of Commerce and Manufac-
tures reported on the need to authorize the president to employ
persons to explore Louisiana. This report defined the area of in-
vestigation as lying west of the Rockies "between the territories
claimed by Great Britain on the one side, and by Spain on the
other, quite to the South Sea." Jefferson, who worked with the
committee, now included not only Texas but also Oregon as
part of Louisiana. A careful scholar of western expansion noted
that thus the Jeffersonian "conception had gradually expanded
until it included West Florida, Texas, and the Oregon country,
a view which was to be the basis of a large part of American
diplomacy for nearly half a century." [19]

Other expansionists concentrated on West Florida and con-
tinued to urge the president to seize it. Robert Livingston, one
of those who had long advised the use of force, now suggested
bribery as a perhaps cheaper means of achieving this goal.

Jefferson himself shifted tactics. On May 30, when he
created the Mobile revenue district, he defined its limits as
"lying *within the boundaries of the United States*," and thus he
seemingly retreated from the more extensive claim of the Mo-
bile Act.[20] Then when he heard that Spanish foreign minister

219

Pedro de Cevallos had denounced the Mobile Act and demanded its revocation before his government would accept the claims convention, the president revived the tactic of coercion. He ordered the secretary of war to pour more troops into the area of the West Florida frontier.

Early in July the cabinet reinforced this hard line, insisting on West Florida and persisting in the claim to Texas. The department heads were willing to pay two million dollars for territory east of the Perdido or proportionate sums for whatever Spain would sell.

In April Madison had instructed Monroe to proceed to Madrid as soon as possible to deal with the boundary issues. Now the secretary of state sent both Monroe and Pinckney fresh instructions embodying the cabinet decisions. All along, Pinckney had been pushing tough tactics. He even menaced the Spaniards with the possibility of hostile action from a United States naval squadron cruising the Mediterranean. "He positively threatens war" and terrifies Cevallos, the French ambassador reported.[21] In this confrontation of nerves, with talk of war in the air, the Spanish policy makers sought French help.

Across the sea where jittery American and Spanish frontier forces faced each other, an uprising of American residents in West Florida added another combustible to the crisis situation. The difficulties began in June 1804 but came to a head in August when two brothers, Nathan and Samuel Kemper, known as frontier roughnecks, and some followers numbering around thirty marched on Baton Rouge. They planned to overthrow the Spanish regime and proclaim independence, but the populace refused to revolt. So "under the pretense of giving freedom to West Florida," the insurgents raided the countryside.[22]

Spanish officials quickly raised a force of about 150 volunteers to crush the rebellion and drove the insurgents into the Mississippi Territory, where they took refuge. Sebastián Casa

Calvo de la Puerta y O'Farrill, the Spanish boundary commissioner in New Orleans, asked Claiborne to extradite them or remove them away from the border. Claiborne refused to apprehend them but promised to inform the president of the problem. Since the Spaniards suspected American officials of encouraging the disturbance, Claiborne's offer did not satisfy them.

Vicente Folch, West Florida's governor general, brought together a professional force much larger than that of the immigrants. But when he arrived at Baton Rouge, all was quiet. Folch later encountered Wilkinson, who still desired and accepted Spanish money, in New Orleans and the two military commanders worked out some kind of agreement that diminished the immediate danger of hostilities between their troops.

During this Spanish and American confrontation Talleyrand reversed the position he had taken earlier, that the United States should make the most of the vagueness in Louisiana's boundaries. He now maintained, in speaking for his government, that the United States could claim only the territory that France had received from Spain and that Louisiana's boundaries should be restricted, not expanded. He instructed General Louis Marie Turreau, the newly appointed French minister to the United States, to divert Americans away from the west and northwest. Spain feared, he said, that "the United States, which are showing their intention to push the boundaries of Louisiana toward the west, are purposing to advance in that direction even to the sea, and of settling along the coasts of America located north of California." [23] At the same time the French leaders sought to profit from American expansionism. On the matter of the Floridas, for example, François Barbé-Marbois asked if the United States would give "sixty millions [francs] for them," and Livingston said that "he even pressed the matter very strongly upon me." [24]

While French policy toward the Louisiana boundary was shifting and the frontier crisis continued, Monroe prepared himself for his rendezvous in Madrid. Reports of possible war spread in Europe. The *Times* of London reported that more than five thousand Spanish troops, with ordnance and military stores, were shortly to embark from Cuba "for the defense of the Floridas." [25] Under the assumption that the French would now support his mission, Monroe left London early in October and stopped off in Paris. There he conferred with Livingston and John Armstrong, the new American minister to France.

Talleyrand told Napoleon, who in May had taken the title of emperor, that "the United States, who wish to negotiate at Madrid under the auspices of France for the acquisition of Florida, have acquired little title to the good offices of the Emperor by the sharpness of tone and the want of civility [*égards*] with which they have conducted themselves toward Spain." He said the "United States should desist from their unjust pretensions to West Florida" and urged the emperor not to recognize "such pretensions." [26]

Not surprisingly, therefore, the American ministers, who talked with Talleyrand, could elicit no French support. When Monroe spoke of his mission to Madrid, Talleyrand said, "Aye, I understand you. You will have much difficulty to succeed there." The American replied, "I hoped not, with the aid of his [Napoleon's] good offices." Though personally cordial, the foreign minister insisted that West Florida did not belong with Louisiana and deplored further American expansion. His chief assistant "observed that both parties must make sacrifices; that Spain must cede territory, and that the U. States must pay money." [27] Armstrong reported that the French, seeking bribes, wanted to convert the negotiations into a "job."

Monroe now seemed to have little reason for proceeding to Madrid and thought of returning to London. Finally, after letting the French know he would pay nothing as a bribe, he decided to try to gain what he could on his own. Leaving Paris in December, after Napoleon's coronation as emperor, he arrived in the Spanish capital early in January 1805.

Within a few weeks of Monroe's departure Armstrong received Napoleon's reply to the American request for support in Madrid. The emperor deplored Jeffersonian imperialism, saying that "he saw with pain the United States commence their differences with Spain in an unusual manner, and conduct themselves toward the Floridas by acts of violence which, not being founded in right, could have no other effect but to injure its lawful owners. Such an aggression" surprised him because the Americans used "their treaty with France as an authority for their proceeding." [28]

This response as well as other developments in relations between France and Spain made Monroe's mission hopeless. Jefferson and his advisers had assumed that Spain, despite her pride and initial resistance, would yield to their demands because she would soon be drawn into the war against England and would be unable to afford to tangle with the United States also. This prognostication proved only partly correct. On December 12, only four days after Monroe had left Paris, Carlos IV declared war on England. Instead of making Spain amenable to American offers, the war increased Carlos's dependence on Napoleon. On January 4, 1805, France concluded an agreement guaranteeing Spain's "territorial integrity" in Europe and the return of colonies she might lose "during the course of the current war." Now Jeffersonian menaces against Spain for territory could bring on a confrontation with France, too.

The altered French position was also evident in Washington, where the French minister, General Turreau, joined Irujo in informing the Jeffersonians that their two governments considered the American claim to West Florida untenable. When Madison told Turreau that "we have a map which probably carries to the Perdido the eastern limit of Louisiana!" the

223

general replied, "I should be curious to see it, sir; the more, because I have one which includes Tennessee and Kentucky in Louisiana. You will agree that maps are not titles." [29]

In Madrid Cevallos, having made his negotiating position secure with pledges of French support, did not open discussions with Monroe until almost a month after his arrival. Monroe, working with Pinckney, sought recognition of the Perdido as Louisiana's eastern boundary, the purchase of East Florida for two million dollars, payment of the spoliation claims, and the surrender of Texas. After discussing these points with the envoys one by one, Cevallos rejected every American demand.

During these negotiations Monroe found that he had to accept terms set by the French or fail. These terms called for a loan of seventy million livres to Spain, really a contribution, which she would immediately give to France. In return, the United States would gain possession of West Florida. Since Jeffersonian dogma maintained that the United States had already bought West Florida, he could not logically agree to buy it a second time. In May Monroe demanded his passports, and he and Pinckney informed Washington of their failure. They were convinced that Spain "would never cede one foot of territory otherwise than by compulsion," and they advised just that. "Take possession of both the Floridas and the whole country west of the Mississippi to the Rio Bravo [Rio Grande]," Monroe wrote.[30]

The president learned of the failure of his boundary strategy during the summer of 1805. "The business at Madrid," Madison informed him, "has had an awkward termination." [31] Jefferson favored breaking relations with Spain and seizing the Floridas and Texas. "I do not," he said, "view peace as within our choice." In the anticipated war to obtain "the acknowledgement by Spain of the rightful boundaries of Louisiana," he was prepared once again to "make common cause" with England.[32] But he listened to contrary counsel before acting.

Albert Gallatin, in advising strongly against war, pointed out the flimsy basis of American boundary claims. He said "that a resort to arms for that cause will, I think, appear unjustifiable in the opinion of mankind and even of America." Furthermore, a settlement of the boundaries "must depend on France, and that it is with her that we ought to negotiate." [33] So even though Jefferson felt that it was a "dangerous error that we are a people whom no injuries can provoke to war," he recognized the weakness of the American position and kept the peace.[34]

This setback did not cause the Jeffersonians to abandon their territorial goals. They merely shifted tactics. Foreign observers, such as General Turreau, were amazed by the poise, self-confidence, and aggressive ambition of the American leaders, especially because they had behind them only a small military establishment. Yet outsiders also recognized that on the North American continent United States expansionism had behind it popular sentiment and was a formidable force that could perhaps be stopped only at great risk.

Chapter XIV

❖

Persisting Coercion

I consider it a base prostration of the national character, to excite one nation by money to bully another nation out of its property.

John Randolph, 1806 [1]

*I*n the spring of 1805 during the crisis of the Louisiana boundary negotiations, Spanish colonial officials began shifting troops from the interior to defend their Texas frontier. Their delineation of the boundary, running from the Gulf of Mexico up the Arroyo Hondo to the vicinity of Natchitoches and along the Red River, differed from the line drawn by the Jeffersonians. Although the American government claimed a more extensive area, it insisted as a minimum that Louisiana's western boundary extended to the Sabine River. When Spanish authorities planted settlers in eastern Texas and established military posts east of the Sabine, the American military commandant on that frontier protested, claiming that they had violated American soil.

William C. C. Claiborne, now governor of the Territory of

Orleans, called out militia units to reinforce Natchitoches, the American outpost nearest Texas. Americans were particularly upset by Spanish activity at Nuestra Señora de los Adaes, a village fourteen miles west of Natchitoches. That summer, as the stress and strain along the frontiers touching Spanish lands increased, a rumor spread through New Orleans that Louisiana was being returned to Spain. Although implausible and certainly not true, the report gained unthinking believers because Jeffersonian border pressures had contributed to a continuing war scare and to a feeling that any kind of change could occur. Claiborne placed military units in his territory on the alert and in August inspected troops and fortifications throughout his jurisdiction. In New Orleans Americans eager for combat and for taking more Spanish land explained that the time was now "favorable to the commencement of a war" and that "the cause of war is ample; and the moment propitious. We deprecate war when it can be avoided with honor, but we never wish to see our country yield an inch." [2]

Spanish administrators in North America believed that war could or would start at any time. They were particularly alarmed by the activities of American planters and settlers in West Florida, most of whom still openly resented not being included within Louisiana. Some of these Americans, as had the Kemper brothers, defied Spanish law, claiming that under the terms of the Louisiana Purchase the province belonged to the United States. They plotted to seize Baton Rouge, to expel the Spaniards, and to take over the province. In August they set their *coup* in motion. It met unexpectedly strong Spanish resistance and failed.

Convinced that the uprisings in West Florida, seemingly coordinated with the American military activity on the frontier, signaled an offensive against the Floridas, Spanish colonial officials stepped up their military preparations. They sent troop reinforcements from Havana and Mexico to West Florida and

eastern Texas. In Havana a squadron of warships awaited the
outbreak of hostilities with orders to blockade various American
ports, mainly those at the mouths of the Mississippi, Potomac,
and Delaware rivers. In October more Spanish soldiers again
crossed the Sabine River, this time to occupy Bayou Pierre,
located just to the north and west of Natchitoches. Elsewhere
along the Texas frontier Spanish troops dug in to repel expected
American attacks.

In Washington Thomas Jefferson and his advisers closely
followed developments along the Louisiana frontiers and inten-
sified their own preparations for possible hostilities. The secre-
tary of war ordered more troops into the forts along the Missis-
sippi, and he also sent reinforcements to Saint Louis and New
Orleans. Despite his earlier decision against war because of the
failed negotiations in Madrid, the president once more became
bellicose and appeared ready to ask Congress for authority to
drive the Spaniards out of West Florida and Texas.

In his annual message to the Ninth Congress on December 3
Jefferson breathed indignation against the Spaniards for their
refusal to pay the spoliation claims, for their resistance to his
boundary and territorial demands, and for their seizure and
plunder of "our citizens" in the Orleans Territory. "I have
therefore found it necessary at length to give orders to our
troops on that frontier to be in readiness to protect our citizens,
and to repel by arms any similar aggression in the future." Fur-
ther diplomatic efforts, he implied, would be useless. Some in-
juries to the national honor could "be met by force only," he
said. He called on Congress to increase the nation's land and
naval forces, to support a call-up of the militia, and to authorize
the construction of ships of war carrying seventy-four guns.[3]

Most Americans considered the message proof of the ad-
ministration's vigor and apparently approved of it. Along the
seaboard people seemed to regard it as the equivalent of a decla-
ration of war against Spain. The Federalist press praised it.

"The message," a Federalist critic commented, "is more energetic and warlike than any he ever sent to Congress." [4] Carlos Martínez de Irujo, whose recall had been requested, protested and questioned the president's assertions.

In Madrid the Spanish government seemed resigned to war. Charles Pinckney, the American minister, had left that city for the United States in October, and George W. Erving took over the legation as *chargé d'affaires*. In December Erving lodged a protest with Manuel de Godoy against Spain's renewed seizure of American ships. "You may choose either peace or war. 'Tis the same thing to me," Godoy said. "I will tell you candidly, that if you go to war this certainly is the moment, and you may take our possessions from us. I advise you to go to war now, if you think that is best for you." [5]

Elsewhere Godoy explained that the United States had brought relations with Spain to such a point as to leave his government indifferent to the consequences. The Jeffersonians were demanding West Florida as the price of peace, he said, yet in a war they would be able to seize only the Floridas anyway. Mexico and Cuba were most likely beyond their reach. So Spain could lose just about as much by appeasement as by war and perhaps less by fighting.

Knowledge of France's support for Spain and concern over their own rising maritime difficulties with England, however, kept the Jeffersonians, despite their menaces, from taking the final step to war. News from Paris that suggested the possibility of gaining the frontier lands through negotiation and perhaps bribery also caused the president to pause once more before using force.

Several months earlier an agent working for Talleyrand had approached the American minister in Paris, John Armstrong, suggesting that Napoleon could serve as arbitrator in America's quarrel with Spain. "The more you refer to the decision of the Emperor," the agent advised, "the more sure & easy will be the settlement." [6] The emperor would decree that the Floridas should go to the United States for ten million dollars, and he would place Louisiana's western boundary deep in Texas at the Colorado River. Armstrong balked at the amount requested. When the agent saw that reluctance, he reduced the amount to seven million; the minister then forwarded the proposal to Washington.

Assuming that more money would be the proper bait, Jefferson told his cabinet "that we should address ourselves to France, informing her that it was a last effort at amicable settlement with Spain." France, "to whom Spain is in arrears for subsidies," would also "be glad to secure us from going into the scale of England." [7] After some debate the president and his department heads decided to accept the French propositions but refused to pay more than five million dollars for the Floridas. They thought they could still get a bargain by agreeing to cancel the spoliation claims against Spain, which they now estimated at three million, as part of the deal. They would go to Congress for the remaining two million dollars.

Considering secrecy essential, Jefferson then gathered selected documents on the territorial controversy with Spain and transmitted them to Congress without hinting about his purpose. He did promise more details later. He also conferred with members of the committee in the House of Representatives who would be most directly involved in the transaction and revealed his purpose to them.

Then on December 6, only three days after his saber-rattling annual message, the president sent another communication and more documents to an anxious and expectant Congress. In keeping with Jefferson's desire for secrecy, the legislators cleared the galleries and listened. Even though the president spoke of Spain's "intention to advance on our possessions," to their surprise he did not ask for a declaration of war. Instead he said that "formal war is not necessary" but that "the

spirit and honor of our country require that force should be in-
terposed to a certain degree." [8] He also revealed his scheme to
work out a collaboration with Napoleon. A few days later he
requested appropriation of the two million dollars he needed to
carry out his plan.

Jefferson was relying on a variation of his earlier strategy of
threatening force with one hand while offering money with the
other. But in this instance, if Spain went along with the scheme,
the money would not go to her. It would go directly to Napoleon's
treasury in payment of subsidies overdue from Madrid. As in
the main Louisiana transaction, Spain would gain nothing directly
except more humiliation.

Before Congress could act, the president's proposal had to
clear a select committee of seven members of the House of Rep-
resentatives headed by John Randolph, the majority leader.
Madison had told him frankly that a peaceful territorial settle-
ment with Spain depended on the payment of the money to
France. This indirect tactic had no appeal for Randolph, a
straightforward expansionist. He denounced the entire scheme
as dishonorable, cowardly, and unworthy of the government.
Let the administration make good its threats, march troops into
Texas if the Spaniards refused to truckle, but it should not
stoop to pawnbrokers' tricks. In his view, as he explained in
public debate several months later, it was "a base prostration of
the national character, to excite one nation by money to bully
another nation out of its property." As a result, "the national
honor has received a stain which all the waters of the Potomac
cannot wash out." [9] Congress should not permit the president
publicly to urge vigorous measures while secretly advising tame
ones and to convey to the public an image of an energetic execu-
tive thwarted by a hesitating legislature.

Some other Republicans, instead of opposing Jefferson be-
cause he was devious rather than openly ruthless as an expan-
sionist, were alarmed by the bellicosity of his annual message.

John Dickinson, a founding father, denounced the idea of war with Spain as unthinkable. He felt that Jefferson's government was trying to cover up its diplomatic blunders "by an excitement of national passion." Its boundary claims were "founded on Arbitrary Inferences from equivocal Premises," he said. "To rush into war at this time for Wildernesses beyond the River Mexicano, or on the remote waters of the Missouri, would be . . . madness. . . . In the natural course of things, we shall, if wise gradually become irresistable, and the people will rise into our population." Warning that "our ambition in acquiring Territory, will destroy our Peace, our welfare, our Reputation," he counseled patience.[10] Whether for or against war at this time, these critics did not denounce expansionism as such. Like most members of Congress, they not only believed in expansionism but also considered it inevitable.

Since majority sentiment in Congress appeared to favor a declaration of war because of the *"Spanish aggressions on our territory,"* as winter deepened, the outlook for peace darkened.[11] But Randolph's opposition to the administration opened a schism in the Republican party. Those on Randolph's side argued that national honor required "chastisement" of the Spaniards, while the administration and its supporters wanted the territory cheaply and without use of force, if that were possible. So the president bypassed Randolph and turned to other more trusted members of the House to sponsor his desired legislation. Finally in February 1806 Congress passed the president's bill "for extraordinary expenses" in foreign relations, usually known as the "Two Million Dollar Act." [12] An accompanying secret resolution explained the purpose of the appropriation—the purchase of the Floridas.

Congress also passed and Jefferson approved an act prohibiting commerce with Santo Domingo. The administration sponsored this law with the hope of gaining Napoleon's favor in the Florida bargaining. A month later instructions went to

Armstrong in Paris and to James Bowdoin, the new American minister in Madrid, to guide them in negotiating under French auspices. They were to seek an arrangement that would not cost more than two million dollars in cash. But the emperor could work up no enthusiasm for pressuring Spain to surrender territory under the niggardly terms the Jeffersonians proposed. Napoleon's scheme had assumed the extraction of a large sum of money from the United States for his own use. When that hope faded, so did his willingness to go along with unabated Jeffersonian expansionism. So he said that he "viewed with pain the conduct of the United States" and urged the Spaniards to reinforce their naval and troop strength in the New World "for encouraging a good and vigorous defence" where the Americans threatened.[13]

Late in March Randolph's continuing opposition forced the administration to remove the cloak of mystery from its two-million-dollar negotiation. Some observers thought the exposure would push Congress into a declaration of war; instead it elicited disappointment, even disgust. Critics charged the president with deception, with submissiveness to France, and with bringing disgrace to the nation.

Regardless of Jefferson's resistance to the war hawks and their criticism that he was not sufficiently tough, he did not slacken his preparations for war. Earlier in the month his government had ordered General James Wilkinson, now governor of the Louisiana Territory and commandant of the United States Army, to send all the troops in the vicinity of Saint Louis, except one company, to Fort Adams. A short time later the cabinet decided to assign nine warships to the Louisiana coast, to erect more fortifications at New Orleans, and to drill militia units. Early in May the secretary of war ordered Wilkinson to leave his headquarters in Saint Louis, go south, and take personal command of the troops in the Territory of Orleans. The administration wanted him to cooperate with Claiborne and to prepare his forces so that they could fight off an invasion and also be strong enough to take and hold all territory east of the Sabine. Essentially, it demanded that the governors of West Florida and Texas respect the *status quo* on Louisiana's frontiers.

Even when the Jeffersonian leaders realized that their two-million-dollar negotiation had failed, they stuck to this strategy. For the time being, it would ensure peace while giving American power a period of unhampered growth. Madison let the French know of this peaceful decision. But they would not let the Florida matter rest. A French officer approached Bowdoin unofficially with another proposal. This agent suggested that the Floridas could be had for six million dollars cash. The American minister thought that his government might go as high as four million and forwarded the proposal to Washington.

Spain decided that she would contribute no more to the Napoleonic war chest and refused to cooperate in the scheme. Nor would the Jeffersonians pay that much cash. They still demanded the Floridas in exchange for their assumption of the spoliation claims against Spain or through negotiation of their border claims. So once more Napoleon's efforts to profit from the Louisiana border conflict failed, and the American confrontation with Spain on the frontier continued.

Earlier in the year, with Americans in the West eager for hostilities, tension along the Texas boundary had seemed ready to explode into violence. The mayor of Natchitoches had asked the Spanish commandant at Nacogdoches to withdraw all his troops from east of the Sabine, as Jeffersonian policy required, and not permit them to patrol on that side of the river. The commandant refused to comply. Anticipating an American attack, he announced to his own people that "the United States, full of ambition and greed, intends to usurp from our sovereign that part of this province between the known limits [the Arroyo Hondo] and the Sabine River." If the Spaniards did not remove their own troops to the west side of the river, he continued, the

Americans would "take that unjust pretext to declare war on us." [14]

Three days later about 150 armed Americans approached the Spanish posts in the disputed area. The Spanish soldiers withdrew without a fight. Still later the Spanish colonial administration ordered Lieutenant Colonel Simón de Herrera y Leyva, governor of the Mexican province of Nuevo León, to proceed to eastern Texas with about twelve hundred men and to fight if Americans crossed the Texas boundary. Herrera arrived on the frontier in June. In July the Spaniards raised their flag at Bayou Pierre, east of the Sabine, and in the next month Herrera's force crossed the river there.

American and Spanish forces faced each other grimly and uneasily. Yet both sides had reason to proceed cautiously. Claiborne knew that in case of hostilities the Creoles would not side with the United States. The Spaniards, aware that they were weak and could gain little through violence, wanted to settle the quarrel peaceably but without conceding the disputed territory. So in September Herrera withdrew his forces to the west side of the Sabine. This retreat removed the basic reason for Wilkinson, in command of superior forces on the American side, to attack an "invader." In October, therefore, Wilkinson proposed a compromise. He told Herrera he would pull back American troops to the east of Arroyo Hondo if the Spanish soldiers would remain west of the Sabine. The territory between them would become neutral ground until officials in Washington and Madrid could settle the dispute. Without consulting his superiors, Herrera agreed to the proposal. He and Wilkinson signed the "neutral ground agreement" on November 5, 1806, and since their governments accepted this informal arrangement, peace again gained the upper hand on the Texas frontier.

Another reason this border crisis of 1806 ended in peace rather than in war can be found in Wilkinson's disenchantment with Aaron Burr, Jefferson's first vice-president and current political enemy. Like Jefferson and other contemporaries, Burr was an expansionist who favored growth at the expense of Indians and Spaniards. In 1805 Burr had also flirted with a scheme for disunion involving Louisiana. He told the British minister in Washington in March "that the inhabitants of Louisiana seem determined to render themselves independent of the United States, along with the Inhabitants of the Western Parts of the United States," and that somehow he would help them achieve that goal.[15] In April Burr met with Wilkinson near the mouth of the Ohio River, where they conferred for several days, apparently about conditions in the West and the probability of war with Spain.

In June, with the collaboration of Wilkinson, Burr floated down the Mississippi in a comfortable barge on a mysterious errand, apparently to investigate and organize Creole discontent in New Orleans. He remained in the city for three weeks, being lavishly entertained by prominent people. When he departed, he promised to return at the head of a military expedition. In September he visited Wilkinson again, this time at his headquarters in Saint Louis, where the two men may have charted plans for an invasion of Mexico.

This plan, plot, or conspiracy was filled with contradictions, and scholars have not been able to pin down its precise objectives. Some contemporaries, as well as historians, believed that with Wilkinson's help Burr planned to detach Louisiana and states along the Mississippi from the Union and create a separate nation. His defenders said no; he merely wished to live in peace on lands he owned in the Territory of Orleans. Others, such as Wilkinson, thought he wanted to raise an army to invade Texas and Mexico, an idea that appealed to the anti-Hispanic prejudices of westerners.

Burr launched his scheme during the war scare while Wilkinson was confronting the Spanish forces on the Sabine fron-

237

tier. A letter from Burr early in October 1806 convinced Wilkinson that the plot would fail and endanger his own political fortunes. So the general turned against Burr, revealed the "deep, dark and widespread conspiracy" to Jefferson, and on his own concluded the "neutral ground agreement." [16] If war had broken out on the Sabine, the army would have been busy fighting Spaniards, and Burr's expedition could have moved south freely without fear of a clash with government troops. As it was, Wilkinson broke camp immediately after his arrangement with the Spaniards and hurried to New Orleans, arriving late in November ready to defend the city against Burr's force. Jefferson expressed approval of Wilkinson's frontier diplomacy because it "permitted him to withdraw his force across the Mississippi, and to enter on measures for opposing the [Burr's] projected enterprise." [17]

Burr's conspiracy, or whatever it was, collapsed when federal officials captured him in Natchez in February 1807. He escaped, was recaptured, tried for treason, and acquitted. Those who at first had supported him because he seemed to be working within the accepted pattern of expansion against Spaniards abandoned him when they saw disunion as part of his program. Andrew Jackson, one of those early supporters, explained this attitude well. "I love my Country and government," he said. "I hate the Dons. I would delight to see Mexico reduced, but I will die in the last Ditch before I would yield a foot to the Dons or see the Union disunited." [18]

During this time of internal tension over the Burr conspiracy, maritime grievances against England multiplied. War seemed likely. So Jefferson put aside his bellicose demands against Spain for expanded Louisiana boundaries, but he did not give them up. In 1807 and 1808 he considered settling accounts with Spain by seizing the Floridas. "I had rather have war against Spain than not, if we go to war against England," he said. He favored extending the "limits of Louisiana" as he

238

saw fit and taking "the residue of the Floridas as reprisals for spoliations." [19]

That autumn rumors reached Spain, which had been occupied by French troops since the beginning of the year, that Napoleon intended to sell the Floridas to the United States. Spanish patriots who were fighting the French protested. Actually, because of the war, neither Spain nor Napoleon had much influence in the Floridas. Without support and leadership from the mother country, those colonies seemed adrift and helpless.

Indians and free blacks attacked white settlements in the Floridas, cutting off the flow of provisions to the inhabitants. American gunboats captured Spanish ships within the jurisdiction of East Florida. Georgians raided settlements in the Floridas, stealing slaves and movable property of all kinds. American military units not only violated Spanish territory but also shut Spanish ships out of the Mississippi in violation of treaty rights and encouraged an uprising at Mobile. In New Orleans Americans plotted revolution in Spain's American colonies and planned filibustering expeditions into Mexico.

Across the border in West Florida in the summer of 1810 American settlers unleashed a full-scale rebellion against what remained of Spanish rule. The rebels marched on Baton Rouge, captured the fort there, and in September declared this part of the province the independent Republic of West Florida. They then sent President James Madison a letter pleading for annexation to the United States. In October the president announced that Claiborne would occupy the territory to the Perdido River, saying it "has at all times, as is well known, been considered and claimed by them [the United States] as being within the colony of Louisiana." In December Claiborne moved in with troops who encountered no opposition, but he took possession only to the Pearl River. Madison then annexed the region to the Territory of Orleans, with the approval of Congress. He defended "the legality and necessity" of this taking of another's property as merely a delayed carrying out of the terms of the Louisiana treaty.[20] Spain, Britain, and other powers protested, but they could or would not do more to stop this latest thrust of American imperialism.

Other encroachments on the Spanish borderlands followed until April 1813, when troops under General Wilkinson occupied the last piece of West Florida, the Mobile district to the Perdido. This annexation completed the Jeffersonian chapter of American expansionism that began with the purchase in 1803. Other chapters, modeled after this "affair of Louisiana," would follow in 1819, 1836, and 1846, until the flag of the American republic flew over a continental empire that spread unbroken from the Atlantic to the Pacific.

Chapter XV

✦

The Imperial Thrust

This great pressure of a people moving always to new frontiers, in search of new lands, new power, the full freedom of a virgin world, has ruled our course and formed our policies like a Fate. It gave us, not Louisiana alone, but Florida also. . . . Who shall say where it will end?

Woodrow Wilson, 1902 [1]

Imperialism, usually a nation's use of power to acquire territory belonging to others, is an emotionally charged word that implies undesirable behavior. So Americans and their historians have seldom employed the term to describe the growth of their country, and most rarely have they applied it to the formative years of the republic. They have preferred to use *expansion, mission,* or other more flattering terms. According to conventional historical theory, American imperialism or something akin to it developed suddenly in the 1840s under a vague but basically beneficent concept called Manifest Destiny. In the era of the Civil War this imperialism virtually disappeared, but it or something like it came to life again in the 1890s to create an empire overseas.

Modern scholarship has just about demolished the idea

that the new Manifest Destiny, or imperialism, of the late nineteenth century was an aberration or something really new in the American experience. In most of the histories dealing with expansion in the early years of the republic, however, the conventional wisdom still prevails. It portrays Americans, at least until mid-nineteenth century, as a peaceful people who shunned the militarism, power politics, and imperialism of European countries but who nonetheless expanded by chance, without much opposition and without causing genuine harm to anyone. They were a people with a sense of mission who when they gobbled territory did so to extend the domain of democracy, to build an empire for liberty, and not to exploit others.

In this interpretation imperialism has no place in the unfolding of early American history. In it the paradigm of peaceful, democratic, fortuitous expansion is the affair of Louisiana. What followed in the nation's history, however, sometimes diverged from the model. In noting this divergence, one scholar argues, for instance, "that Manifest Destiny and imperialism were traps into which the nation was led in 1846 and 1899." [2] This conventional thesis has not reigned without challenge. A diverse group of scholars have depicted imperialism, or expansionism, as a main theme, even as a determining force, in the history of the United States. They contend that from the beginning the leaders of the republic had the imperial urge and that the founding fathers intended the United States to possess adjacent and even distant lands.

In this book the process of analyzing expansionism takes the questioning of the conventional interpretation a step further. It places the origin of the imperial thrust in the colonial period and in Europe, but especially in England, and hence American expansionism fits into a context wider than that depicted in most histories. If we separate rationale from true motivation and from events, or from what happened in the New World since the time of the first European settlements, we can discern the Europeans as venturesome expansionists. We can, in the large context, perceive American expansionism as part of the rise of Western nationalism and imperialism. We can note also that the Anglo-Americans brought with them from England an especially compelling imperialist creed. For example, the eminent English philosopher Francis Bacon stressed the importance of "imperial expansion" as a duty for a people who sought "greatness." [3]

The powerful national states of western Europe pursued imperial greatness in the New World by planting colonies. In the process they systematically reduced, absorbed, or annihilated tribal or other native peoples. In no other people was the racism implicit in this imperial process more deeply rooted than among Anglo-Americans. The sixteenth-century Oxford geographer Richard Hakluyt and others maintained that Englishmen, like the Romans of the ancient world, were predestined to take over, colonize, and rule the New World. Imbued with the concept that native Americans were an inferior people who had to give way before a superior race, Anglo-Americans felt no compunctions in dispossessing Indians. They did all this while using the rationale that they were advancing the frontier of civilization and doing so more capably than any other people.

So it was that descendants of those who settled Jamestown, Plymouth, and Massachusetts Bay inherited an imperialist ideology along with their language, politics, religion, and culture. Motivated by a tough, ruthless acquisitiveness that drove them westward in an unrelenting quest for empire, they accepted territorial expansion in conflict with Indians as an intrinsic part of their experience. Considering themselves a chosen people, the Puritans of New England even rationalized their conquest of Indians in the place of converting them to Christianity as the will of God. Two of the leading Puritan divines, Increase and Cotton Mather, defended wars against Indians and Frenchmen, too, as just and proper. Sometimes these Anglo-

243

American colonists were more aggressively expansionist than were the policy makers of empire in London.

The imperial ideology that accompanied the Anglo-American experience runs through the thinking of a number of pre-Revolutionary leaders, but it stands out most vividly in the thought of Benjamin Franklin, the foremost believer in the idea of an expanding American empire. Another who shared this idea, John Adams, spoke in 1755 while not yet twenty of a time when Anglo-Americans would transfer "the great seat of empire into America. It looks likely to me," he added, "for if we can remove the turbulent Gallicks, our people, according to the exactest computations, will in another century become more numerous than England itself." [4]

Three years later Brigadier General James Wolfe, the British hero of the French and Indian War, was impressed with the presence of this imperial urge and with the general aggressiveness in the Anglo-American colonies. He thought that they had acquired "the vices and bad qualities of the mother country." Nonetheless, he prognosticated that those colonies "will some time hence, be a vast empire, the seat of power and learning, . . . and there will grow a people out of our little spot, England, that will fill this vast space, and divide this great portion of the globe with the Spaniards." [5]

After benefiting from the British conquests in the French and Indian War, Anglo-Americans expanded their horizon in their quest for imperial greatness. Even college students could join in praising such a quest. At the Princeton commencement of 1771 two seniors envisioned the time

> . . . *when we shall spread*
> *Dominion from the north, and south, and west,*
> *Far from the Atlantic to Pacific shores,*
> *And people half the convex of the main!—*
> *A glorious theme!—* [6]

The patriot victories of the American Revolution enhanced this imperial view of the future, which now became part of the heritage of the new nation. At the Paris peace negotiations in 1782 and 1783 Benjamin Franklin sought, along with England's recognition of the independence of the United States, acquisition of Canada and the Floridas, or essentially all of continental British North America. He was convinced that eventually all this territory must become part of the empire of the United States. Like Franklin and other Revolutionary leaders, J. Hector St. John de Crèvecoeur, the popular French observer of the American scene, took for granted the indefinite westward expansion of American society. "Who can tell how far it extends?" he wrote. "Who can tell the millions of men whom it will feed and contain?" [7]

Immediately after independence the leaders of the new nation fixed their eyes on Louisiana. They replaced British policy makers and their Anglo-American representatives as the prime imperialists in the Mississippi Valley. Independent Americans were confident that the imperial thrust that had brought them possession of the trans-Appalachian West would make the territory west of the Mississippi the heartland of the American empire.

Those in the ruling establishment, as well as other Americans, unabashedly thought of themselves as expansionists and proudly tried to justify their imperialist ideology with pious assertions of a hazy continental destiny. Their foes, whether Indians, Spaniards, Frenchmen, or Englishmen, also considered them aggressive expansionists, essentially imperialists. Through infiltration, immigration, and trade, American hunters, farmers, and merchants began dominating parts of Spanish Louisiana and West Florida. Retaining their loyalty to the United States, these settlers not only refused allegiance to Spain but also brought with them an undisguised contempt for the

Spanish rulers of their new homeland. More than the rhetoric or theories of statesmen, the inexorable pressure of these Americans expanding into the Ohio and Mississippi valleys and then into the territory held by Spain gave substance to the imperial thrust.

While this American vanguard moved across Louisiana's frontiers, prominent and well-to-do men of the republic in 1787 framed a new constitution that could or could not sanction imperialism, depending on the attitude of the interpreter. James Madison, one of the Constitution's most perceptive original interpreters, viewed it as congenial to empire building. In support of this view he advanced a theory that justified American territorial expansion as a means of extending the boundaries of freedom. In discussing the advantages of a republic over a democracy, for example, he argued that "the greater the number of citizens and extent of territory," the less the oppression and the more the security for republican government. "Extend the sphere," he said, "and . . . you make it less probable that a majority of the whole will have a common motive to invade the rights of other citizens." [8] This kind of government required, in his analysis, a strong union or "one great, respectable, and flourishing empire." [9] So he married the idea of freedom with that of expansionism, a duality that American leaders such as Thomas Jefferson used often in the quest for empire.

This theme, taken from the words of the founding fathers themselves, formed a foundation for the conventional wisdom. It gave historians a ready-made analysis based on original sources. They could depict American expansion in moral terms as the peaceful extension of democracy into wilderness or into sparsely settled land and as bringing considerable benefit to lesser peoples. What the expounders of this thesis often overlook or put aside is that early continental expansionism had behind it a thrust of force, a coercive energy, something that its victims—mainly Indians and Spaniards—well understood.

Actually, the thinking of early national leaders as it pertained to empire was less altruistic and tougher than is usually depicted in the conventional analysis. Patrick Henry, for one, argued that "Some way or other we must be a great and mighty empire; we must have an army, and a navy, and a number of things." [10] Publicists stressed the same aggressive theme. Jedidiah Morse, a New Englander, in 1789 published a widely read *American Geography* in which he anticipated American expansion across the Mississippi into Louisiana. Since these were not "merely the visions of fancy," he wrote, "we cannot but anticipate the period, as not far distant, when the AMERICAN EMPIRE will comprehend millions of souls, west of the Mississippi. . . . the Mississippi was never designed as the western boundary of the American empire." [11]

Federalist leaders in the 1790s supported the westward push of "pioneers" and were willing to coerce a weak Spain into relinquishing at least part of Louisiana and the Floridas. A western publicist predicted in 1792 that "posterity will not deem it extraordinary, should they find the country settled quite across to the Pacific ocean, in less than another century." [12]

Eager to extend American dominion toward the Pacific, Federalists debated the various means of acquiring Louisiana. In 1796 Federalist newspapers expressed hope that the United States could someday obtain the province "by purchase or amicable means." Other Federalist shapers of opinion, such as Alexander Hamilton, were willing, even eager, to conquer for empire.

When the Republicans gained control of the federal government, they thought and acted toward Louisiana as had their Federalist predecessors, but they showed more caution in pressuring powerful France than in badgering weak Spain. Despite their periods of restraint, these Jeffersonian leaders, too, were confident expansionists, men with an unquestioning faith in America's destined right to conquer, whether by sword or diplomacy. They played power politics, as they saw it, from a position of strength because they were convinced that the future belonged to them. They viewed the United States as a "rising power," and looked down on rivals such as Spain as "declining powers." Those in decline had no choice. The reality of power compelled them, as it had forced Indian tribes, to recognize the predominance of the United States in North America and to give way before it.

Regardless of the contradictions and inconsistencies in the expansionist ideology, few of the leaders of American society, whether Federalist or Republican, questioned it. They justified their land hunger as the dictate of highest morality. Yet their actions, rather than their rhetoric, indicated that anything goes in constructing an empire for liberty.

According to the conventional view, Thomas Jefferson, the builder of the empire for liberty, was a man who considered war the "greatest scourge of mankind," believed only in defensive measures, and sought peaceful solutions to all foreign problems. Yet historians point out his willingness to use offensive tactics to gain territory. They call him "the greatest of American expansionists," "the architect of orderly expansion," "the first apostle of Manifest Destiny," "the grand agrarian imperialist," the "expansionist of freedom, not of empire," and "America's first great expansionist." Regardless of the accuracy or flaws in the conventional view, he clearly thought in imperial terms.[13]

Unlike contemporaries who often used the rhetoric of expansion without having power, Jefferson as president possessed power; he had the opportunity to act decisively as well as to talk. Continuing desire, ideology, a rhetoric and a program of expansion, no matter how widespread, do not necessarily translate into national policy. A program that becomes policy and a foreign policy that produces imperialist action are shaped by definable forces, usually by men in positions of power.

In the case of Louisiana both external and internal forces,

men of power in Europe and America, brought about the acquisition. In the United States Jeffersonians felt the expansionist ideology with such intensity that they considered the transformation of rhetoric and policy into action as the working of Providence. In their thinking the Indians, the French, and the Spaniards held Louisiana temporarily as trustees. Jeffersonians saw themselves as taking rightful possession, regardless of the clouded legal title, of what had been destined to be theirs anyway. With their program of deliberate expansionism, these confident activists merely hastened the work of this inevitable destiny.

In working out this program, Jefferson took over the ideas of Benjamin Franklin, John Adams, James Madison, and other founding fathers, fused expansion with destiny and freedom, and rationalized the whole process as the building of an empire for liberty. Capitalizing on the westward surge of population and using a mixture of threat and restraint in diplomacy, he never lost sight of his desired objective: territory. With the acquisition of Louisiana he converted the idea of empire into reality and made it the finest achievement of his presidency. Henry Adams, a historian often critical of Jefferson, called this affair of Louisiana an unparalleled piece of diplomacy, "the greatest diplomatic success recorded in American history." He ranked its importance "next to the Declaration of Independence and the adoption of the Constitution." [14]

The Jeffersonian concept of empire did not emerge suddenly or haphazardly a full-blown success. It reflected a well-developed expansionist tradition and a conscious vision of a national future. Yet the immediate circumstances of the president's decision to try to buy New Orleans and of Bonaparte's decision to sell Louisiana give the appearance of stemming more from expediency than from plan. So the conventional wisdom usually depicts Louisiana as coming to the Jeffersonians unexpectedly, "out of the blue," as "an accident of fate," a "diplomatic miracle," as being suddenly thrust upon "indifferent hands," virtually "forced on the United States," or tossed "into the lap of Americans." [15] This aspect of conventional history echoes Federalist reactions. Federalists wanted to deny Jefferson credit for the achievement, and so they argued that he really did nothing more than profit from fortuitous circumstances.

Jefferson's political maneuvering lends credence to this thesis. Although committed to a doctrine of expansion, he appeared to act more to placate aggressive Westerners, to preserve his party's power, and perhaps to prevent disunion than to carry out a national mission. Destiny may work in strange, but not necessarily inexplicable, ways. If the president and his advisers had not been heirs of an imperial tradition and believers in an expansionist ideology, they probably would not have acted as they did when they did.

American policy makers and opinion makers and others had long coveted Louisiana, had schemed to obtain it, had within a decade converted at least part of the province into an economic dependent, and had all along assumed that it was destined in the long pull for no hands but their own. When the prize appeared within their grasp, they did not hesitate; they moved swiftly and confidently to possess it.

Bonaparte, too, had a commitment to a concept of western empire. Chance and expediency, according to conventional interpretations, forced him to abandon that commitment. He found it expedient to sell Louisiana to the United States rather than lose it in war to England. Chance, shaped by the struggle for power in Europe, brought him suddenly to the decision to sell.

Actually, the idea of the sale to the United States had many antecedents. Federalists discussed the possibility of purchase as well as of conquest; Joseph Bonaparte hinted at selling it in 1802; Jefferson alluded to it after hearing of the retrocession to France; and Robert R. Livingston suggested purchase to

Bonaparte before Pierre Samuel Du Pont de Nemours and Jefferson had discussed it.

The evidence also suggests that the First Consul decided to sell because of the pressure Americans exerted on him as much as for any other reason. Jefferson, his advisers and diplomats, and Congress all joined the campaign against the French. The Jeffersonians threatened to use force if Bonaparte did not offer concessions in Louisiana, and the evidence indicates they meant it. Bonaparte's own diplomats and advisers, as well as the Jeffersonian leaders, pointed out to him that his plan of empire in North America was turning a friend into an enemy. At the least it was driving the United States into an alliance with England.

Despite this American pressure, according to some scholars, Bonaparte did not have to sell to the United States. He could have disposed of Louisiana in some other way. Actually, he had little real choice. If he had held on, either England or the United States would have conquered the province. Why not turn it over to the United States in exchange for profit and goodwill? He knew that Americans were driven, as much as he was, by a virtually compulsive expansionism. Sooner or later they would take Louisiana anyway. Why not "spare the continent of North America from the war that threatened" to erupt because of clashing French and American imperialisms? [16]

Even the actions of James Monroe and Livingston stemmed more from dedication to the imperial concept than from mere expediency. They committed their government to buy Louisiana, even though they had no authority to do so, because they instantly recognized a great bargain, knew it fitted the American program of empire, and were convinced that the Jeffersonian leadership would support them. They did not think that the affair of Louisiana all hinged on chance. Nor did other Jeffersonian partisans. They gave credit to the president's "wise & firm tho moderate measures," or his masterly statesmanship, as the essential factor that influenced Bonaparte to sell. [17]

Jefferson himself, in retrospect, stressed the inevitability of Louisiana's fate. "I very early saw that Louisiana was indeed a speck in our horizon which was to burst in a tornado," he said. Napoleon's "good sense" in perceiving this as well as the unavoidable sequence between "causes and effects," he added, "saved us from that storm." [18] The acquisition of Louisiana, as the frontier historian Frederick Jackson Turner hypothesized, was thus "no sudden or unrelated episode. . . . It was the dramatic culmination of a long struggle" that began in the colonial era. [19]

The president's shift in constitutional principles can also be viewed as culminating in his desire to gain and hold Louisiana. Since his strict-constructionist principles clashed with his imperial concept, he switched to broad construction, or to the use of implied powers of government to justify the acquisition. This shift, the argument goes, exemplifies gross expediency, or that the end justifies the means. There is truth in this assessment, but in addition the evidence suggests that Jefferson moved as he did not just out of expediency but also because he felt that now he could carry out the imperial idea that had been important in his thinking for years. He never really retreated from his expansionist program; he never questioned the acquisition or considered relinquishing it. He merely sought the best constitutional means of carrying it out, especially a formula that would blunt the criticism of Federalists and antiexpansionists. In doing so, he established a precedent for use of the Constitution as an instrument sanctioning, even sanctifying, expansionism.

This constitutional sanction helped make the Jeffersonian empire for liberty successful and lasting. Independence had given the United States a sound foundation for growth in the trans-Appalachian West. Louisiana provided Americans with room for more growth with a sense of legal and physical security. Its acquisition not only removed "a fearful cause of war with France" and eliminated a powerful barrier to expansion, but also placed the force of the Constitution behind the imperial thrust.[20] American society and institutions, as a result, fashioned no lasting legal barriers to the absorption of nearly a million square miles to the national domain. This area, larger than Great Britain, France, Germany, Italy, Spain, and Portugal lumped together, doubled the size of the nation.

There were, of course, initial difficulties. To the consternation of the Jeffersonians, the Creoles for a while preferred Spanish sovereignty to incorporation within the benevolent empire for liberty. So the president violated the principle he had himself inscribed in the Declaration of Independence—that governments derive "their just powers from the consent of the governed." He used troops in ruling the new empire.

Some critics feared that such tactics, the apparatus of imperial government, or just expansion itself would endanger American democracy as it was evolving within existing geographical limits. In his second inaugural address Jefferson took note of such criticism and restated his old imperial argument. "I know that the acquisition of Louisiana has been disapproved by some from a candid apprehension that the enlargement of our territory would endanger its union," he said. "But who can limit the extent to which the federative principle may operate effectively? The larger our association, the less will it be shaken by local passions; and in any view, is it not better that the opposite bank of the Mississippi should be settled by our own brethren and children than by strangers of another family?" [21]

Disputes within the American family over the governing and status of Louisiana did produce long-lasting political strain and recurring conflicts over constitutional interpretation. Despite these problems, the enlarged nation, as Jefferson hoped, did hold together. Out of the western empire eventually came the states of Louisiana, Arkansas, Missouri, Nebraska, North and South Dakota, Oklahoma, and much of Kansas, Minnesota,

Colorado, Montana, and Wyoming. The difficulty of fitting these territories into the nation's previous sectional pattern, however, contributed to the coming of the Civil War.

Regardless of the internal difficulties that Louisiana stimulated, Jefferson considered it—the largest acquisition in the nation's history—a personal and national triumph, a proper monument to the imperial idea. When he left office, he expressed an old desire, expansion into the Floridas, Cuba, Mexico's provinces, and Canada. Then, he said, "we should have such an empire for liberty as she has never surveyed since the creation." He was convinced that his fellow Americans had fashioned an instrument of government uniquely suited for this continuing imperial thrust. "I am persuaded," he added, "no constitution was ever before so well calculated as ours for extensive empire and self-government." [22]

More than a decade later John Quincy Adams, who believed that all of North America was "destined by Divine Providence to be peopled by one *nation*," the United States, looked back upon this affair of Louisiana and expressed similar sentiments. Within it he saw "an assumption of implied power greater in itself and more comprehensive in its consequences than all the assumptions of implied powers in the twelve years of the Washington and Adams Administrations put together." [23]

In even broader perspective, with the acquisition of Louisiana the Jeffersonians carried on the imperial creed of their Anglo-American forefathers. With it they accelerated the dismantling of Spain's New World empire and the emergence of the United States as one of the truly powerful nations in the world. Although the United States did not immediately achieve the status or influence of a great power, its size and wealth after the incorporation of Louisiana were such that other nations could not ignore it or threaten it with impunity in its own North American neighborhood.

While anchored in the past of the Anglo-American imperial tradition, this affair of Louisiana also faced the future. It fitted comfortably within the nationalistic and expansionist ideology of America's political leaders, regardless of party affiliation, and met the desires of the many Americans who felt that sooner or later the entire North American continent must be theirs. With minor variations it gave form to the idea of Manifest Destiny and served as a model for future expansion.

Notes

Chapter I

1. "Mémoire sur les affaires de l'Amérique, Janvier 1684," in Pierre Margry, ed., *Découvertes et établissements des français dans l'ouest et dans le sud de l'Amérique Septentrionale (1614–1754): Memoires et documents originaux* (6 vols., Paris, 1879–88), III, 56.

2. Quoted in Antoine Simon Le Page du Pratz, *Histoire de la Louisiane . . .* (3 vols., Paris, 1758), I, 203.

3. *Procès verbal* of the Taking Possession of Louisiana, in *The Journeys of René Robert Cavelier, Sieur de La Salle,* ed. Isaac J. Cox (2 vols., New York, 1922), I, 167.

4. Minister of Marine to M. Ducasse, April 8, 1699, quoted in Andrew M. Davis, "Canada and Louisiana," in *Narrative and Critical History of America,* ed. Justin Winsor (8 vols., Boston, 1884–89), V, 13.

5. "Mémoire sur l'État présent de la Province de la Louisiana en l'année 1720," *Archives Nationales,* series Colonies, 13 A/6 fols. 99–110, cited in Max Savelle, *The Origins of American Diplomacy: The International History of Anglo-America, 1492–1763* (New York, 1967), p. 367.

6. Robert Livingston, a New York merchant, to Jacob Wendall of Massachusetts, Jan. 14, 1746, Livingston Collection of the City of New York, quoted in John A. Schutz, "Imperialism in Massachusetts during the Governorship of William Shirley, 1741–1756," *The Huntington Library Quarterly,* XXIII (May 1960), 222–24.

Chapter II

1. William Henry Drayton, *A Charge on the Rise of the American Empire* ([Charlestown, S.C.], 1776), pamphlet.

2. "Observations concerning the Increase of Mankind, Peopling of Countries, &c," written in 1751. Printed in *The Papers of Benjamin Franklin,* ed.

Leonard W. Labaree et al. (18 vols., New Haven, Conn., 1959–74), IV, 231.

3. "Memoir on English Aggression," Oct. 1750, and "Memoir of La Galissonière, 1751," in Theodore C. Pease, ed., *Anglo-French Boundary Disputes in the West, 1749–1763* (Springfield, Ill., 1936), pp. 1–2, 11.

4. Benjamin Franklin, "A Plan for Settling Two Western Colonies," 1754, in Labaree et al., ed., *Papers of Franklin,* V, 458.

5. Nathaniel Ames, "America—Its Past, Present, and Future State," *Astronomical Diary and Almanac* (Boston, 1758).

6. Pierre Paul, marquis d'Ossun, to Choiseul, July 4, 1760, *Archives des Affaires Étrangères, Correspondance Politique, Espagne,* 529, fols. 22–34, quoted in Savelle, *Origins of American Diplomacy,* p. 461.

7. "Mémoire on Terms of Peace, April 13, 1761," in Pease, ed., *Anglo-French Boundary Disputes,* p. 290.

8. Quoted in William R. Shepherd, "The Cession of Louisiana to Spain," *Political Science Quarterly,* XIX (Sept. 1904), 449.

9. Lawrence H. Gipson, "The American Revolution as an Aftermath of the Great War for Empire, 1754–1763," *Political Science Quarterly,* LXV (March 1950), 102.

10. "Sentiments of a Frenchman on the Preliminaries of Fontainebleau, November 3, 1762," in *The South Carolina Gazette* (Charleston), Feb. 5–12, 1793, p. 1.

11. Quoted in Charles E. A. Gayarré, *History of Louisiana* (3rd ed., 4 vols., New Orleans, 1885), II, 129.

12. Report of a conference with Shawnee and Miami delegates, held at New Orleans, March 1765, Francis Parkman, Jr., *History of the Conspiracy of Pontiac* (Boston, 1855), p. 536.

13. Oct. 26, 1774, quoted in Simeon E. Baldwin, "The Historic Policy of the United States as to Annexation," *American Historical Association Annual Report for the Year 1893* (Washington, D.C., 1894), p. 369.

14. To James Warren, Feb. 18, 1776, "Warren-Adams Letters . . . 1743–1814," *Massachusetts Historical Society Collections,* LXXII (2 vols., Boston, 1917–25), I, 208.

15. Adams to James Warren, Philadelphia, Nov. 3, 1778, Edmund C. Burnett, ed., *Letters of Members of the Continental Congress* (8 vols., Washington, D.C., 1921–36), III, 476.

16. Ellery to William Whipple, York Town, May 31, 1778, *ibid.,* 269.

17. Jefferson to Clark, Williamsburg, Jan. 29, 1780, *Papers of Thomas Jefferson,* ed. Julian P. Boyd (19 vols., Princeton, N.J., 1950–74), III, 276, and

Notes

Julian P. Boyd, "Thomas Jefferson's 'Empire of Liberty,' " *Virginia Quarterly Review,* XXIV (Autumn 1948), 550.

18. Franklin to John Jay, Passy, Oct. 2, 1780, *The Works of Benjamin Franklin,* ed. Jared Sparks (10 vols., Boston, 1836–40), VIII, 501.

19. Aranda to Conde de Florida Blanca, Sept. 1, 1782, *Archivo Histórico Nacional,* Estado series (Madrid), 6609, quoted in Richard B. Morris, *The Peacemakers: The Great Powers and American Independence* (New York, 1965), pp. 321–22, and in a slightly different version in Samuel F. Bemis, "The Rayneval Memoranda of 1782 on Western Boundaries and Some Comments on the French Historian Doniel," *American Antiquarian Society Proceedings,* n.s. XLVII (1937), 35–36.

20. Samuel F. Bemis, *The Diplomacy of the American Revolution* (Washington, D.C., 1935; reprint ed., Bloomington, Ind., 1957), p. 99.

21. Anne César, chevalier de la Luzerne, to Vergennes, n.d., quoted in Justin Winsor, *The Westward Movement: The Colonies and the Republic West of the Alleghenies, 1763–1798* (Boston, 1897), p. 216.

22. The quotations are from *The Morning Post* (London), Aug. 21 and Nov. 7, 1782, cited in Eunice Wead, "British Public Opinion of the Peace with America in 1782," *American Historical Review,* XXXIV (April 1929), 520, 522.

23. Martín de Navarro, "Political Reflections on the present condition of the province of Louisiana" [New Orleans, ca. 1785], in *Louisiana under the Rule of Spain, France, and the United States, 1785–1807,* James A. Robertson, ed. (2 vols., Cleveland, 1911), I, 247.

Chapter III

1. Jedidiah Morse, *The American Geography; or View of the Present Situation of the United States of America* (Elizabethtown, N.J., 1789), p. 469.

2. Jefferson to Bernardo de Gálvez, Williamsburg, Nov. 8, 1779, Boyd, ed., *Jefferson Papers,* III, 168.

3. *The Autobiography of James Monroe,* ed. Stuart Gerry Brown (Syracuse, N.Y., 1959), p. 45.

4. Thomas Hutchins, *An Historical Narrative and Topographical Description of Louisiana and West-Florida* (Philadelphia, 1784), pp. 93–94.

5. John Adams to John Jay, Auteuil, May 8, 1785, *The Works of John Adams,* ed. Charles Francis Adams (10 vols., Boston, 1850–56), VIII, 246.

6. John Jay to Count de Florida Blanca, St. Ildefonso, Sept. 22, 1781, *The Correspondence and Public Papers of John Jay,* ed. Henry P. Johnston (4 vols., New York, 1890–93; reprint ed., 1970), II, 126.

7. John Jay to Congress, Aug. 3, 1786, U.S. Continental Congress, *Secret Journal of the Acts and Proceedings of Congress* (4 vols., Boston, 1820–21), IV, 53–54.

8. Anonymous letter from Louisville, Dec. 4, 1786, *ibid.*, pp. 320–23.

9. Jefferson to Archibald Stuart, Paris, Jan. 25, 1786, Boyd, ed., *Jefferson Papers*, IX, 218.

10. Navarro to the Spanish crown, Madrid, Feb. 12, 1787, in Gayarré, *History of Louisiana*, III, 182–83.

11. Jefferson to Washington, Philadelphia, April 2, 1791, *The Writings of Thomas Jefferson*, ed. Paul L. Ford (10 vols., New York, 1892–99), VI, 239.

12. *Boston Gazette*, May 11, 1789, p. 3.

13. Queries to the Heads of the Departments, United States, Aug. 27, 1790, in *The Writings of George Washington from the Original Manuscript Sources, 1745–1799*, ed. John C. Fitzpatrick (39 vols., Washington, D.C., 1931–44), XXXI, 102–3.

14. Answers to the Questions proposed by the President . . . to the Secretary of the Treasury [New York, Sept. 15, 1790], *Papers of Alexander Hamilton*, ed. Harold C. Syrett and Jacob E. Cooke (19 vols., New York, 1961–73), VII, 51, 53.

15. The quotations are from Jefferson to William Short, New York, Aug. 10, 1790, Mr. [William] Carmichael [Aug. 22, 1790], and Washington [Aug. 28, 1790], Ford, ed., *Jefferson's Writings*, VI, 116, 123, and 141.

Chapter IV

1. Baron de Carondelet, Military Report on Louisiana and West Florida, New Orleans, Nov. 24, 1794, Robertson, ed., *Louisiana*, I, 298.

2. Carondelet to Juan Delavillebeuvre, New Orleans, April 13, 1794, *Spain in the Mississippi Valley, 1765–94: Translations of Materials from the Spanish Archives in the Bancroft Library*, ed. Lawrence Kinnaird, vols. II–IV of *Annual Report of the American Historical Association for the Year 1945* (4 vols., Washington, D.C., 1946–49), IV, 271.

3. Timothy Dwight, *Greenfield Hill: A Poem* (New York, 1794), pp. 52–53.

4. Luis de las Casas to del Campo de Alange (minister of war), Havana, May 19, 1794, *Archives of the Indies*, quoted in James A. James, *The Life of George Rogers Clark* (Chicago, 1928), p. 428; Carondelet, Report on Louisiana, New Orleans, Nov. 24, 1794, Robertson, ed., *Louisiana*, I, 297–98.

5. Jefferson to United States Commissioners, March 23, 1793, Ford, ed., *Jefferson's Writings*, VII, 268.

6. *Porcupine's Gazette* (Philadelphia), July 15, 1797, William Cobbett, *Porcupine's Works* (12 vols., London, 1801), VI, 270.

7. Pickering to Hamilton, Philadelphia, March 25, 1798, *Works of Alexander Hamilton,* ed. John C. Hamilton (7 vols., New York, 1850–51), VI, 275–76.

8. Don Luis de Peñalvert y Cardenas 1799, quoted in Gayarré, *History of Louisiana,* III, 407–409.

9. Hamilton to George Washington, New York, June 15, 1799, *The Works of Alexander Hamilton,* ed. Henry Cabot Lodge (9 vols., New York, 1885–86), VIII, 535.

10. Hamilton to Harrison Gray Otis, New York, Jan. 26, 1799, Hamilton, ed., *Works of Hamilton,* VI, 391.

11. William Cobbett, July 1797, quoted in Alexander DeConde, *The Quasi-War* (New York, 1966), p. 116.

12. Quoted in William S. Robertson, *The Life of Miranda* (2 vols., Chapel Hill, N.C., 1929), I, 168.

13. Grenville to Robert Liston, Downing Street, June 8, 1798, *Instructions to the British Ministers to the United States, 1791–1812,* ed. Bernard Mayo, *Annual Report of the American Historical Association for the Year 1936* (3 vols., Washington, D.C., 1941), III, 158.

Chapter V

1. Instructions données aux Citoyen Guillemardet, Prairial, An VI (May 20–June 19, 1798), in Henry Adams, *History of the United States of America during the Administrations of Jefferson and Madison* (9 vols., New York, 1891–96), I, 356–57.

2. Louis-Guillaume Otto to Vergennes, New York, April 23, 1786, and Vergennes to Otto, Versailles, Aug. 25, 1786, in George Bancroft, *History of the Formation of the Constitution of the United States of America* (2 vols., New York, 1882), I, 498, and II, 387.

3. Quoted in Howard C. Rice, *Barthélemi Tardiveau: A French Trader in the West* (Baltimore, 1938), p. 14.

4. Instructions to Genêt, Dec. 1792, *Correspondence of the French Ministers to the United States, 1791–1797,* ed. Frederick J. Turner, *Annual Report of the American Historical Association for the Year 1903* (2 vols., Washington, D.C., 1904), II, 205. Subsequent instructions, written after France went to war against Spain and England, directed Genêt to attack Louisiana.

5. Fauchet to Commissioners of Foreign Relations, Philadelphia, Feb. 4, 1795, *ibid.,* p. 567.

6. Brown, ed., *Monroe's Autobiography,* p. 136.

7. *The New York Herald,* reprinted in the *New Hampshire and Vermont Journal: Or the Farmer's Weekly Museum* (Walpole, N.H.), Sept. 6, 1796.

8. Oliver Wolcott, Jr., to Oliver Wolcott, Sr., Philadelphia, Oct. 17, 1796, *Memoirs of the Administrations of Washington and John Adams, Edited from the Papers of Oliver Wolcott, Secretary of the Treasury,* ed. George Gibbs (2 vols., New York, 1846), I, 387–88.

9. The first quotation is from Instructions données au Général Pérignon par le Directoire [July 8, 1796], in François P. Renaut, *La Question de la Louisiane, 1796–1806* (Paris, 1918), p. 198; and the second quotation is from Frederick J. Turner, "The Diplomatic Contest for the Mississippi Valley," *Atlantic Monthly,* XCIII (June 1904), 810.

10. The quotations are from Georges Henri Victor Collot, *A Journey in North America* . . . (2 vols., Paris, 1826), I, v, and II, 246; and "General Collot's Plan for a Reconnaissance of the Ohio and Mississippi Valleys, 1796," trans. Durand Echeverria, *William and Mary Quarterly,* 3rd ser. IX (Oct. 1952), 518.

11. Quoted in Turner, "Diplomatic Contest for the Mississippi Valley," p. 812.

12. William Cobbett, "Porcupine's Political Censor for November 1796," quoted in Pierce W. Gaines, *William Cobbett and the United States, 1792–1835: A Bibliography with Notes and Extracts* (Worcester, Mass., 1971), p. 70.

13. Pickering to Rufus King, Department of State, Feb. 15, 1797, Timothy Pickering Papers, Massachusetts Historical Society, Boston (microfilm copy).

14. Pickering to Charles C. Pinckney, Philadelphia, Feb. 25, 1797, National Archives, Department of State, Diplomatic and Consular Instructions.

15. Pickering to Rufus King, June 20, 1797, Pickering Papers, cited in Gerard H. Clarfield, "Victory in the West: A Study of the Role of Timothy Pickering in the Successful Consummation of Pinckney's Treaty," *Essex Institute Historical Collections,* CI (Oct. 1965), 335.

16. Quoted in Raymond Guyot, *Le Directoire et la Paix de l'Europe des Traités de Bâle à Deuxième Coalition 1795–99* (Paris, 1912), p. 409–410n. Italics in Guyot.

17. Létombe to Talleyrand, Philadelphia, April 19, 1798, *Archives des Affaires Etrangères, Correspondance Politique, Etats-Unis,* vol. 49, *ff.* 328–29. Photostats in the Library of Congress.

18. Instructions to Guillemardet, May 20–June 29, 1798, Adams, *History of the U.S.,* I, 356.

19. Letter of Collot, Philadelphia, June 26, 1798, *Archives nationales, relations extérieures, U.S.A.,* AF III, 64, dossier 263, pp. 5–6 (microfilm copy).

Létombe to Directory, Philadelphia, July 18, 1798, Turner, ed., *Correspondence of French Ministers,* p. 1051.
20. Rufus King Memorandum Book, summary of a conversation, Sept. 22, 1798, *The Life and Correspondence of Rufus King,* ed. Charles R. King (6 vols., New York, 1894–1900), III, 572.

Chapter VI

1. As reported by Louis A. Pichon to Talleyrand, Georgetown, July 20, 1801, *Archives des Affaires Etrangères, Correspondance Politique, Etats Unis,* vol. LIII, pt. 3, p. 171.
2. Urquijo to Hervas, Aranjuez, June 22, 1800, in Arthur P. Whitaker, "The Retrocession of Louisiana in Spanish Policy," *American Historical Review,* XXXIX (April 1934), 455, and Whitaker, *The Mississippi Question, 1795–1803* (New York, 1934), p. 176.
3. Charles-Jean-Marie Alquier, to the First Secretary of State of Spain, Aug. 3, 1800, *Archives des Affaires Etrangères, Correspondance Politique, Etats-Unis,* trans. in Adams, *History of the U.S.,* I, 366.
4. The quotations from Pontalba's memoir, dated Sept. 15, 1800, are translated in Gayarré, *History of Louisiana,* III, 410–11, 426.
5. Quoted in Adams, *History of the U.S.,* I, 369.
6. Manuel de Godoy Alvarez de Faría Ríos Sanchez y Zarzosa, *Principe de la Paz Memorias,* ed. Carlos Seco Serrano (2 vols., Madrid, 1956), I, 292.
7. William Vans Murray to John Quincy Adams, The Hague, March 30, 1801, "Letters of William Vans Murray to John Quincy Adams, 1797–1803," ed. Worthington C. Ford, *Annual Report of the American Historical Association for the Year 1812* (Washington, D.C., 1914), p. 693.
8. Pichon to Talleyrand, Georgetown, July 22, 1801, *Archives des Affaires Etrangères, Correspondance Politique, Etats-Unis,* vol. LIII, pt. 3, p. 178.
9. Carl L. Lokke, "The Leclerc Instructions," *Journal of Negro History,* X (Jan. 1925), 93.
10. Madison to Tobias Lear, Washington, D.C., Feb. 28, 1802, State Department Consular Dispatches, Cap-Haitien Series, vol. 4 (microfilm copy).
11. Quoted in Irving Brant, *James Madison: Secretary of State, 1800–1809* (Indianapolis, 1953), p. 89.
12. Letter published in Washington, D.C., in Aug. 1802, quoted in *ibid.,* p. 93.
13. Bonaparte to Decrès, Paris, June 4, 1802 (presumed date), *Corre-*

spondance de Napoléon Ier, ed. Albert Du Casse (32 vols., Paris, 1858–70), VII, 485.

14. Bonaparte to Gouvion St. Cyr, quoted in E. Wilson Lyon, *Louisiana in French Diplomacy, 1759–1804* (Norman, Okla., 1934), p. 122.

15. Cevallos to St. Cyr, May 26, 1802, Jerónimo Bécker, *Historia de las relaciones exteriores de España durante el siglo XIX* (3 vols., Madrid, 1924–26), I, 73.

16. St. Cyr to Cevallos, July 12, 1802, *American State Papers, Foreign Relations,* II, 569.

Chapter VII

1. King to R. R. Livingston, London, March 23, 1802, King, ed., *Life of Rufus King,* IV, 89.

2. King to Secretary of State, London, March 29, 1801, June 1, 1801, *American State Papers, Foreign Relations,* II, 509.

3. Jefferson to Thomas Mann Randolph, Jr., May 14, 1801, Jefferson Papers, Massachusetts Historical Society, quoted in Dumas Malone, *Jefferson the President: First Term, 1801–1805* (Boston, 1970), p. 248.

4. Pichon to Talleyrand, Georgetown, July 20, 1801, *Archives des Affaires Etrangères, Correspondance Politique, Etats Unis,* vol. LIII, pt. 3, p. 172.

5. King to Madison, London, June 1, 1801, *American State Papers, Foreign Relations,* II, 510.

6. Madison to King, Washington, D.C., July 24, 1801, *The Writings of James Madison,* ed. Gaillard Hunt (9 vols., New York, 1900–10), VI, 435.

7. Madison to Livingston, Washington, D.C., Sept. 28, 1801, *American State Papers, Foreign Relations,* II, 510.

8. Pichon to Talleyrand, Georgetown, October 25, 1801, *Archives des Affaires Etrangères, Correspondance Politique, Etats Unis,* vol. LIII, 343–45.

9. Jefferson to Monroe, Washington, D.C., Nov. 24, 1801, Ford, ed., *Jefferson's Writings,* IX, 317.

10. Rufus King Memorandum Book, conference of Nov. 25, 1801, King, ed., *Life of Rufus King,* IV, 19.

11. Livingston to Madison, Paris, Dec. 12, 1801, *American State Papers, Foreign Relations,* II, 512.

12. Livingston to Madison, Paris, Dec. 31, 1801, *ibid.,* p. 513.

13. Pichon to Talleyrand, Georgetown, Dec. 3, 1801, *Archives des Affaires Etrangères, Correspondance Politique, Etats Unis,* vol. LIII, pt. 3, p. 437.

14. King to Livingston, London, March 23, 1802, King, ed., *Rufus King,* IV, 87.

15. Hawkesbury is quoted in *The Annual Register . . . for the Year 1802* (London, 1803), p. 264.
16. Jefferson to Livingston, Washington, D.C., April 18, 1802, Ford, ed., *Jefferson's Writings,* IX, 363–68.
17. Jefferson to Du Pont, Washington, D.C., April 25, 1802, *The Correspondence of Thomas Jefferson and Du Pont de Nemours,* ed. Gilbert Chinard (Baltimore and Paris, 1931), 46–47.
18. Du Pont to Jefferson, New York, April 30, 1802, *ibid.,* pp. 49–52.
19. Madison to Jefferson, May 7, 1802, quoted in Brant, *Madison: Secretary of State,* p. 78.
20. The quotations come from Albert K. Weinberg, *Manifest Destiny: A Study of Nationalist Expansion in American History* (Baltimore, 1935), p. 40; New York *Commercial Advertiser,* March 12, 1802; and Brant, *Madison: Secretary of State,* p. 78.
21. Thornton to Hawkesbury, no. 29, Philadelphia, July 3, 1802, Public Record Office, Foreign Office, America, 55, XXXV. Transcript, Library of Congress.
22. Pichon to Talleyrand, July 7, 31, 1802, quoted in Brant, *Madison: Secretary of State,* pp. 90–91.
23. The memoir, transmitted to Madison on Aug. 10 and to Talleyrand on Aug. 19, 1802, is titled "Is it advantageous to France to take possession of Louisiana?" *American State Papers, Foreign Relations,* II, 520–24.
24. Livingston to Madison, Paris, Sept. 1, 1802, *ibid.,* p. 525.
25. Pichon to Talleyrand, Oct. 16, 1802, *Archives des Affaires Étrangères, Correspondance Politique, États Unis,* LI, quoted in Brant, *Madison: Secretary of State,* pp. 104–105.
26. Livingston to Jefferson, Paris, Oct. 28, 1802, *American State Papers, Foreign Relations,* II, 525–26.
27. Pierre Clément Laussat to Decrès, New Orleans, April 18, 1803, Robertson, ed., *Louisiana,* II, 33.
28. Brown, ed., *Monroe's Autobiography,* p. 153.
29. *Charleston Courier,* Jan. 11, 1803, p. 3, italics in original.
30. James Madison to Charles Pinckney, Department of State, Nov. 27, 1802, Hunt, ed., *Madison's Writings,* VI, 462.
31. Phineas Bond to Lord Hawkesbury, Jan. 3, 1803, Public Record Office, Foreign Office, America, 5, XXXVIII.
32. The first quotations come from [Charles Brockden Brown], *An Address to the Government of the United States on the Cession of Louisiana to the French* (Philadelphia, 1803), pp. 48, 52, and 56. This pamphlet was published anony-

mously. The latter quotation comes from William Duane, ed., *The Missis-sippi Question Fairly Stated, and the Views and Arguments of Those Who Clamor for War Examined in Seven Letters* (Philadelphia, 1803), p. 1.

33. Madison to Livingston, Haverford, Dec. 16, 1802, quoted in Brant, *Madison: Secretary of State,* p. 99.

34. Talleyrand to José Nicolas Azara [Feb. 10, 1803], and to Jean B. J. Bernadotte, Jan. 11, 1803, *Archives des Affaires Etrangères, Correspondance Politique, Etats Unis,* cited in Arthur B. Darling, *Our Rising Empire, 1763–1803* (New Haven, Conn., 1940), p. 452.

Chapter VIII

1. William Coleman's *New York Evening Post,* Jan. 28, 1803.

2. Hamilton to Charles C. Pinckney, Grange, New York, Dec. 29, 1802, and "Pericles," *New York Evening Post* (no month or day), 1803, Lodge, ed., *Hamilton's Works,* VIII, 606, and V, 465–67.

3. Thomas Paine to Jefferson, Dec. 25, 1802, *The Complete Writings of Thomas Paine,* ed. Philip S. Foner (2 vols., New York, 1945), II, 1431–32.

4. R. R. Livingston to Talleyrand, Paris, Jan. 10, 1803, *American State Papers, Foreign Relations,* II, 532.

5. Pichon to Talleyrand, Jan. 4, 1803, quoted in Brant, *Madison: Secretary of State,* p. 105.

6. Edward Thornton to Lord Hawkesbury, Washington, D.C., Jan. 3, 1803, Robertson, ed., *Louisiana,* II, 15.

7. Claiborne to Madison, Natchez, Jan. 3, 1803, *Official Letter Books of W. C. C. Claiborne, 1801–1816,* ed. Dunbar Rowland (6 vols., Jackson, Miss., 1917), I, 253.

8. "Hints on the Subject of Indian Boundaries," Jefferson to Henry Dearborn, Dec. 29, 1802; Jefferson to Horatio Gates, Jan. 27, 1803, Thomas Jefferson Papers, Library of Congress.

9. Jefferson to William Henry Harrison, Washington, D.C., Feb. 27, 1803, *Writings of Thomas Jefferson,* ed. Henry A. Washington (9 vols., Washington, 1853–54), IV, 473–74.

10. *Frankfort Palladium* (Kentucky), March 3, 1803, quoted in Stuart S. Sprague, "Jefferson, Kentucky and the Closing of the Port of New Orleans, 1802–1803," *Register of the Kentucky Historical Society,* LXX (Oct. 1972), 316.

11. Jan. 4, 5, 1803, 7th Cong., 2d sess., *Annals of the Congress of the United States 1789–1824* (42 vols., Washington, D.C., 1834–56), pp. 312–14.

12. Jefferson to Monroe, Washington, D.C., Jan. 10, 1803, Ford, ed., *Jefferson's Writings,* IX, 416.

13. Jefferson to Monroe, Washington, D.C., Jan. 13, 1803, *ibid.*, 418–19.
14. Jefferson to Thomas M. Randolph, Jr., Jan. 17, 1803, quoted in Brant, *Madison: Secretary of State,* p. 107.
15. Thornton to Lord Hawkesbury, Washington, D.C., May 30, 1803, Robertson, ed., *Louisiana,* II, 20–21.
16. The substance of the instructions, Madison to Livingston and Monroe, was decided upon in February but they were dated, Department of State, March 2, 1803, *American State Papers, Foreign Relations,* II, 540–44. The quotation comes from p. 541.
17. Carlos Martínez de Irujo to Pedro Cevallos, Dec. 1802, *Letters of the Lewis and Clark Expedition with Related Documents, 1783–1854,* ed. Donald Jackson (Urbana, Ill., 1962), pp. 4–5.
18. "Confidential Message on Expedition to the Pacific," Jan. 18, 1803, Ford, ed., *Jefferson's Writings,* IX, 421–34.
19. William Plumer Repository, Anecdotes, January 19, 1803, Library of Congress, quoted in Brant, *Madison: Secretary of State,* p. 108.
20. Gallatin to Jefferson [April 13, 1803], Jackson, ed., *Letters of Lewis and Clark Expedition,* pp. 32–33.
21. Meriwether Lewis to William Clark, Washington, D.C., June 19, 1803, *ibid.,* p. 59.
22. *New York Evening Post,* Jan. 28, 1803.
23. "Pericles" for the *New York Evening Post,* Feb. 8, 1803, Lodge, ed., *Hamilton's Works,* V, 465.
24. [Charles Brockden Brown], *Monroe's Embassy, or The Conduct of the Government, in Relation to Our Claims to the Navigation of the Mississippi* (Philadelphia, 1803), pp. 4, 7, 12.
25. Manasseh Cutler to Joseph Torrey, Washington, D.C., Jan. 15, 1803, William P. and Julia P. Cutler, *Life Journals and Correspondence of Rev. Manasseh Cutler, LL.D.* (2 vols., Cincinnati, 1888), II, 122; and Jefferson to Thomas McKean, Washington, D.C., Feb. 19, 1803, Ford, ed., *Jefferson's Writings,* IX, 450.
26. Feb. 16, 1803, *Annals of Congress,* 7th Cong., 2d sess., pp. 83–88.
27. Madison to Monroe, Washington, D.C., March 1, 1803, Hunt, ed., *Madison's Writings,* VII, 30n, and Stevens T. Mason of Virginia, Feb. 25, 1803, *Annals of Congress,* 7th Cong. 2d sess., pp. 222–23.
28. Senator James Jackson of Georgia, Feb. 23, 1803, *Annals of Congress,* 7th Cong. 2d sess., p. 150.
29. Jefferson to P. S. Du Pont de Nemours, Washington, D.C., Feb. 1, 1803, Ford, ed., *Jefferson's Writings,* IX, 436–41.
30. *Charleston Courier,* March 22, 1803, p. 2.

31. Livingston to Jefferson, Paris, March 12, 1803, *American State Papers, Foreign Relations,* II, 547.

32. Irujo to Cevallos, Washington, Jan. 3, 1803, *Archivo Histórico Nacional* (Madrid), Est. 5538, exp. 16, fol. 570–85, photostat.

33. Rufus King to Madison, London, April 2, 1803, *American State Papers, Foreign Relations,* II, 551.

34. *Ibid.,* p. 552.

35. Cabinet Memorandum, April 8, 1803, *The Complete ANAS of Thomas Jefferson,* ed. Franklin B. Sawvel (New York, 1903; reprint ed., 1970), p. 219.

36. Supplemental Instructions, Department of State, Madison to Livingston and Monroe, April 18, 20, 1803, *American State Papers, Foreign Relations,* II, 555–56.

37. Jefferson to Dr. Hugh Williamson, Washington, D.C., April 30, 1803, Washington, ed., *Writings of Jefferson,* IV, 484.

38. *Scíoto Gazette* (Chillicothe, Ohio), May 7, 1803, p. 2.

39. Quoted in Merrill D. Peterson, *Thomas Jefferson and the New Nation* (New York, 1970), p. 759.

40. Laussat to Decrès, New Orleans, May 17, 1803, Robertson, ed., *Louisiana,* II, 39.

Chapter IX

1. Collot, *Journey in North America,* II, 233.

2. Decrès to Victor, Nov. 29, 1802, quoted in Lyon, *Louisiana in French Diplomacy,* pp. 134–35.

3. Secret Instructions for the Captain-General of Louisiana, Nov. 26, 1802, Robertson, ed., *Louisiana,* I, 361–74. These instructions, although signed by Decrès, were never issued.

4. Decrès to Victor, Dec. 18, 1802, quoted in Lyon, *Louisiana in French Diplomacy,* pp. 138–39.

5. Talleyrand to Bernadotte, Jan. 14, 1803, *Archives des Affaires Etrangères, Correspondance Politique, Etats Unis,* cited in Adams, *History of the U.S.,* II, 11.

6. Spoken on Jan. 11, 1803, *Oeuvres du comte P. L. Roederer,* ed. A. M. Roederer (8 vols., Paris, 1853–59), III, 461. Recorded on Jan. 12 as the *"Propres paroles du premier consul."*

7. Bonaparte to Decrès, Paris, Feb. 3, 1803, *Correspondance de Napoleon Ier,* VIII, 199.

8. Quoted in M. J. Louis Adolphe Thiers, *The History of the Consulate and the*

Empire of France under Napoleon, trans. from the French (2 vols. in 1, London, 1875), I, 455.

9. Whitworth to Hawkesbury, Paris, March 14, 1803, *England and Napoleon in 1803; Being the Despatches of Lord Whitworth and Others,* ed. Oscar Browning (London, 1887), p. 116.

10. Whitworth to Hawkesbury, Paris, March 17, 1803, *ibid.,* p. 128.

11. Pichon to Talleyrand, Jan. 21, 24, 1803, *Archives des Affaires Étrangères, Correspondance Politique, États Unis,* cited in Brant, *Madison: Secretary of State,* p. 117.

12. Brown, ed., *Monroe's Autobiography,* p. 167.

13. Darling, *Our Rising Empire,* p. 531.

14. Quoted in Irving Brant, "James Madison and His Times," *American Historical Review,* LVII (July 1952), 863.

15. Thiers, *History of the Consulate and Empire,* p. 458.

16. James Smith to James Findlay, New Orleans, April 13, 1803, Isaac J. Cox, ed., "The Transfer of Louisiana and the Burr Conspiracy, as Illustrated by the Findlay Letters," *Quarterly Publication of the Historical and Philosophical Society of Ohio,* IV (July–Sept. 1909), 101.

17. Collot, *Journey in North America,* II, 233.

Chapter X

1. James Smith to James Findlay, New Orleans, April 13, 1803, Cox, ed., "The Transfer of Louisiana and the Burr Conspiracy," p. 101.

2. Madison to Livingston, Department of State, Jan. 18, 1803, *American State Papers, Foreign Relations,* II, 529.

3. Livingston to Monroe, April 10, 1803, Robert R. Livingston Papers, quoted in George Dangerfield, *Chancellor Robert R. Livingston of New York, 1746–1813* (New York, 1960), p. 358.

4. Francois Barbé-Marbois, *The History of Louisiana,* trans. from the French (Philadelphia, 1830), pp. 264–65. This conversation, recalled in old age, is uncorroborated by other sources and is probably inaccurate in detail, but it is the only record available and is apparently sound in substance. E. Wilson Lyon, in *The Man Who Sold Louisiana: The Career of Barbé-Marbois* (Norman, Okla., 1942), p. 19, says that in a manuscript memoir Barbé-Marbois gives a different version of his reply and sets the date of the conversation as April 8. The confusion may be the result of faulty memory, or perhaps a doctored *Histoire.*

5. Barbé-Marbois, *History of Louisiana,* pp. 270–71, 274–75. The sum was the equivalent of $9,375,000.

6. Livingston to Madison, Paris, April 11, 1803, *American State Papers, Foreign Relations,* II, 552.

7. The conversational excerpts are from *Lucien Bonaparte et ses mémoires, 1775–1840,* ed. Théodore Iung (3 vols., Paris, 1882--83), II, 146–52.

8. Brown, ed., *Monroe's Autobiography,* p. 158.

9. Livingston to Madison, Paris, April 13, 1803, *American State Papers, Foreign Relations,* II, 552–53.

10. Brown, ed., *Monroe's Autobiography,* p. 164.

11. Monroe to Madison, Paris, April 15, 1803, *The Writings of James Monroe,* ed. Stanislaus M. Hamilton (7 vols., New York, 1898–1903), IV, 10.

12. Livingston to Gouverneur Morris, April 18, 1803, quoted in Brant, *Madison: Secretary of State,* pp. 111–12.

13. This wording comes from the final draft printed in *Treaties and Other International Acts of the United States of America,* ed. David Hunter Miller (8 vols., Washington, D.C., 1931–48), II, 499.

14. Monroe to Madison, April 19, 1803, quoted in Adams, *History of the U.S.,* II, 44, and Monroe, "Journal or Memoranda—Louisiana," May 1, 1803, Hamilton, ed., *Writings of Monroe,* IV, 16.

15. Livingston to Madison, May 3, 1804, *ibid.,* p. 46.

16. Quoted in Brant, *Madison: Secretary of State,* p. 140.

17. Barbé-Marbois, *History of Louisiana,* pp. 310–11, and Livingston to Rufus King, May 7, 1803, *The Original Letters of Robert R. Livingston, 1801–1803, Written during His Negotiations of the Purchase of Louisiana,* ed. Edward A. Parsons (New Orleans, 1953), p. 60.

18. Du Pont to Jefferson, Paris, May 12, 1803, Chinard, ed., *Jefferson–Du Pont Correspondence,* pp. 72–73.

19. Quoted in Barbé-Marbois, *History of Louisiana,* p. 312.

20. The Livingston and Talleyrand quotations are from Livingston to Madison, Paris, May 20, 1803, *State Papers and Correspondence Bearing upon the Purchase of the Territory of Louisiana,* 57th Cong., 2d sess., H.R. Doc. no. 431 (Washington, D.C., 1903), p. 200. Napoleon is quoted in Barbé-Marbois, *History of Louisiana,* p. 286.

21. Barbé-Marbois, *History of Louisiana,* p. 316.

Chapter XI

1. Nov. 25, 1803, *The Diary and Letters of Gouverneur Morris,* ed. Anne C. Morris (2 vols., New York), II, 442.

2. Madison to Monroe, June 25, 1803, Monroe Papers, quoted in Brant, *Madison: Secretary of State,* p. 132.

3. *National Intelligencer and Washington Advertiser,* July 8, 1803.

4. Cabot to King, Boston, July 1, 1803, King, *Life of Rufus King,* IV, 279, and "Fabricus" in the *Boston Columbian Centinel,* July 13, 1803, quoted in Jerry W. Knudson, "Newspaper Reaction to the Louisiana Purchase: 'This New Immense, Unbounded World,' " *Missouri Historical Review,* LXIII (Jan. 1969), 198–99.

5. *New York Evening Post,* July 5, 1803, quoted in Douglas Adair, ed., "Hamilton on the Louisiana Purchase: A Newly Identified Editorial from the New York *Evening Post," William and Mary Quarterly,* 3rd ser. XII (April 1955), 274–75.

6. *Boston Independent Chronicle,* July 14, 1803, quoted in Knudson, "Newspaper Reaction to the Louisiana Purchase," pp. 200–201.

7. Jackson to Jefferson, Nashville, Aug. 7, 1803, *Correspondence of Andrew Jackson,* ed. John S. Bassett (7 vols., Washington, D.C., 1926–35), I, 68; Madison to Monroe, Washington, D.C., July 30, 1803, Hunt, ed., *Madison's Writings,* VII, 60.

8. Jefferson to P. J. G. Cabanis, New York, July 12, 1803, *The Writings of Thomas Jefferson,* ed. Andrew S. Lipscomb and Albert E. Bergh (20 vols., Washington, D.C., 1903–4), X, 405.

9. Jefferson to William Dunbar, July 17, 1803, Ford, ed., *Jefferson's Writings,* X, 19n.

10. Lincoln to Jefferson, Jan. 10, 1803, in Everett S. Brown, *The Constitutional History of the Louisiana Purchase, 1803–1812* (Berkeley, Calif., 1920), pp. 18–20.

11. Gallatin to Jefferson, Department of Treasury, Jan. 13, 1803, *The Writings of Albert Gallatin,* ed. Henry Adams (3 vols., Philadelphia, 1879; reprint ed., 1960), I, 113.

12. Jefferson to Gallatin, Washington, D.C., Jan. 18, 1803, *ibid.,* p. 115.

13. Jefferson to John Dickinson, Monticello, Aug. 9, 1803, Ford, ed., *Jefferson's Writings,* X, 29.

14. Jefferson to John Breckinridge, Monticello, Aug. 12, 1803, *ibid.,* p. 7.

15. Livingston to Madison, Paris, June 25, 1803, *American State Papers, Foreign Relations,* II, 566.

16. Jefferson to Gallatin, Monticello, Aug. 23, 1803, Adams, ed., *Gallatin's Writings,* I, 144–45.

17. Paine to Jefferson, Stonington, Conn., Sept. 23, 1803, Foner, ed., *Paine's Writings,* pp. 1447–48.

18. Jefferson to Wilson C. Nicholas, Monticello, Sept. 7, 1803, Ford, ed., *Jefferson's Writings,* X, 11, and Jefferson to Andrew Jackson, Sept. 19, 1803, quoted in Malone, *Jefferson the President: First Term,* p. 348.

19. John Rutledge to H. G. Otis, Oct. 1, 1803, Samuel Eliot Morison, *Harrison Gray Otis, 1765–1848: The Urbane Federalist* (Boston, 1969), p. 269.
20. Fisher Ames to Christopher Gore, Oct. 31, 1803, *Works of Fisher Ames . . . ,* ed. Seth Ames (2 vols., Boston, 1854), I, 323–24.
21. Third Annual Message, Oct. 17, 1803, Ford, ed., *Jefferson's Writings,* X, 37.
22. Entry of Oct. 20, 1803, *William Plumer's Memorandum of Proceedings in the United States Senate, 1803–1807,* ed. Everett S. Brown (New York, 1923), p. 13.
23. David Campbell to Jefferson, Oct. 27, 1803, quoted in Malone, *Jefferson the President: First Term,* p. 325.
24. Entry of Oct. 24, 1803, *Plumer's Memorandum,* ed. Brown, p. 24, and William Fessenden, *The Political Farrago, or a Miscellaneous Review of Politics in the United States* (Brattleboro, Vt., 1807), p. 47.
25. Nov. 25, 1803, Anne C. Morris, ed., *Diary and Letters of Gouverneur Morris,* II, 442.
26. Nov. 3, 1803, *Annals of Congress,* 8th Cong., 1st sess., p. 60.
27. Fisher Ames to Timothy Pickering, Dedham, Mass., Jan. 7, 1804, in Charles W. Upham and Octavius T. Pickering, *The Life of Timothy Pickering* (4 vols., Boston, 1867–73), IV, 79.

Chapter XII
1. Jefferson to Du Pont, Washington, D.C., Nov. 1, 1803, Chinard, ed., *Jefferson–Du Pont Correspondence,* p. 80.
2. José Nicolas D'Azara to Cevallos, May 19, 1803, in Bécker, *Historia de las relaciones exteriores de España,* I, 94n.
3. Beurnonville to Talleyrand, June 2, 1803, *Archives des Affairs Etrangères, Correspondance Politique, Etats Unis,* Sup. 7: 377.
4. Laussat to Decrès, New Orleans, July 1803, Robertson, ed., *Louisiana,* II, 46–47.
5. Laussat to Decrès, New Orleans, Aug. 17, 1803, *ibid.,* pp. 50–51.
6. Jackson's General Order to the Militia, Hunter's Hill, August 7, 1803, Bassett, ed., *Jackson Correspondence,* I, 68.
7. Irujo to Cevallos, Philadelphia, Aug. 3, 1803, Robertson, ed., *Louisiana,* II, 69–70.
8. Gallatin to Jefferson, New York, Sept. 5, 1803, Adams, ed., *Gallatin's Writings,* I, 153.
9. Memorandum of a meeting of Oct. 4, 1803, Sawvel, ed., *Anas of Jefferson,* p. 222.

Notes

10. Madison to Robert R. Livingston, Washington, D.C., Oct. 6, 1803, *American State Papers, Foreign Relations,* II, 568, and Irujo to Cevallos, Germantown, Sept. 30, 1803, Robertson, ed., *Louisiana,* II, 84.

11. *New York Evening Post,* Nov. 1803, in Knudson, "Newspaper Reaction to the Louisiana Purchase," p. 208.

12. Madison to Pinckney, Washington, D.C., Oct. 12, 1803, *American State Papers, Foreign Relations,* II, 571.

13. Irujo to Cevallos, Washington, D.C., Nov. 4, 1803, Robertson, ed., *Louisiana,* II, 110.

14. Jefferson to Livingston, Washington, D.C., Nov. 4, 1803, Ford, ed., *Jefferson's Writings,* X, 50.

15. Irujo to Cevallos, Washington, D.C., Nov. 5, 1803, Robertson, ed., *Louisiana,* II, 121.

16. *Ibid.,* 118, but in a separate letter written earlier in the day.

17. Jefferson to Du Pont, Washington, D.C., Nov. 1, 1803, Chinard, ed., *Jefferson–Du Pont Correspondence,* p. 80.

18. The proclamation is dated Nov. 15, 1803, Robertson, ed., *Louisiana,* II, 124–27.

19. *Maryland Gazette* (Baltimore), Jan. 26, p. 2, and Feb. 9, p. 1, and Marc de Villiers du Terrage, *Les dernières années de la Louisiane française* (Paris, 1904), pp. 432–38.

20. *National Intelligencer and Washington Advertiser* (Washington, D.C.), Jan. 16, 1804.

21. Pichon to Talleyrand, Jan. 30, 1804, quoted in Brant, *Madison: Secretary of State,* p. 159, and Edward Thornton to George Hammond, Washington, D.C., Jan. 29, 1804, Robertson, ed., *Louisiana,* II, 24.

22. Manasseh Cutler to Francis Low, Washington, D.C., Jan. 21, 1804, "Seven Letters Written by Manasseh Cutler. . . ," *Historical Collections of the Essex Institute,* XXXIX (Oct. 1903), 325.

23. *Scíoto Gazette* (Chillicothe, Ohio), March 12, 1804.

24. The French were informed on Jan. 19, 1804. Cevallos to Pinckney, Pardo, Feb. 10, and Irujo to Madison, Philadelphia, May 15, 1804, *American State Papers, Foreign Relations,* II, 583.

Chapter XIII

1. Sebastián Calvo de la Puerta y O'Farrill, Marqués de Casa Calvo, to Pierre Clément Laussat, New Orleans, March 31, 1804, Robertson, ed., *Louisiana,* II, 184.

2. Morris to Henry W. Livingston, Morrisania, Dec. 4, 1803, Jared Sparks,

The Life of Gouverneur Morris with Selections from His Correspondence (3 vols., Boston, 1833), III, 192.

3. Jefferson to De Witt Clinton, Washington, D.C., Dec. 2, 1803, Ford ed., *Jefferson's Writings*, X, 55.

4. Jan. 24, 1804, quoted in Malone, *Jefferson the President: First Term*, p. 354.

5. George W. Campbell of Tennessee, Feb. 28, 1804, and Dr. William Eustis of Boston, Feb. 28, 1804, *Annals of Congress*, 8th Cong., 1st sess., pp. 1058, 1063.

6. Madison to R. R. Livingston, Washington, D.C., Jan. 31, 1804, Hunt, ed., *Madison's Writings*, VII, 116.

7. *Plumer's Memorandum*, ed. Brown, entry of February 18, 1804, p. 145.

8. *New York Herald*, Oct. 20, 1804.

9. The quotations are from Livingston to Jefferson, May 2, 1803, Brant, *Madison: Secretary of State*, p. 146, and Livingston to Madison, Paris, May 20, 1803, *American State Papers, Foreign Relations*, II, 561.

10. The orator is Joseph Chandler, quoted in Weinberg, *Manifest Destiny*, p. 48, and the diplomat quoted is Louis A. F., baron de Beaujour, *Sketch of the United States of North America, at the Commencement of the 19th Century, from 1800 to 1810*, trans. William Walton (London, 1814), p. 284.

11. Jefferson to John Breckinridge, Monticello, Aug. 12, 1803, Ford, ed., *Jefferson's Writings*, X, 5n.

12. Madison to Monroe, Washington, D.C., July 29, 1803, *American State Papers, Foreign Relations*, II, 626–27.

13. Brown, ed., *Monroe's Autobiography*, p. 171.

14. Quoted in Monroe to Madison, London, July 20, 1803, Hamilton, ed., *Writings of Monroe*, IV, 45.

15. Madison to Livingston, Washington, D.C., Jan. 31 and March 31, 1804, Hunt, ed., *Madison's Writings*, VII, 117, 127.

16. Gallatin to Hore B. Trist, Washington, D.C., Feb. 27, 1804, *The Territorial Papers of the United States*, ed. Clarence E. Carter (27 vols., Washington, D.C., 1934–69), IX, 193.

17. Irujo to Madison, March 7, 1804, quoted in Hubert B. Fuller, *The Purchase of Florida* (Cleveland, 1906; reprint ed., 1964), pp. 122–24.

18. Gallatin to Jefferson, Oct. 1804, Adams, ed., *Gallatin's Writings*, I, 212.

19. The congressman was Samuel L. Mitchell. The quotations come from Thomas M. Marshall, *A History of the Western Boundary of the Louisiana Purchase, 1819–1841* (Berkeley, Calif., 1914), p. 14.

Notes

20. Proclamation by Jefferson, May 30, 1804, *American State Papers, Foreign Relations,* II, p. 583. Italics in original.
21. Vandeul to Talleyrand, July 26, 1804, *Archives des Affaires Étrangères, Correspondance Politique, États Unis,* cited in Adams, *History of the U.S.,* II, 284.
22. Carlos de Grand Pré to Casa Calvo, Aug. 8, 1804, quoted in Isaac J. Cox, *The West Florida Controversy, 1798–1813* (Baltimore, 1918), p. 157.
23. Talleyrand to Turreau, Aug. 8, 1804, Robertson, ed., *Louisiana,* II, 193.
24. Livingston to Madison, Sept. 21, 1804, Hamilton, ed., *Writings of Monroe,* IV, 305n.
25. *The Times* (London), Oct. 23, 1804, p. 4.
26. Report to the Emperor, Nov. 19, 1804, *Archives des Affaires Étrangères, Correspondance Politique,* cited in Renaut, *Question de la Louisiane,* pp. 227–33.
27. Monroe to Madison, Bordeaux, Dec. 16, 1804, Hamilton, ed., *Writings of Monroe,* IV, 280–82. The assistant to Talleyrand was Alexander Maurice Blanc de La Nautte, comte d'Hauterive.
28. Talleyrand to Armstrong, Paris, Dec. 21, 1804, *American State Papers, Foreign Relations,* II, 635.
29. Turreau to Talleyrand, Jan. 27, 1805, *Archives des Affaires Étrangères, Correspondance Politique, États Unis,* cited in Adams, *History of the U.S.,* II, 276.
30. Monroe to Madison, May 25, 1805, quoted in Fuller, *Purchase of Florida,* p. 146.
31. Madison to Jefferson, Aug. 2, 1805, quoted in Adams, *History of the U.S.,* III, 59.
32. Jefferson to Madison, Aug. 17, 1805, quoted in Malone, *Jefferson the President: Second Term,* p. 56; Jefferson to Madison, Monticello, Aug. 27, 1805, Lipscomb and Bergh, eds., *Writings of Jefferson,* XI, 87.
33. Gallatin to Jefferson, New York, Sept. 12, 1805, Adams, ed., *Gallatin's Writings,* I, 244, 247.
34. Jefferson to Madison, Sept. 18, 1805, quoted in Adams, *History of the U.S.,* III, 72.

Chapter XIV
1. April 5, 1806, *Annals of Congress,* 9 Cong., 1 sess., p. 947.
2. Report from New Orleans dated Sept. 21 in the *Scioto Gazette* (Chillicothe, Ohio), Oct. 31, 1805, p. 2.

3. Fifth Annual Message, Dec. 3, 1805, Lipscomb and Bergh, eds., *Jefferson's Writings,* III, 388–90.

4. Entry of Dec. 3, 1805, *Plumer's Memorandum,* ed. Brown, p. 339.

5. George W. Erving, Dec. 7, 1805, quoted in Adams, *History of the U.S.,* III, 38.

6. Armstrong to Madison, Sept. 14, 1805, quoted in Clifford L. Egan, "The United States, France, and West Florida, 1803–1807," *Florida Historical Quarterly,* XLVII (Jan. 1969), 238.

7. Entry of Nov. 12, 1805, Sawvel, ed., *Anas of Jefferson,* pp. 232–33.

8. Message of Dec. 6, 1805, Confidential, *American State Papers, Foreign Relations,* II, 613.

9. April 5, 1806, *Annals of Congress,* 9th Cong., 1st sess., p. 947; April 8, p. 960.

10. John Dickinson to George Logan, Wilmington, Dec. 19, 1805, Deborah Norris Logan, *Memoir of Dr. George Logan of Stenton,* ed. Frances A. Logan (Philadelphia, 1899), pp. 152–54.

11. Entry of Jan. 14, 1806, *Plumer's Memorandum,* ed. Brown, p. 373.

12. January 16, 1806, passed by the House, *Annals of Congress,* 9th Cong., 1st sess., p. 1133. The Senate concurred on Feb. 7; the president signed the act on Feb. 13.

13. Napoleon to Talleyrand, Saint-Cloud, June 23, 1806, *Correspondance de Napoléon Ier,* ed. Du Casse, XII, 484–85.

14. Manifesto of Sebastian Rodriguez, Nacogdoches, Feb. 2, 1806, quoted in Odie B. Faulk, *The Last Years of Spanish Texas, 1778–1821* (The Hague, 1964), p. 123.

15. Anthony Merry to Lord Harrowby, Washington, March 29, 1805, Great Britain Public Record Office, Foreign Office, 5, Vol. 45, no. 15.

16. Wilkinson to Jefferson, Seat of Major Minor, near Natchez, Nov. 12, 1806, James Wilkinson, *Memoirs of My Own Times,* (4 vols. Philadelphia, 1816), II, app. C.

17. Special Message to Congress, Jan. 22, 1807, Lipscomb and Bergh, eds., *Jefferson's Writings,* III, 430.

18. Jackson to Claiborne, Hermitage, Tennessee, Nov. 12, 1806, Bassett, ed., *Jackson Correspondence,* I, 153.

19. Jefferson to Madison, Monticello, August 16, 1807, and to Secretary of War, Monticello, August 12, 1808, Ford, ed., *Jefferson's Writings,* X, 476, and XI, 43.

20. Proclamation of October 27, 1810, and Second Annual Message of Dec. 5, 1810, Hunt, ed., *Madison's Writings,* VIII, 113, 126.

Notes

Chapter XV

1. Woodrow Wilson, "The Ideals of America," *Atlantic Monthly,* XC (Dec. 1902), p. 726.
2. Frederick Merk, *Manifest Destiny and Mission in American History: An Interpretation* (New York, 1963), p. 261.
3. Howard B. White, "Bacon's Imperialism," *American Political Science Review,* LIII (June 1958), 475.
4. John Adams to Nathan Webb, Worcester, Oct. 12, 1755, Charles F. Adams, ed., *John Adams's Works,* I, 23.
5. James Wolfe to his mother, Louisbourg, Aug. 11, 1758, Beckles Wilson, *The Life and Letters of James Wolfe* (New York, 1909), p. 395.
6. "The Rising Glory of America," written in 1771, published in 1775, by Philip Freneau and Hugh Henry Brackenridge, *Poems of Freneau,* ed. Harry H. Clark (New York, 1929), p. 13.
7. Hector St. John de Crèvecoeur, *Letters from an American Farmer* (London, 1782), p. 41.
8. Alexander Hamilton, James Madison, and John Jay, *The Federalist,* ed. Benjamin F. Wright (Cambridge, Mass., 1961), no. 10, p. 135.
9. *Ibid.,* no. 14, p. 154.
10. Richmond, Va., June 5, 1788, *The Debates in the Several State Conventions on the Adoption of the Federal Constitution,* ed. Jonathan Elliot (5 vols., Washington, D.C., 1836–45), III, 53.
11. Jedidiah Morse, *The American Geography; or View of the Present Situation of the United States of America* (Elizabethtown, N.J., 1789; reprint ed., 1970), p. 469.
12. Gilbert Imlay, *A Topographical Description of the Western Territory of North America* (3rd ed., London 1797; reprint ed., 1968), p. vii. The quotation is from the introduction written for the 1792 edition.
13. See Paul A. Varg, *Foreign Policies of the Founding Fathers* (East Lansing, Mich., 1963), p. 150; Henry Nash Smith, *Virgin Land: The American West as Symbol and Myth* (New York, 1957), p. 15; Malone, *Jefferson the President: First Term,* p. 241; Merrill D. Peterson, *The Jefferson Image in the American Mind* (New York, 1960), p. 267; Gilbert Chinard, *Thomas Jefferson: The Apostle of Americanism* (2nd ed. rev., Ann Arbor, 1957), p. 396; Charles A. Beard, *The Idea of National Interest: An Analytical Study in American Foreign Policy* (New York, 1935), p. 52; and Darling, *Our Rising Empire,* p. 402.
14. Adams, *History of the U.S.,* II, 48–49.
15. See Samuel F. Bemis, *John Quincy Adams and the Foundations of American Foreign Policy* (New York, 1949), p. 118; Charles F. Robertson, "The Loui-

siana Purchase in Its Influence upon the American System," *Papers of the American Historical Association* (5 vols., New York, 1886–91), I, 254; Frederic A. Ogg, *The Opening of the Mississippi* (New York, 1904; reprint ed., 1968), p. 539; Charles A. Barker, *American Convictions: Cycles of Public Thought, 1600–1850* (Philadelphia, 1970), p. 318; Arthur P. Whitaker, *The Spanish-American Frontier 1783–1795* (Boston, 1927, reprint ed., 1962), p. 220, but in *The Mississippi Question, 1795–1803* (New York, 1934; reprint ed., 1962), p. vii, Whitaker refutes the accident theory; Oscar Handlin, *Chance or Destiny: Turning Points in American History* (Boston, 1955), pp. 27–48; and Gerald Stourzh, *Alexander Hamilton and the Idea of Republican Government* (Stanford, Calif., 1970), p. 194.

16. Talleyrand to Decrès, Paris, May 23, 1803, Robertson, ed., *Louisiana,* II, 63.

17. See, for example, James Monroe to Virginia senators, Paris, May 25, 1803, Hamilton, ed., *Writings of Monroe,* IV, 31.

18. Jefferson to Dr. Joseph Priestley, Washington, D.C., Jan. 29, 1804, Lipscomb and Bergh, eds., *Writings of Jefferson,* X, 446.

19. Frederick Jackson Turner, "The Diplomatic Contest for the Mississippi Valley," *Atlantic Monthly,* XCIII (May 1904), 676.

20. John Quincy Adams, "Reply to the Appeal of the Massachusetts Federalists," *Documents Relating to New England Federalism, 1800–1815,* ed. Henry Adams (Boston, 1877), p. 148.

21. Second Inaugural Address, March 4, 1805, Lipscomb and Bergh, ed., *Writings of Jefferson,* III, 377–78.

22. Jefferson to Madison, Monticello, April 27, 1809, Washington, ed., *Writings of Jefferson,* V, 444.

23. First quotation, John Quincy Adams to John Adams, St. Petersburg, Aug. 31, 1811, *The Writings of John Quincy Adams,* ed. Worthington C. Ford (7 vols., New York, 1913–17), IV, 209. Second quotation, entry of Oct. 20, 1821, *Memoirs of John Quincy Adams, Comprising Portions of His Diary from 1795 to 1848,* ed. Charles F. Adams (12 vols., Philadelphia, 1874–77), V, 364–65.

Bibliographical Essay

❧

I have used notes only to indicate the sources of the quotations within the narrative. In this essay I identify and evaluate some of the scholarly literature used in my synthesis and analyses. I also indicate main interpretations, points of controversial scholarship, and major sources on the Louisiana Purchase and early expansionism. Since most of the documentary materials on this subject are in print, or when in manuscript are available to the researcher on film of some kind, and can be traced through a number of bibliographical guides, I have not appended an extensive list of such sources. Because the secondary literature on the subject is well known and also readily available in major libraries, I have limited my discussion to the more important books and articles. I have also included those whose ideas, analyses, or facts are at odds with the conventional interpretations or otherwise merit special attention.

General Sources

For manuscript sources on this subject one must search the archives of at least four nations: the United States, France, Spain, and Great Britain. The records of the Department of State are in the National Archives, Washington, D.C.; those touching on the Louisiana affair are available on microfilm.

France's *Archives des Affairs Etrangères, Correspondance Politique, Etats Unis,* are deposited in the Ministry of Foreign Affairs in Paris, and photocopies are available in the Manuscripts Division of the Library of Congress. Spain's relevant documents are in *Archivo Histórico Nacional, Sección de Estado* (Madrid) and *Archivo General de Indias* (Seville), some of which have been filmed and are available in the Library of Congress and the Bancroft Library, University of California, Berkeley. The manuscript documents of the British Foreign Office are housed in the Public Records Office, London; transcripts are in the Library of Congress.

The major figures in this study have left collections of correspondence and papers, and these are available to scholars in various repositories. Much, if not most, of this correspondence has been published, and I have usually relied on the printed works. Thomas Jefferson's writings, for instance, are available in a number of editions. This is also true for others such as Benjamin Franklin, Alexander Hamilton, James Madison, and Napoleon Bonaparte. Among the published government documents, the most valuable for this study are: *American State Papers, Class I; Foreign Relations,* ed. Walter Lowrie and Matthew St. Clair Clarke (6 vols., Washington, D.C., 1832–59), and *Annals of the Congress of the United States, 1789–1824* (42 vols., Washington, D.C., 1834–56).

Although biased against the Jeffersonians, flawed by errors uncovered by later scholars, repetitious, and dubious in a number of judgments, Henry Adams's volumes two and three of his *History of the United States of America during the Administrations of Jefferson and Madison* (9 vols., New York, 1889–91) still offer the fullest, most readable, and most scholarly general account of the Louisiana Purchase. He delved deeply into European as well as American archives, and his copious quotations make his work a source book as well as a synthesis. Just as basic as Adams's *History* are two volumes by Arthur P. Whitaker, *The*

Spanish-American Frontier, 1783–1795: The Westward Movement and The Spanish Retreat in the Mississippi Valley (Boston, 1927) and *The Mississippi Question, 1795–1803: A Study in Trade, Politics, and Diplomacy* (New York, 1934). These studies are based on an extensive use of Spanish documents. Unlike Adams, who focuses on European causes, Whitaker stresses the theme that American frontier pressure contributed to diplomatic triumphs in Europe and that the Louisiana Purchase resulted from such pressure. E. Wilson Lyon, *Louisiana in French Diplomacy, 1759–1804* (Norman, Okla., 1974), is the best study of the purchase from the perspective of French colonial and foreign policy and contains much on American foreign policy also. Doris Graber, *Public Opinion, the President, and Foreign Policy: Four Case Studies from the Formative Years* (New York, 1968), depicts Jefferson as dominating the Louisiana affair and enhancing presidential power. *Louisiana under the Rule of Spain, France, and the United States, 1785–1807*, ed. James A. Robertson (2 vols., Cleveland, 1911), is an excellent selection of documents arranged chronologically with foreign materials translated into English. Jack D. L. Holmes, ed., *Documentos inéditos para la historia de la Lusiana, 1792–1810* (Madrid, 1963), offers material, much of it descriptive, from Spanish sources. François Barbé-Marbois, *Histoire de la Louisiane et de la cession de cette colonie par la France aux Etats-Unis* (Paris, 1829), with an 1830 translation, reprinted, E. Wilson Lyon, ed., with an Introduction (Baton Rouge: Louisiana State University Press, 1977), provides the only view of Bonaparte on the sale of Louisiana.

Most of the popular histories offer little to the serious reader, not because they are popular, make limited use even of secondary sources, and attempt to tell an interesting story, but because often they distort and are inaccurate. Works of this genre include Marshall Sprague, *So Vast So Beautiful a Land: Louisiana and the Purchase* (Boston, 1974), one of the better popular accounts; John Keats, *Eminent Domain: The Louisiana Pur-*

chase and the Making of America (New York, 1973); Donald B. Chidsey, *The Louisiana Purchase: The Story of the Biggest Real Estate Deal in History* (New York, 1972); Charles L. Dufour, *Ten Flags in the Wind: The Story of Louisiana* (New York, 1967); John F. Bannon, ed., *The Greatest Real Estate Deal in History: The Louisiana Purchase—1803* (St. Louis, 1953), a series of lectures that are generally sound; Robert Tallant, *The Louisiana Purchase* (New York, 1952), an inadequate account for juveniles; Emile Lauvrière, *Histoire de la Louisiane Français, 1673–1939* (Baton Rouge, La., 1940); Henry E. Chambers, *A History of Louisiana: Wilderness-Colony-Province-State-People* (3 vols., Chicago, 1925); Curtis M. Geer, *The Louisiana Purchase and the Westward Movement* (Philadelphia, 1904), a clear, sound narrative; Ripley Hitchcock, *The Louisiana Purchase and the Exploration, Early History and Building of the West* (Boston, 1904); Albert E. Winship and Robert Wallace, *The Louisiana Purchase As It Was and As It Is* (Chicago, 1903); James K. Hosmer, *The History of the Louisiana Purchase* (New York, 1902); and James Q. Howard, *History of the Louisiana Purchase* (Chicago, 1902). Viña Delmar, *A Time for Titans* (New York, 1974), is a simplistic novel about the Louisiana Purchase in which the titans are Jefferson, Napoleon, and Toussaint.

Biographies of the men involved are important for understanding the personal and psychological aspects of the Louisiana affair, but most of the biographies suffer from biases in favor of the subject, sometimes so much so that they distort the record. Three of the best biographies for this study are Dumas Malone, *Jefferson and His Time* (5 vols., Boston, 1948–74), vols. IV and V; Irving Brant, *James Madison* (6 vols., Indianapolis, 1941–61), which in vol. IV covers the Louisiana affair; and George Dangerfield, *Chancellor Robert R. Livingston of New York* (New York, 1960). Other important biographical studies are Harry Ammon, *James Monroe: The Quest for National Identity* (New York, 1971); E. Wilson Lyon, *The Man Who Sold Loui-*

siana: The Career of François Barbé-Marbois (Norman, Okla., 1942).

The biographies of Napoleon and Talleyrand usually concentrate on European events and virtually ignore Louisiana. For background the following studies, among many, are useful: August Fournier, *Napoleon I: A Biography,* trans. Annie E. Adams (2nd ed., 2 vols., London, 1912); William M. Sloane, *The Life of Napoleon Bonaparte* (4 vols., London, 1909); John H. Rose, *The Life of Napoleon I* (2 vols., London, 1902); Emile Dard, *Napoléon et Talleyrand* (Paris, 1935); Jack F. Bernard, *Talleyrand: A Biography* (New York, 1973); Jean Orieux, *Talleyrand: Le Sphinx incompris* (Paris, 1971), published in English in 1974 as *Talleyrand: The Art of Survival;* Gilbert L. Lycan, *Alexander Hamilton and American Foreign Policy: A Design for Greatness* (Norman, Okla., 1970); and James R. Jacobs, *Tarnished Warrior: Major-General James Wilkinson* (New York, 1938). Among the numerous other biographical studies of Jefferson, the best brief analysis based on recent scholarship is Merrill D. Peterson, *Thomas Jefferson and the New Nation: A Biography* (New York, 1970), while Peterson's *The Jefferson Image in the American Mind* (New York, 1960) is useful for its assessment of the effect of the Louisiana Purchase on Jefferson's reputation and place in the histories.

Chapter I

The latest, and also best, full scholarly study for the early period under the French is Marcel Giraud, *Histoire de la Louisiane Française* (3 vols., Paris, 1953–65). The first volume has been translated by Joseph C. Lambert and published in English as *A History of French Louisiana: The Reign of Louis XIV* (Baton Rouge, La., 1973). Giraud concentrates on the relationship of the colony with France but also includes much on foreign relations. Although dated, Charles E. A. Gayarré, *History of Louisiana* (3rd ed., 4 vols., New Orleans, 1885), is written largely from original sources and contains information not readily available elsewhere. Gayarré's *Romance of the History of Louisiana* (New York, 1848), published two years after the first edition of his larger work, is also useful. Alcée Fortier, *A History of Louisiana* (4 vols., New York, 1904), is also based on archival sources and reproduces documents. François-Xavier Martin, *The History of Louisiana from the Earliest Period* (2 vols., New Orleans, 1827–29) is flawed but is also the first noteworthy history of the colony. Martin borrowed extensively from Pierre François Xavier de Charlevoix, *History and General Description of New France,* trans. and ed. John G. Shea (6 vols., New York, 1866–72), and *Journal of a Voyage to North America,* trans. and ed. Louise P. Kellogg (2 vols., Chicago, 1923), first published in Paris in 1744 and the most complete history of Louisiana that had yet appeared. Other important early histories are Antoine Simon Le Page du Pratz, *Histoire de la Louisiane* (3 vols., Paris, 1758), and Jean Baptiste Benard de la Harpe, *Journal historique de l'établissement des français à la Louisiane* (New Orleans, 1831). There are inadequate English translations. An important collection of documents and narratives is Pierre Margry, ed., *Mémoires et documents pour servir à l'histoire des origines françaises des pays d'outre-mer. Découvertes et établissements des Français dans l'ouest et dans le sud de l'Amérique Septentrionale (1614–1754)* (6 vols., Paris, 1879–88).

Other useful studies are: William J. Eccles, *France in America* (New York, 1972), which emphasizes Canada but contains important insights on French policy in Louisiana; John F. Bannon, *The Spanish Borderlands Frontier: 1513–1821* (New York, 1970); John F. McDermott, ed., *Frenchmen and French Ways in the Mississippi Valley* (Urbana, Ill., 1969) and *The French in the Mississippi Valley* (Urbana, Ill., 1965), which are collections of scholarly essays; John A. Caruso, *The Mississippi*

Valley Frontier: The Age of French Exploration and Settlement (Indianapolis, 1966); Henri Blet, *Histoire de la colonisation française* (3 vols., Paris, 1946–50); Jean-Louis Aujol, *L'Empire français du Mississippi* (Paris, 1954), an uncritical secondary account; Antoine Bernard, *Histoire de la Louisiane de ses origines à nos jours* (Quebec, 1953); Norman W. Caldwell, *The French in the Mississippi Valley, 1740–1750* (Urbana, Ill., 1941), which stresses Anglo-French commercial rivalry; Regine M. G. Hubert-Robert, *L'Histoire Merveilluse de la Louisiane* (New York, 1941), a popular account; Herbert I. Priestley, *France Overseas Through the Old Régime: A Study of European Expansion* (New York, 1939), one of the better general accounts; John B. Brebner, *The Explorers of North America, 1492–1806* (London, 1933), which emphasizes a theme of westward imperialism; Georges Oudard, *Four Cents an Acre: The Story of Louisiana under the French,* trans. Margery Bianco (New York, 1931), an inadequate popular account; Joseph H. Schlarman, *From Quebec to New Orleans: The Story of the French in America* (Belleville, Ill., 1929); Herbert E. Bolton, *Texas in the Middle Eighteenth Century* (Berkeley, Calif., 1915); John G. Shea, *Discovery and Exploration of the Mississippi Valley* (Albany, N.Y., 1903); Isaac J. Cox, *The Early Exploration of Louisiana* (Cincinnati, 1906); Joseph Wallace, *The History of Illinois and Louisiana under French Rule* (Cincinnati, 1893); John W. Monette, *History of the Discovery and Settlement of the Valley of the Mississippi by the Three Great European Powers, Spain, France, and Great Britain* . . . (New York, 1846); George W. Cable, *The Creoles of Louisiana* (New York, 1884), delightful essays summarizing Louisiana's history; Louis Pauliat, *La politique coloniale sous l'Ancien Régime* (Paris, 1887); Francis Parkman, *Pioneers of France in the New World* (Boston, 1865), and Marcel Trudel, *The Beginnings of New France, 1524–1663,* trans. Patricia Claxton (Toronto, 1973), which have little on Louisiana proper but are useful for background; Richbourg G. McWilliams, *Fleur de Lys and Calumet* (Baton Rouge, La., 1953); Marc

Villiers du Terrage, *Histoire de la fondation de la Nouvelle Orleans (1717–1722)* (Paris, 1917); Pierre Heinrich, *La Louisiane sous la Compagnie des Indes, 1717–1731* (Paris, 1908); and Henri Gravier, *La colonisation de la Louisiane à l'époque de Law: Octobre, 1717–Janvier, 1721* (Paris, 1904).

The following, in one way or another, stress imperial conflict: Max Savelle, *The Origins of American Diplomacy: The International History of Angloamerica, 1492–1763* (New York, 1967) and *Empires to Nations: Expansion in America, 1713–1824* (Minneapolis, 1974); Verner W. Crane, *The Southern Frontier, 1670–1732* (Ann Arbor, Mich., 1929), which plays up the theme of an Anglo-American imperialist ethos; Francis Parkman, *A Half-Century of Conflict* (2 vols., Boston, 1892); Robert S. Weddle, *Wilderness Manhunt: The Spanish Search for La Salle* (Austin, Tex., 1973); Ernest F. Dibble and Earle W. Newton, eds., *Spain and Her Rivals on the Gulf Coast* (Pensacola, Fla., 1971), a collection of conference papers; J. Leitch Wright, *Anglo-Spanish Rivalry in North America* (Athens, Ga., 1971); Howard H. Peckham, *The Colonial Wars, 1689–1762* (Chicago, 1964); Henri Folmer, *Franco-Spanish Rivalry in North America, 1524–1763* (Glendale, Calif., 1953); Theodore C. Pease, ed., *Anglo-French Boundary Disputes in the West, 1749–1763* (Springfield, Ill., 1936), a valuable collection of documents; William E. Dunn, *Spanish and French Rivalry in the Gulf Region of the United States, 1678–1702* (Austin, Tex., 1917); Frederic A. Ogg, *The Opening of the Mississippi: A Struggle for Supremacy in the American Interior* (New York, 1904); and Justin Winsor, *The Mississippi Basin: The Struggle in America between England and France, 1697–1763* (Boston, 1895).

A few of the biographical studies that give flavor and the background of the personalities involved are: Samuel E. Morison, *Samuel de Champlain: Father of New France* (Boston, 1972); Noel M. Loomis and Abraham P. Nasatir, *Pedro Vial and the Roads to Santa Fe* (Norman, Okla., 1967); Henri Joutel, *A Jour-*

nal of La Salle's Last Voyage (New York, 1962), an account by one of the explorer's soldiers; Mellis M. Crouse, *Le Moyne d'Iberville: Soldier of New France* (Ithaca, N.Y., 1954); Guy Fregault, *Le Grand Marquis: Pierre de Rigaud de Vaudreuil et la Louisiane* (Montreal, 1952); Ross Phares, *Cavalier in the Wilderness: The Story of the Explorer and Trader Louis Juchereau de St. Denis* (Baton Rouge, La., 1952); Edmund R. Murphy, *Henry de Tonty: Fur Trader of the Mississippi* (Baltimore, 1941); Georges Oudard, *The Amazing Life of John Law: The Man Behind the Mississippi Bubble,* trans. G. E. C. Massé (New York, 1928); and Francis Parkman, *La Salle and the Discovery of the Great West* (Boston, 1885).

For general information on the native Americans who held the land before the Europeans see Harold E. Driver, *Indians of North America* (2nd ed., Chicago, 1969); Alvin M. Josephy, Jr., *The Indian Heritage of America* (New York, 1966); Wendell H. Oswalt, *This Land Was Theirs: A Study of the North American Indian* (New York, 1966); William Brandon, *The Last Americans: The Indian in American Culture* (New York, 1974); William C. Macleod, *The American Indian Frontier* (New York, 1928); and John R. Swanton, *The Indians of the Southeastern United States* (Washington, D.C., 1946), a specialized basic study. The following discuss or touch on the theme of European despoiling of the Indians: Francis Jennings, *The Invasion of America: Indians, Colonialism, and the Cant of Conquest* (Chapel Hill, N.C., 1975), which stresses that Europeans "did not settle a virgin land. They invaded and displaced a resident population"; Wilbur R. Jacobs, *Dispossessing the American Indian: Indians and Whites on the Colonial Frontier* (New York, 1972), particularly stimulating in its theses; Wilcomb E. Washburn, *Red Man's Land—White Man's Law: A Study of the Past and Present Status of the American Indian* (New York, 1971); and Roy Harvey Pearce, *The Savages of America: A Study of the Indian and the Idea of Civilization* (rev. ed., Baltimore, 1965).

Particularly useful articles are: T. H. Watkins, "Discoverers of the Mississippi: European Explorers' 158-Year Quest Across the Heartland of America," *American West,* XI (March 1974), 4–11, a well-written, sound, popular account; David B. Quinn, "James I and the Beginnings of Empire in America," *Journal of Imperial and Commonwealth History,* II (Jan. 1974), 135–52, an account of English expansion against Spanish possessions; Wilbur R. Jacobs, "The Tip of an Iceberg: Pre-Columbian Indian Demography and Some Implications for Revisionism," *William and Mary Quarterly,* 3rd ser., XXXI (Jan. 1974), 123–32, which points to depopulation of Indian peoples; Robert S. Weddle, "La Salle's Survivors," *Southwestern Historical Quarterly,* LXXV (April 1972), 413–33; Marcel Giraud, "Un aspect de la rivalité franco-espagnole au début du XVIIIᵉ siècle (1713–1717)," *Revue historique,* CCXVII (1957), 250–69, and "France and Louisiana in the Early Eighteenth Century," *Mississippi Valley Historical Review,* XXXVI (March 1950), 657–74; Andrew C. Albrecht, "Indian-French Relations at Natchez," *American Anthropologist,* n.s. XLVIII (July–Sept. 1946), 321–54; Charmion Shelby, "The Effect of the Spanish Reoccupation of Eastern Texas upon French Policy in Louisiana, 1715–1717," *Hispanic American Historical Review,* XXIV (Nov. 1944), 605–13; Henri Folmer, "Contraband Trade Between Louisiana and New Mexico in the Eighteenth Century," *New Mexico Historical Review,* XVI (July 1941), 249–74, and "The Mallet Expedition of 1739 through Nebraska, Kansas and Colorado to Santa Fé," *Colorado Magazine,* XVI (Sept. 1939), 161–73; Francis Parkman, "French Policy in the Lower Mississippi Valley, 1697–1712," *The Colonial Society of Massachusetts Publications,* XXVIII (Boston, 1935), 225–38; Charles W. Hackett, "Policy of the Spanish Crown Regarding French Encroachments from Louisiana, 1721–1762," in Charles W. Hackett et al., eds., *New Spain and the Anglo-American West* (2 vols., Los Angeles, 1932), I, 107–45; Louise P. Kellogg, "France and the Mississippi Valley: A Résumé," *Mississippi Val-*

ley Historical Review, XVIII (June 1931), 3–22; Emile Lauvrière, "Les premières expéditions en Louisiane," *Revue de l'histoire des colonies françaises,* IV, no. 55 (1926), 305–76; and Herbert E. Bolton, "French Intrusions into New Mexico, 1749–1752," in *The Pacific Ocean in History,* ed. H. Morse Stephens and Herbert E. Bolton (New York, 1917), pp. 389–407.

Chapter II

A number of the titles cited for the previous chapter are pertinent to this one. Some books overlap in that they cover periods or topics discussed in more than one chapter, but in order to avoid repetition I cite them only once.

The following books are valuable for the European background of events in North America: Rupert Furneaux, *The Seven Years' War* (London, 1973), a popular history; Jean Tarrade, *Le commerce colonial de la France à la fin de l'Ancien Régime* (2 vols., Paris, 1972); John H. Parry, *Trade and Dominion: The European Overseas Empires in the Eighteenth Century* (New York, 1971); Vincent Harlow, *The Founding of the Second British Empire, 1763–1793* (2 vols., London, 1952, 1964), which shows the influence of American westward expansionists on British policy; Zenab E. Rashed, *The Peace of Paris, 1763* (Liverpool, 1951), the best overall treatment; Vicente Palacio Atard, *El Tercero Pacta de Familia* (Madrid, 1945); François P. Renaut, *Le pact de famille et l'Amérique* (Paris, 1922); Julian S. Corbett, *England in the Seven Years' War* (2nd ed., 2 vols., London, 1918); Louis Blart, *Les rapports de la France et l'Espagne après le Pacte de famille, jusqu'à la fin du ministere de duc de Choiseul* (Paris, 1915); Alfred Bourguet, *Le duc de Choiseul et l'alliance espagnole* (Paris, 1906); Richard Waddington, *La Guerre de Sept Ans* (5 vols., Paris, 1899–1914), although dated, valuable for the French side; and

Antonio Ferrer del Rio, *Historia del reinado de Carlos III en España* (4 vols., Madrid, 1856).

For Spanish rule in Louisiana and adjoining areas, see Francis D. McDermott, ed., *The Spanish in the Mississippi Valley, 1762–1804* (Urbana, Ill., 1974), especially valuable for bibliographical pieces; Robert L. Gold, *Borderland Empires in Transition: The Triple-Nation Transfer of Florida* (Carbondale, Ill., 1969); Vicente Rodriguez Casado, *Primeros años de dominación española en la Luisiana* (Madrid, 1942), the most thorough Spanish treatment based on archival sources; John W. Caughey, *Bernardo de Galvéz in Louisiana, 1776–1783* (Berkeley, Calif., 1934); Ameda R. King, "Social and Economic Life in Spanish Louisiana, 1763–1783" (Ph.D. diss., University of Illinois, 1931); David K. Bjork, "The Establishment of Spanish Rule in the Province of Louisiana, 1762–1770" (Ph.D. diss., University of California, Berkeley, 1923); Herbert E. Bolton, ed., *Athanase de Mézières and the Louisiana-Texas Frontier, 1768–1780* (2 vols., Cleveland, 1914); and Marc de Villiers du Terrage, *Les dernières années de la Louisiane française* (Paris, 1904), which covers the transition to Spanish rule.

The following touch upon or explain developing American expansionism or nationalism: Lawrence S. Kaplan, *Colonies into Nation: American Diplomacy, 1763–1801* (New York, 1972), which shows the long-term American interest in Louisiana; John G. Clark, *New Orleans, 1718–1812: An Economic History* (Baton Rouge, La., 1970), which synthesizes the scholarship on the subject; Richard W. Van Alstyne, *Genesis of American Nationalism* (Waltham, Mass., 1970), which contains a discussion of the idea of empire in the eighteenth century; Allan W. Eckert, *Wilderness Empire* (Boston, 1969), which deals with the French and Indian War; Ian Mugridge, "The Old West in Anglo-American Relations, 1783–1803" (Ph.D. diss., University of California, Santa Barbara, 1969), which emphasizes British interest in Louisiana; William C. Stinchcombe, *The Ameri-*

can Revolution and the French Alliance (Syracuse, N.Y., 1969), which stresses the expansionist theme; Gustave Lanctot, *Canada and the American Revolution, 1774–1783,* trans. Margaret M. Cameron (Toronto, 1967); Richard B. Morris, *The Peacemakers: The Great Powers and American Independence* (New York, 1965), the basic work on its subject; Francis S. Philbrick, *The Rise of the West, 1754–1830* (New York, 1965); Richard W. Van Alstyne, *Empire and Independence: The International History of the American Revolution* (New York, 1965); Jack M. Sosin, *Whitehall and the Wilderness: The Middle West in British Colonial Policy, 1760–1775* (Lincoln, Neb., 1969); Gerald Stourzh, *Benjamin Franklin and American Foreign Policy* (Chicago, 1954), the fullest and most scholarly treatment of Franklin's expansionist ideas; Marcel Trudel, *Louis XVI, le congrès américain et le Canada* (Quebec, 1949); William E. O'Donnell, *The Chevalier de la Luzerne: French Minister to the United States, 1779–1784* (Bruges, 1938); Samuel F. Bemis, *The Diplomacy of the American Revolution* (2nd ed., Bloomington, Ind., 1957), the basic study; Thomas P. Abernethy, *Western Lands and the American Revolution* (New York, 1937); James A. James, *Oliver Pollock: The Life and Times of an Unknown Patriot* (New York, 1937; reprint ed., 1970); Wilbur H. Siebert, *Loyalists in East Florida, 1774–1785* (2 vols., De Land, Fla., 1929); Juan Francisco Yela Utrilla, *España ante la independencia de los Estados Unidos* (2 vols., Lérida, 1925); Clarence W. Alvord, *The Illinois Country, 1673–1818* (Chicago, 1922; reprint ed., 1965); Valentín Urtasun, *Historia diplomática de América* (2 vols., Pamplona, 1920–24), which covers only the period of the American Revolution; Manuel Conrotte, *La intervención de España en la independencia de los Estados Unidos de la América del Norte* (Madrid, 1920); Clarence W. Alvord, *The Mississippi Valley in British Politics* (2 vols., Cleveland, 1917); Edward S. Corwin, *French Policy and the American Alliance of 1778* (Princeton, N.J., 1916; reprint ed., 1962), which on pages 9–13 and 57 exposes Vergennes's *Mémoire* on

Louisiana as a forgery; Paul C. Phillips, *The West in the Diplomacy of the American Revolution* (Urbana, Ill., 1913); Clarence E. Carter, *Great Britain and the Illinois Country, 1763–1774* (Washington, D.C., 1910); Justin H. Smith, *Our Struggle for the Fourteenth Colony: Canada and the American Revolution* (2 vols., New York, 1907); Henri Doniol, *Histoire de la participation de la France à l'établissement des Etats-Unis d'Amérique* (5 vols., Paris, 1886–92), which, although flawed, is still the most important printed source on the subject; Justin Winsor, *The Westward Movement: The Colonies and the Republic West of the Alleghenies, 1763–1798* (Boston, 1897); and Thomas Balch, *The French in America during the War of Independence of the United States, 1777–1783,* trans. Thomas W. Balch (Philadelphia, 1891).

The articles that follow offer special details or analyses: James H. Hutson, "Benjamin Franklin and the West," *Western Historical Quarterly,* IV (Oct. 1973), 425–34, which concentrates on Franklin's ethnocentric expansionism; Robert R. Rea, "Assault on the Mississippi—The Loftus Expedition, 1764," *Alabama Review,* XXVI (July 1973), 173–93; Richard I. Matthews, "The New Orleans Revolution of 1768: A Reappraisal," *Louisiana Studies,* IV (Summer 1965), 124–67; Fernando de Armas Medina, "Luisiana y Florida en el reinado de Carlos III," *Estudios Americanos,* XIX, no. 100 (Seville, 1960), 67–92; Fernando Solano Costa, "Los problemas diplomáticos de las fronteras de la Luisiana," *Cuadernos de Historia Diplomática* (Zaragoza: Institucion Fernando el Catolico, 1956), III, 51–95, and IV, 121–54, a scholarly treatment that stresses Anglo-American expansion; Lawrence H. Gipson, "The American Revolution as an Aftermath of the Great War for the Empire, 1754–1763," *Political Science Quarterly,* LXV (March 1950), 86–104; Richard W. Van Alstyne, "The Significance of the Mississippi Valley in American Diplomatic History, 1686–1890," *Mississippi Valley Historical Review,* XXXVI (Sept. 1949), 215–38, which argues that the first half of the nineteenth century "witnessed the most concentrated period of American empire building"; Gilbert Chinard, "Looking Westward," in Franklin Institute, *Meet Dr. Franklin* (Philadelphia, 1943), a brief account of Franklin's expansionism; Herbert E. Bolton, "Defensive Spanish Expansion and the Significance of the Borderlands," in his *Wider Horizons of American History* (New York, 1939), pp. 55–106, a theory on expansionism; Samuel F. Bemis, "The Rayneval Memoranda of 1782 on Western Boundaries and Some Comments on the French Historian Doniol," *American Antiquarian Society Proceedings*, XLVII, no. 3 (1937), 15–92; Theodore C. Pease, "The Mississippi Boundary of 1763: A Reappraisal of Responsibility," *American Historical Review*, XL (Jan. 1935), 278–86; Robert R. Stenberg, "The Louisiana Cession and the Family Compact," *Louisiana Historical Quarterly*, XIX (Jan. 1936), 204–9; Cecil Johnson, "Expansion in West Florida, 1770–1779," *Mississippi Valley Historical Review*, XX (March 1934), 481–96; Arthur S. Aiton, "The Diplomacy of the Louisiana Cession," *American Historical Review*, XXXVI (July 1931), 701–20, which says the cession of 1763 resulted from a peace bribe; David K. Bjork, "Alexander O'Reilly and the Spanish Occupation of Louisiana, 1769–1770," in Hackett and Hammond, eds., *New Spain and the Anglo-American West*, I, 165–82; James E. Winston, "The Causes and Results of the Revolution of 1768 in Louisiana," *Louisiana Historical Quarterly*, XV (April 1932), 182–213; V. M. Scramuzza, "Galveztown: A Spanish Settlement of Colonial Louisiana," *ibid.*, XIII (Oct. 1930), 553–609; James A. James, "An Appraisal of the Contributions of George Rogers Clark to the History of the West," *Mississippi Valley Historical Review*, XVIII (June 1930), 98–115; Kathryn J. Abbey, "Spanish Projects for the Reoccupation of the Floridas during the American Revolution," *Hispanic American Historical Review*, IX (Aug. 1929), 265–85; Abraham P. Nasatir, "Anglo-Spanish Rivalry on the Upper Missouri," *Mississippi Valley Historical*

Review, XVI (Dec. 1929), 359–82 (March 1930), 507–28; Eunice Wead, "British Public Opinion of the Peace with America in 1782," *American Historical Review,* XXXIV (April 1929), 513–31, which is really selected newspaper opinion; Abraham P. Nasatir, "The Anglo-Spanish Frontier in the Illinois Country during the American Revolution, 1779–1783," *Journal of the Illinois State Historical Society,* XXI (Oct. 1928), 291–358; George A. Wood, "Celoron de Blainville and French Expansion into the Ohio Valley," *Mississippi Valley Historical Review,* IX (March 1923), 302–19; Vera Lee Brown, "Anglo-Spanish Relations in America in the Closing Years of the Colonial Era," *Hispanic American Historical Review,* V (Aug. 1922), 325–483; Clarence E. Carter, "British Policy Towards the American Indians in the South, 1763–8," *English Historical Review,* XXXIII (Jan. 1918), 37–56, which reveals Indian fear of Anglo-American expansion; James A. James, "Spanish Influence in the West during the American Revolution," *Mississippi Valley Historical Review,* IV (Sept. 1917), 193–208, which explains British plans to capture Louisiana; Kate Hotblack, "The Peace of Paris, 1763," *Transactions of the Royal Historical Society,* II (3rd ser., London, 1908), 234–67; and William R. Shepherd, "The Cession of Louisiana to Spain," *Political Science Quarterly,* XIX (Sept. 1904), 439–58.

Chapter III

Many of the entries for the previous chapters apply also to this one. The books that follow touch in particular on the subject of this chapter: Warren L. Cook, *Flood Tide of Empire: Spain and the Pacific Northwest, 1543–1819* (New Haven, Conn., 1973), which gives a detailed account of the Nootka Sound controversy; Frederick W. Marks III, *Independence on Trial: Foreign Affairs and the Making of the Constitution* (Baton Rouge, La.,

1973), which shows southern concern over the future of the Mississippi; Jack D. L. Holmes, *Gayoso: The Life of a Spanish Governor in the Mississippi Valley, 1789–1799* (Baton Rouge, La., 1965), a careful piece of scholarship that illuminates much in Spanish Louisiana; Paul A. Varg, *Foreign Policies of the Founding Fathers* (East Lansing, Mich., 1963); Lawrence Kinnaird, ed., *Spain in the Mississippi Valley, 1765–94* in *Annual Report of the American Historical Association for the Year 1945* (4 vols., Washington, D.C., 1946–49), translated documents, well-indexed, easy to use; José Navarro Latorre and Fernando Solano Costa, *¿ Conspiración Española? 1787–1789* (Zaragoza, 1949), which considers the alleged conspiracy an Anglo-American plot; Michael A. Otero, "The American Mission of Diego de Gardoqui, 1785–1789" (Ph.D. diss., University of California, Los Angeles, 1948), useful for the Spanish point of view in the Jay-Gardoqui negotiations; Miguel Gómez del Campillo, *Relaciones diplomaticas entre España y los Estados Unidos segun los documentos del Archivo Historico Nacional* (2 vols., Madrid, 1945); Caroline M. Burson, *The Stewardship of Don Esteban Mirò, 1782–1792* (New Orleans, 1940), useful for facts, not analysis; Arthur B. Darling, *Our Rising Empire, 1763–1803* (New Haven, Conn., 1940), scholarly, detailed, stressing the expansionist theme; Howard C. Rice, *Barthélemi Tardiveau: A French Trader in the West* (Baltimore, 1938); Lawrence Kinnaird, "The Beginnings of American Penetration into the Louisiana Country: A Study of Anglo-American Expansion, 1763–1800" (M.A. thesis, University of California, Berkeley, 1927), dated and based on limited sources, but perceptive and still useful; Manuel Serrano y Sanz, *El Brigadier James Wilkinson y sus tratos con España para la independencia del Kentucky (años 1787 á 1797)* (Madrid, 1915); and Thomas M. Green, *The Spanish Conspiracy* (Cincinnati, ca. 1891; reprint ed., 1967).

For this chapter the periodical literature is especially helpful. Gilbert C. Din has written a number of articles on immigration. See "Spain's Immigration Policy in Louisiana and the American Penetration, 1792–1803," *Southwestern Historical Quarterly*, LXXVI (Jan. 1973), 255–76; "Pierre Wouves d'Argès in North America: Spanish Commissioner, Adventurer, or French Spy?" *Louisiana Studies*, XII (Spring 1973), 354–75; "Early Spanish Colonization Efforts in Louisiana," *ibid.*, XI (Spring 1972), 31–49; "Proposals and Plans for Colonization in Spanish Louisiana, 1787–1790," *Louisiana History*, XI (Summer 1970), 197–214; and "The Immigration Policy of Governor Esteban Miró in Spanish Louisiana," *Southwestern Historical Quarterly*, LXXIII (Oct. 1969), 155–75. Other articles relating to this chapter include: James H. Mast, "Hugh Henry Brackenridge and the Mississippi Question, 1786–1787," *Western Pennsylvania Historical Magazine*, LIV (Oct. 1971), 375–83, which discusses reaction to Spain's closure of the Mississippi; J. Leitch Wright, Jr., "Creek-American Treaty of 1790: Alexander McGillivray and the Diplomacy of the Old Southwest," *Georgia Historical Quarterly*, LI (Dec. 1967), 389–400; Jack D. L. Holmes, "Spanish-American Rivalry Over the Chickasaw Bluffs, 1780–1795," *The East Tennessee Historical Society's Publications*, XXIV (1962), 26–57; Carmelo R. Arena, "Philadelphia–Spanish New Orleans Trade in the 1790's," *Louisiana History*, III (Fall 1961), 429–45; Randolph C. Downes, "Indian Affairs in the Southwest Territory, 1790–1796," *Tennessee Historical Magazine*, 2nd ser. III (Jan. 1937), 240–68, which stresses United States "imperial" policy toward Creeks and Cherokees; John W. Caughey, "Alexander McGillivray and the Creek Crisis, 1783–1784," in Hackett and Hammond, eds., *New Spain and the Anglo-American West*, I, 263–88; Lawrence Kinnaird, "American Penetration into Spanish Louisiana," in *ibid.*, 211–37, which says this experience marked the beginning of United States expansionism; Abraham P. Nasatir, "The Anglo-Spanish Frontier on the Upper Mississippi, 1786–1796," *Iowa Journal of History and Politics*, XXIX (April 1931),

155–232; Arthur P. Whitaker, "Alexander McGillivray, 1783–1793," *North Carolina Historical Review,* V (April and July 1928), 181–203, 289–309, portrays McGillivray as a symbol of the hopeless resistance of both Indian and Spaniard to American expansionism, and "Spanish Intrigue in the Old Southwest; An Episode, 1788–89," *Mississippi Valley Historical Review,* XII (Sept. 1925), 155–76; Jane M. Berry, "The Indian Policy of Spain in the Southwest, 1783–1795," *ibid.,* III (March 1917), 462–77; Isaac J. Cox, "The New Invasion of the Goths and Vandals," *Proceedings of the Mississippi Valley Historical Association,* VIII (1914–15), 176–200; William R. Manning, "The Nootka Sound Controversy," in *Annual Report of the American Historical Association for the Year 1904* (Washington, D.C., 1905), pp. 279–478; William R. Shepherd, "Wilkinson and the Beginnings of the Spanish Conspiracy," *American Historical Review,* IX (April 1904), 490–506; and Frederick J. Turner, "The Origins of Genet's Projected Attack on Louisiana and the Floridas," *ibid.,* III (July 1898), 650–71.

Chapter IV

Gerald Stourzh, *Alexander Hamilton and the Idea of Republican Government* (Stanford, Calif., 1970), valuable for its analysis of empire and American expansionism; Jerald A. Combs, *The Jay Treaty: Political Battleground of the Founding Fathers* (Berkeley, Calif., 1970); Gerard H. Clarfield, *Timothy Pickering and American Diplomacy, 1795–1800* (Columbia, Mo., 1969); Abraham P. Nasatir, *Spanish War Vessels on the Mississippi, 1792–1796* (New Haven, Conn., 1968); Samuel F. Bemis, *Jay's Treaty: A Study in Commerce and Diplomacy* (2nd. ed., New Haven, Conn., 1962), and *Pinckney's Treaty: America's Advantage from Europe's Distress, 1783–1800* (rev. ed., New Haven, Conn., 1960); Carmelo R. Arena, "Philadelphia–Spanish New Orleans

Trade: 1789–1803" (Ph.D. diss., University of Pennsylvania, 1959); Bradford Perkins, *The First Rapprochement: England and the United States, 1795–1805* (Berkeley, Calif., 1957); Abraham P. Nasatir, ed., *Before Lewis and Clark: Documents Illustrating the History of the Missouri, 1785–1804* (2 vols., St. Louis, 1952); Mary A. M. O'Callaghan, "The Indian Policy of Carondelet in Spanish Louisiana, 1792–1797" (Ph.D. diss., University of California, Berkeley, 1942); James A. James, *The Life of George Rogers Clark* (Chicago, 1928); Jerónimo Bécker, *Historia de las relaciones exteriores de España durante el siglo XIX* (3 vols., Madrid, 1924–26), of which the first volume covers the Louisiana diplomacy; French E. Chadwick, *The Relations of the United States and Spain: Diplomacy* (New York, 1909); and Charles W. Upham and Octavius T. Pickering, *The Life of Timothy Pickering* (4 vols., Boston, 1867–73).

Pertinent articles are: Douglas Hilt, "Manuel Godoy, Prince of Peace," *History Today,* XXI (Dec. 1971), 833–41, a well-written brief sketch; Gerard H. Clarfield, "Victory in the West: A Study of the Role of Timothy Pickering in the Successful Consummation of Pinckney's Treaty," *Essex Institute Historical Collections,* CI (Oct. 1965), 333–53, valuable for its explanation of Pickering's concern over possible French reacquisition of Louisiana; Jack D. L. Holmes, "The Ebb-Tide of Spanish Military Power on the Mississippi: Fort San Fernando de las Barrancas, 1795–1798," *The East Tennessee Historical Society's Publications,* no. 36 (1964), 22–44; Raymond A. Young, "Pinckney's Treaty—A New Perspective," *Hispanic American Historical Review,* XLIII (Nov. 1963), 526–35; Jack D. L. Holmes, "La última barrera: la Lusiana y la Nueva España," *Historia Mexicana,* X (April–June, 1961), 637–49; Ernest R. Liljegren, "Jacobinism in Spanish Louisiana, 1792–1797," *Louisiana Historical Quarterly,* XXII (Jan. 1939), 47–97; several articles by Arthur P. Whitaker, "Louisiana in the Treaty of Basel," *Journal of Modern History,* VIII (March 1936), 1–26, "Godoy's Knowledge of the Terms of Jay's Treaty," *American Historical Review,* XXXV (July 1930), 804–10, "New Light on the Treaty of San Lorenzo: An Essay in Historical Criticism," *Mississippi Valley Historical Review,* XV (March 1929), 435–54, "Harry Innes and the Spanish Intrigue, 1794–1795," *ibid.,* XV (Sept. 1928), 236–48, and "The Commerce of Louisiana and the Floridas at the End of the Eighteenth Century," *Hispanic American Historical Review,* VIII (May 1928), 190–203; John C. Parish, "The Intrigues of Doctor James O'Fallon," *Mississippi Valley Historical Review,* XVII (Sept. 1930), 230–63; F. R. Hall, "Genet's Western Intrigue, 1793–1794," *Journal of the Illinois State Historical Society,* XXI (Oct. 1928), 359–81; E. Merton Coulter, "The Efforts of the Democratic Societies of the West to Open the Navigation of the Mississippi," *Mississippi Valley Historical Review,* XI (Dec. 1924), 376–89; Frederick J. Turner, "The Policy of France Toward the Mississippi Valley in the Period of Washington and Adams," *American Historical Review,* X (Jan. 1905), 249–79; David Y. Thomas, "The Diplomatic Struggle for the Mississippi and the Southern Boundary," *The Gulf States Historical Magazine,* II (1904), 343–63; George L. Rives, "Spain and the United States in 1795," *American Historical Review,* IV (Oct. 1898), 62–79; Franklin L. Riley, "Spanish Policy in Mississippi after the Treaty of San Lorenzo," in *Annual Report of the American Historical Association for the Year 1897* (Washington, D.C., 1898), pp. 177–91; and B. A. Hinsdale, "The Establishment of the First Southern Boundary of the United States," in *ibid.* for 1893 (Washington, D.C., 1894), pp. 331–65. Consult the citations for the previous chapter for other pertinent studies.

Chapters V and VI

The books that follow deal with French politics, foreign policy, colonial policy, and/or the French connection to the

United States. Jacques Godechot, *L'Europe et l'Amérique à l'époque Napoléonienne (1800–1815)* (Paris, 1967), a convenient survey; Ronald D. Smith, "French Interests in Louisiana: From Choiseul to Napoleon" (Ph.D. diss., University of Southern California, 1964), which sees French interest as never flagging; Ulane Bonnel, *La France, les Etats-Unis, et la guerre de course (1797–1815)* (Paris, 1961); Durand Echeverria, *Mirage in the West: A History of the French Image of American Society to 1815* (Princeton, N.J., 1957); Harold C. Deutsch, *The Genesis of Napoleonic Imperialism* (Cambridge, Mass., 1938), which deals with European background; Gabriel L. Jaray, *L'empire français d'Amérique (1534–1803)* (Paris, 1938), which says United States hostility to Napoleon's Louisiana venture persuaded him to sell; Célestin-Pierre Cambiaire, *Le rôle de la France dans l'expansion des Etats-Unis* (Paris, 1935), a popular account; Carl L. Lokke, *France and the Colonial Question: A Study of Contemporary French Opinion, 1763–1801* (New York, 1932); J. Saintoyant, *La colonisation française pendant la période Napoléonienne (1799–1815)* (Paris, 1931); André Fugier, *Napoléon et l'Espagne, 1799–1808* (2 vols., Paris, 1930); Bernard Faÿ, *The Revolutionary Spirit in France and America*, trans. Ramon Guthrie (New York, 1927); Albert Sorel, *L'Europe et la révolution française* (11th ed., 8 vols., Paris, 1921); François P. Renaut, *La question de la Louisiane, 1796–1806* (Paris, 1918); Alfred Schalck de la Faverie, *Napoléon et l'Amérique* (Paris, 1917); Raymond Guyot, *Le Directoire et la paix de l'Europe des Traités de Bâle à Deuxième Coalition, 1795–1799* (Paris, 1911), which explains French efforts to recover Louisiana; Paul L. J. Gaffarel, *La politique coloniale en France de 1789 à 1830* (Paris, 1908); Charles A. Geoffroy de Grandmaison, *L'ambassade française en Espagne pendant la revolution, (1789–1804)* (Paris, 1892); Frédéric Masson, *Le département des affaires étrangères pendant la révolution, 1787–1804* (Paris, 1877), which explains the relationship between Napoleon and Talleyrand; and Maria J. L. A. Thiers, *The History of the Consulate and the Empire of France under Napoleon,* trans. from the French (2 vols. in 1, London, 1875).

For the French-American relationship and its influence on American politics see: Albert H. Bowman, *The Struggle for Neutrality: Franco-American Diplomacy during the Federalist Era* (Knoxville, Tenn., 1974); Peter P. Hill, *William Vans Murray, Federalist Diplomat: The Shaping of Peace with France, 1797–1801* (Syracuse, N.Y., 1971); Alexander DeConde, *Entangling Alliance: Politics and Diplomacy under George Washington* (Durham, N.C., 1958) and *The Quasi-War: The Politics and Diplomacy of the Undeclared War with France, 1797–1801* (New York, 1966); Joseph I. Shulim, *The Old Dominion and Napoleon Bonaparte: A Study in American Opinion* (New York, 1952); and Beckles Willson, *America's Ambassadors to France (1777–1927): A Narrative of Franco-American Diplomatic Relations* (New York, 1927).

Important in the periodical literature are: Durand Echeverria, trans., "General Collot's Plan for a Reconnaissance of the Ohio and Mississippi Valleys, 1796," *William and Mary Quarterly,* 3rd ser. IX (Oct. 1952), 512–20; Wendell G. Schaeffer, "The Delayed Cession of Spanish Santo Domingo to France, 1795–1801," *Hispanic-American Historical Review,* XXIX (Feb. 1949), 46–68; Arthur P. Whitaker, "The Retrocession of Louisiana in Spanish Policy," *American Historical Review,* XXXIX (April 1934), 454–76, which points out that Spain sought the best bargain possible; Mildred S. Fletcher, "Louisiana as a Factor in French Diplomacy from 1763 to 1800," *Mississippi Valley Historical Review,* XVII (Dec. 1930), 367–70, which argues that French desire for reacquisition did not antedate 1793; James A. James, "French Opinion as a Factor in Preventing War between France and the United States, 1795–1800," *American Historical Review,* XXX (Oct. 1924), 44–45, and "Louisiana as a Factor in American Diplomacy, 1795–1800," *Mississippi Valley Historical Review,* I (June 1914), 44–56, which say that the French desire for Louisiana contributed to peace in 1800; Frederick J. Turner, ed., "Correspondence of French Ministers to the United States, 1791–97," in *Annual Report of the American Historical Association for the Year 1903* (2 vols., Washington, D.C., 1904), II, and "Documents on the Relations of France to Louisiana, 1792–1795," *American Historical Review*, III (Jan. 1898), 490–516; William M. Sloane, "Napoleon's Plans for a Colonial System," *ibid.*, IV (April 1899), 439–55; and Albert Sorel, "La diplomatie française et l'Espagnole de 1792–96," *Revue Historique*, XI (Sept.–Dec. 1879), 298–330, XII (Jan.–April 1880), 279–313, and XIII (May–Aug. 1880), 41–80, 241–78.

Chapters VII and VIII

In addition to the items cited for previous chapters, the following offer background material and analyses: Marshall Smelser, *The Democratic Republic, 1801–1815* (New York, 1968); Lawrence S. Kaplan, *Jefferson and France: An Essay on Politics and Political Ideas* (New Haven, Conn., 1967), which contains insight on Jefferson's motivation in the crisis; Reginald Horseman, *Expansion and American Indian Policy, 1783–1812* (East Lansing, Mich., 1967); Ambrose Saricks, *Pierre Samuel du Pont de Nemours* (Lawrence, Kans., 1965); Noble E. Cunningham, Jr., *The Jeffersonians in Power: Party Operations, 1801–1807* (Chapel Hill, N.C., 1963); William D. Barber, "The West in National Politics, 1784–1804" (Ph.D. diss., University of Wisconsin, 1961), which documents the Jeffersonian view of expansion as a basic force in American society; Raymond Walters, Jr., *Albert Gallatin: Jeffersonian Financier and Diplomat* (New York, 1957); Adrienne Koch, *Jefferson and Madison: The Great Collaboration* (New York, 1950), and *The Philosophy of Thomas Jefferson* (New York, 1943); John E. Bakeless, *Lewis and Clark: Partners in Discovery* (New York, 1947); and

Charles M. Wiltse, *The Jeffersonian Tradition in American Democracy* (Chapel Hill, N.C., 1935).

Significant in the periodical literature are: Stuart S. Sprague, "Jefferson, Kentucky and the Closing of the Port of New Orleans, 1802–1803," *Register of the Kentucky Historical Society,* LXX (Oct. 1972), 312–17; Dumas Malone, "Presidential Leadership and National Unity: The Jeffersonian Example," *Journal of Southern History,* XXXV (Feb. 1969), 3–17; Mary P. Adams, "Jefferson's Reaction to the Treaty of San Ildefonso," *ibid.,* XXI (May 1955), 173–88, which points out that Jefferson made extensive military preparations and considered resorting to war; Irving Brant, "James Madison and His Times," *American Historical Review,* LVII (July 1952), 853–70, which argues that Jefferson followed Madison's policies in dealing with France; Edwin W. Hemphill, "The Jeffersonian Background of the Louisiana Purchase," *Mississippi Valley Historical Review,* XXII (April 1935), 177–90; Ralph B. Guinness, "The Purpose of the Lewis and Clark Expedition," *ibid.,* XX (June 1933), 90–100, which argues that Jefferson's motives were commercial and political; E. Wilson Lyon, ed., "The Closing of the Port of New Orleans," *American Historical Review,* XXXVII (Jan. 1932), 280–86, the text of the report to the Spanish king; and Arthur P. Whitaker, "France and the American Deposit at New Orleans," *Hispanic American Historical Review,* XI (Nov. 1931), 485–802, which explains that there was no French-Spanish collusion on the closure.

Chapter IX

J. Leitch Wright, Jr., *Britain and the American Frontier, 1783–1815* (Athens, Ga., 1975) gives a full account of British policy toward Louisiana and French repossession; Thomas O.

Ott, *The Haitian Revolution, 1789–1804* (Knoxville, Tenn., 1973), a balanced analysis that provides insight on the Louisiana affair as well; Hubert Cole, *Christophe: King of Haiti* (New York, 1967); Ralph Korngold, *Citizen Toussaint* (2nd ed., New York, 1965); Aimé Césaire, *Toussaint Louverture: la révolution française et le problème colonial* (Paris, 1961); Oscar Handlin, *Chance or Destiny: Turning Points in American History* (Boston, 1955), in which the Louisiana turning point, linked with Haiti, is discussed in pages 27–48; W. Adolphe Roberts, *The French in the West Indies* (New York, 1942); Rayford W. Logan, *The Diplomatic Relations of the United States with Haiti, 1776–1891* (Chapel Hill, N.C., 1941); Ludwell L. Montague, *Haiti and the United States, 1714–1938* (Durham, N.C., 1940); Charles C. Tansill, *The United States and Santo Domingo, 1798–1873* (Baltimore, 1938); T. Lothrop Stoddard, *The French Revolution in San Domingo* (Boston, 1914); P. Coquelle, *Napoleon and England, 1803–1813: A Study from Unprinted Documents*, trans. Gordon D. Knox (London, 1904); Antoine Metral, *Histoire de l'expedition des français à Saint Domingue sous le consulat de Napoléon Bonaparte* (Paris, 1825); and James Stephen, *The Crisis of the Sugar Colonies; or, An Enquiry into the Objects and Probable Effects of the French Expedition to the West Indies* (London, 1802).

Valuable articles are: Carl L. Lokke, "Secret Negotiations to Maintain the Peace of Amiens," *American Historical Review,* XLIX (Oct. 1943), 55–64, which recounts the British efforts to bribe Joseph Bonaparte, Talleyrand, and others for peace, "Jefferson and the Leclerc Expedition," *ibid.,* XXXIII (Jan. 1928), 322–28, and "The Leclerc Instructions," *Journal of Negro History,* X (Jan. 1925), 80–98; Richard R. Stenberg, "Napoleon's Cession of Louisiana: A Suggestion," *Louisiana Historical Quarterly,* XXI (April 1938), 354–61, which suggests that Bonaparte's failure to acquire the Floridas was the main cause for the cession; Jacques Leger, "Le rôle de Toussaint Louverture dans la cession de la Louisiane aux Etats-Unis," *La Relève,* II (Jan. 1934), 16–18; Mary W. Treudley, "The United States and Santo Domingo, 1798–1866," *Journal of Race Development,* VII (1916–17), 83–145, 220–74; Martin Philippson, "La Paix d'Amiens et la politique générale de Napoléon Ier," *Revue Historique,* LXXV (Jan.–April 1901), 286–318, and LXXVI (May–Aug. 1901), 48–78; and Henry Adams, "Napoleon Ier et Saint Domingue," *ibid.,* XXIV (Jan.–April 1884), 92–130. See also pertinent references cited for previous chapters.

Chapters X and XI

In addition to previously cited literature, the following specialized studies are valuable. Robert A. McCaughey, *Josiah Quincy, 1772–1864: The Last Federalist* (Cambridge, Mass., 1974), which argues that Federalist opposition was based on antiexpansionism as a principle; Hervey P. Prentiss, *Timothy Pickering as the Leader of New England Federalism, 1800–1815* (New York, 1972), a reprint of articles published in 1933 and 1934; Linda K. Kerber, *Federalists in Dissent: Imagery and Ideology in Jeffersonian America* (Ithaca, N.Y., 1970); Robert C. Alberts, *The Golden Voyage: The Life and Times of William Bingham, 1752–1804* (Boston, 1969), a Federalist merchant who helped finance the Louisiana purchase; Lowell H. Harrison, *John Breckinridge: Jeffersonian Republican* (Louisville, Ky., 1969); Jerry W. Knudson, "The Jefferson Years: Response by the Press, 1801–1809" (Ph.D. diss., University of Virginia, 1962), which says the purchase of Louisiana was an act that easily gained widespread popular approval; Lynn W. Turner, *William Plumer of New Hampshire, 1759–1850* (Chapel Hill, N.C., 1962); Charles W. Meinert, "The American Periodic Press and Napoleonic France, 1800–1815" (D.SS. diss., Syracuse University, 1960), asserts that the "topic of Louisiana received more space in the periodical literature during 1800–1803 than any other subject"; Caleb P. Patterson, *The Constitutional Principles of Thomas Jefferson* (Austin, Tex., 1953); Samuel F. Bemis, *John Quincy Adams and the Foundations of American Foreign Policy* (New York, 1949); Ralph W. Hidy, *The House of Baring in American Trade and Finance* (Cambridge, Mass., 1949); Charles K. Burdick, *The Law of the American Constitution: Origin and Development* (New York, 1922); Everett S. Brown, *The Constitutional History of the Louisiana Purchase, 1803–1812* (Berkeley, Calif., 1920), a basic book, but poorly structured; Charles R. Brown, *The Northern Confederacy According to the Plans of the "Essex Junto," 1796–1814* (Princeton, N.J., 1915), which points out that Louisiana's acquisition gave immediate impetus to plans for disunion; Albert Phelps, *Louisiana: A Record of Expansion* (Boston, 1905), "the final conflict of Latin against Saxon for the domination of North America" (p. vi); Shosuke Sato, *History of the Land Question in the United States* (Baltimore, 1886); and William Plumer, Jr., *Life of William Plumer,* ed. A. P. Peabody (Boston, 1856).

Useful articles are: Jerry W. Knudson, "Newspaper Reaction to the Louisiana Purchase: 'This New, Immense, Unbounded World,' " *Missouri Historical Review,* LXIII (Jan. 1969), 182–213; Thomas J. Farnham, "The Federal-State Issue and the Louisiana Purchase," *Louisiana History,* VI (Winter 1965), 5–25, which discusses New England separatism; Elisha P. Douglass, "Fisher Ames, Spokesman for New England Federalism," *Proceedings of the American Philosophical Society,* CIII (Oct. 1959), 693–715, which also discusses secessionist plans; Bradford Perkins, "England and the Louisiana Question," *Huntington Library Quarterly,* XVIII (May 1955), 279–95; Floyd C. Shoemaker, "The Louisiana Purchase, 1803, and the Transfer of Upper Louisiana to the United States, 1804," *Missouri Historical Review,* XLVIII (Oct. 1953), 1–22; L. Lafargue, "The Louisiana Purchase: The French Viewpoint," *Louisiana Historical Quar-*

terly, XXIII (Jan. 1940), 107–17; Edward L. Tinker, "Louisiana Changes Flags: The Tribulations of a Préfet Colonial," *Légion d'Honneur Magazine,* IX (1939), 375–84; Richard A. McLemore, "Jeffersonian Diplomacy in the Purchase of Louisiana, 1803," *Louisiana Historical Quarterly,* XVIII (April 1935), 346–53, which argues against the acquisition-by-chance theory; James E. Winston and R. W. Colomb, "How the Louisiana Purchase Was Financed," *ibid.,* XII (April 1929), 189–237; André Lafargue, " 'A Reign of Twenty Days': Pierre Clément de Laussat," *ibid.,* VIII (July 1925), 398–410; Edna F. Campbell, "New Orleans at the Time of the Louisiana Purchase," *Geographical Review,* XI (July 1921), 414–25; G. Labouchère, "L'annexion de la Louisiane aux Etats-Unis et les maisons Hope et Baring," *Revue d'histoire diplomatique,* XXX (1916), 423–55; Louis Pelzer, "Economic Factors in the Acquisition of Louisiana," *Mississippi Valley Historical Association Proceedings,* VI (Cedar Rapids, Iowa, 1912), 109–28; D. D. Wallace, "Jefferson's Part in the Purchase of Louisiana," *Sewanee Review* XIX (July 1911), 328–38, which denies Jefferson credit for the acquisition; Josiah P. Quincy, "The Louisiana Purchase; and the Appeal to Posterity," *Massachusetts Historical Society Proceedings 1903, 1904,* 2nd ser. XVIII (Boston, 1905), 48–59, which points out that the Massachusetts legislature condemned the acquisition; William A. Sloane, "The World Aspects of the Louisiana Purchase," *American Historical Review,* IX (April 1904), 507–21; Max Farrand, "The Commercial Privileges of the Treaty of 1803," *ibid.,* VII (April 1902), 494–99, which argues that these privileges were in conflict with the Constitution; Daniel R. Goodloe, "The Purchase of Louisiana and How It Was Brought About," *Southern History Association Publications,* IV (1900), 149–71; Marcus J. Wright, "Some Account of the Transfer of the Territory of Louisiana from France to the United States," *ibid.,* II (1898), 17–28; Thomas M. Cooley, "The Acquisition of Louisiana," *Indiana Historical Pub-*

lication, II (1887), 65–93, stimulating for its constitutional analysis; Sylvestris [St. George Tucker], *Reflections on the Cession of Louisiana to the United States* (Washington, D.C., 1803), a brief pamphlet.

Chapters XII, XIII, and XIV

George Dargo, *Jefferson's Louisiana: Politics and the Clash of Legal Traditions* (Cambridge, Mass., 1975), which concentrates on the conflict between Louisiana civil law and Anglo-American common law; Jack E. Eblen, *The First and Second United States Empires: Governors and Territorial Government* (Pittsburgh, 1968); William H. Goetzmann, *When the Eagle Screamed: The Romantic Horizon in American Diplomacy, 1800–1860* (New York, 1966), which views the Louisiana Purchase as "Jefferson's ultimate master stroke as an expansionist"; Odie B. Faulk, *The Last Years of Spanish Texas, 1778–1821* (The Hague, 1964); Mary P. Adams, "Jefferson's Military Policy with Special Reference to the Frontier, 1805–1809" (Ph.D. diss., University of Virginia, 1958); Russell Kirk, *Randolph of Roanoke: A Study in Conservative Thought* (Chicago, 1951); Stanley C. Arthur, *The Story of the West Florida Rebellion* (St. Francisville, La., 1935), a series of detailed newspaper articles; José Antonio Pichardo, *Pichardo's Treatise on the Limits of Louisiana and Texas: An Argumentative Historical Treatise with Reference to the Verification of the True Limits of the Provinces of Louisiana and Texas; written . . . to Disprove the Claim of the United States that Texas Was Included in the Louisiana Purchase of 1803,* ed. and trans. Charles W. Hackett (4 vols., Austin, Tex., 1931–46), written between 1808 and 1812; Mattie A. Hatcher, *The Opening of Texas to Foreign Settlement, 1801–1821* (Austin, Tex., 1927); William C. Bruce, *John Randolph of Roanoke, 1773–1833* (2 vols., New York, 1922); John S. Kendall, *History of New Orleans* (3 vols., Chicago, 1922), of which vol. I contains a good account of transition to American rule; Isaac J. Cox, *The West Florida Controversy, 1798–1813: A Study in American Diplomacy* (Baltimore, 1918), the basic study; Thomas M. Marshall, *A History of the Western Boundary of the Louisiana Purchase, 1819–1841* (Berkeley, Calif., 1914); Herbert B. Fuller, *The Purchase of Florida: Its History and Diplomacy* (Cleveland, 1906; reprint ed., 1964); David Y. Thomas, *A History of Military Government in Newly Acquired Territory of the United States* (New York, 1904); Louis Houck, *The Boundaries of the Louisiana Purchase* (St. Louis, 1901); Binger Hermann, *The Louisiana Purchase and Our Title West of the Rocky Mountains* (Washington, D.C., 1900); and Amos Stoddard, *Sketches Historical and Descriptive of Louisiana* (Philadelphia, 1812).

Among the specialized articles these are useful: Yves Auguste, "Jefferson et Haiti (1804–1810)," *Revue d'histoire diplomatique,* LXXXVI (Oct.–Dec. 1972), 333–48; Raymond A. Mohl, "Britain and the Aaron Burr Conspiracy," *History Today,* XXI (June 1971), 391–98, which views the "conspiracy" as an expression of American expansionism; Gilbert L. Lycan, "Alexander Hamilton's Florida Policy," *Florida Historical Quarterly,* XLIX (Oct. 1971), 143–57; Clifford L. Egan, "The United States, France, and West Florida, 1803–1807," *ibid.,* XLVIII (Jan. 1969), 227–52, an insightful analysis critical of American policy; James E. Scanlon, "A Sudden Conceit: Jefferson and the Louisiana Government Bill of 1804," *Louisiana History,* IX (Spring 1968), 139–62; Jack D. L. Holmes, "The Marqués de Casa-Calvo, Nicolás de Finiels, and the 1805 Spanish Expedition through East Texas and Louisiana," *Southwestern Historical Quarterly,* LXIX (Jan. 1966), 324–39, which deals with the Spanish boundary commission that mapped the area; Fabius Dunn, "The Concern of the Spanish Government of Texas over United States Expansionism, 1805–1808," *Louisiana Studies,* IV (Spring 1965), 45–61; Jack D. L. Holmes, "Showdown on the

Sabine: General James Wilkinson vs. Lieutenant-Colonel Simón de Herrera," *ibid.*, III (Spring 1964), 46–76, the best account; Elizabeth G. Brown, "Law and Government in the 'Louisiana Purchase,' 1803–1804," *Wayne Law Review,* II (Summer 1956), 169–89; Lawrence S. Kaplan, "Jefferson, the Napoleonic Wars, and the Balance of Power," *William and Mary Quarterly,* 3rd ser. XIV (April 1957), 196–217; Walter Prichard, "Selecting a Governor for the Territory of Orleans," *Louisiana Historical Quarterly,* XXXI (April 1948), 269–393; Jaime Delgado, "Una Polémica en 1805 sobre los límites de la Luisiana (La mision en España de Jaime Monroe)," *Revista de Archivos, Bibliotecas y Museos,* LIV (Madrid, Sept.–Dec., 1948), 403–33, critical of American expansionism; J. Villasana Haggard, "The Neutral Ground Between Louisiana and Texas, 1807–1821," *Louisiana Historical Quarterly,* XXVIII (Oct. 1945), 1001–1128; William C. Holmes, "The Exalted Enterprise (The Mississippi Question: The Louisiana Answer)," *ibid.*, XXIII (Jan. 1940), 78–106; James A. Padgett, ed., "The West Florida Revolution of 1810, As Told in the Letters of John Rhea, Fulwar Skipwith, Reuben Kemper, and Others," *ibid.*, XXI (Jan. 1938), 76–202; Philip C. Brooks, "Spain's Farewell to Louisiana, 1803–1821," *Mississippi Valley Historical Review,* XXVII (June 1940), 29–42, and "Pichardo's Treatise and the Adams-Onis Treaty," *Hispanic-American Historical Review,* XV (Feb. 1935), 94–99; Richard R. Stenberg, "The Boundaries of the Louisiana Purchase," *ibid.*, XIV (Feb. 1934), 32–64, and "The Western Boundary of Louisiana, 1762–1803," *Southwestern Historical Quarterly,* XXXV (Oct. 1931), 95–108; Francis P. Burns, "West Florida and the Louisiana Purchase: An Examination into the Question of Whether It Was Included in the Territory Ceded by the Treaty of 1803," *Louisiana Historical Quarterly,* XV (July 1932), 391–416; Dunbar Rowland, "Mississippi in the Transfer of the Louisiana Purchase," *ibid.*, XIII (April 1930), 235–45; Everett S. Brown, "Jefferson's Plan for a Military Colony in Orleans

Territory," *Mississippi Valley Historical Review,* VIII (March 1922), 373–76, and "The Orleans Territory Memorialists to Congress, 1804," *Louisiana Historical Quarterly,* I (Jan. 1917), 99–102; Mattie A. Hatcher, "The Louisiana Background of the Colonization of Texas, 1763–1803," *Southwestern Historical Quarterly,* XXIV (Jan. 1921), 169–94; Isaac J. Cox, "The Louisiana-Texas Frontier During the Burr Conspiracy," *Mississippi Valley Historical Review,* X (Dec. 1923), 274–84, "The Pan-American Policy of Jefferson and Wilkinson," *ibid.,* I (Sept. 1914), 212–39, "The Louisiana-Texas Frontier," *Southwestern Historical Quarterly,* X (July 1906), 1–75, XVII (July 1913), 1–42, "The American Intervention in West Florida," *American Historical Review,* XVII (Jan. 1912), 290–311, and "The Exploration of the Louisiana Frontier, 1803–1806," in *Annual Report of the American Historical Association for the Year 1904* (Washington, D.C., 1905), pp. 149–74; Jonas Viles, "Population and Extent of Settlement in Missouri Before 1804," *Missouri Historical Review,* V (July 1911), 189–213, which explains Americanization of upper Louisiana; John R. Ficklen, "Was Texas Included in the Louisiana Purchase?" *Publications of the Southern History Association,* V (Sept. 1901), 351–87; Henry E. Chambers, "West Florida and Its Relation to the Historical Cartography of the United States," *Johns Hopkins University Studies in History and Political Science,* ser. 16, no. 5 (May 1898), 201–59, which maintains that Jefferson and Madison were wrong; and Simeon E. Baldwin, "The Historic Policy of the United States as to Annexation," *Annual Report of the American Historical Association for the Year 1893* (Washington, D.C., 1894), pp. 369–90.

Chapter XV

The titles cited for this chapter are generally more important for their ideas and interpretations than for factual content.

H. M. Drucker, *The Political Uses of Ideology* (New York, 1974), which has a chapter on the Idéologues; Immanuel M. Wallerstein, *The Modern World System: Capitalist Agriculture and the Origins of the European World-Economy in the Sixteenth Century* (New York, 1974), which analyzes early European imperialism; William A. Williams, *The Roots of Modern American Empire* (New York, 1969), which views expansion as the central theme in the nation's history; Sidney Lens, *The Forging of the American Empire* (New York, 1971); George Lictheim, *Imperialism* (New York, 1971), a stimulating theoretical analysis; Amaury de Riencourt, *The American Empire* (New York, 1968); Frederick Merk, *Manifest Destiny and Mission in American History* (New York, 1963), which tries to distinguish between "mission" and imperialism; Richard W. Van Alstyne, *The Rising American Empire* (New York, 1960), which discusses American imperialism in its early setting; Edward M. Burns, *The American Idea of Mission: Concepts of National Purpose and Destiny* (New Brunswick, N.J., 1957); Henry Nash Smith, *Virgin Land: The American West as Symbol and Myth* (2nd ed., New York, 1957), which assesses the intellectual basis of westward expansion; Hans Kohn, *American Nationalism: An Interpretive Essay* (New York, 1957); Bernard A. De Voto, *The Course of Empire* (Boston, 1952), which stresses the continuity of the imperial theme from the eighteenth century; Merle E. Curti, *The Roots of American Loyalty* (New York, 1946), which links patriotism to expansionism; Ramiro Guerra y Sánchez, *La expansión territorial de los Estados Unidos a expensas de España y de los paises Hispano-americanos* (Havana, 1935), a critical analysis of early American imperialism; Albert K. Weinberg, *Manifest Destiny: A Study of Nationalist Expansionism in American History* (Baltimore, 1935), a pioneer study showing the continuity of expansionism, a basic work; Charles A. Beard, *The Idea of National Interest: An Analytical Study in American Foreign Policy* (New York, 1934); Alpheus H. Snow, *The Administration of Dependencies: A Study of the Evolution of the Federal*

Empire, with Special Reference to American Colonial Problems (New York, 1902), which advances the concept of the United States as an expanding empire; and Franklin H. Giddings, *Democracy and Empire* (New York, 1900), written by a sociologist who maintains that expansion is natural for "superior" peoples, such as Americans.

Jacob W. Cooke, "Jefferson on Liberty," *Journal of the History of Ideas,* XXXIV (Oct.–Dec. 1973), which emphasizes "liberty" rather than "empire"; Nicholas P. Canny, "The Ideology of English Colonization: From Ireland to America," *William and Mary Quarterly,* 3rd ser. XXX (Oct. 1973), 575–98, which shows similarity in the rationale of English and American expansionism; Juan A. Ortega y Medina, "Fundamentos Doctrinales del *Manifest Destiny,*" *Anglia: Anuario de Estudios Angloamericanos,* V (1973), 11–50; Reginald Horsman, "American Indian Policy and the Origins of Manifest Destiny," *University of Birmingham Historical Journal,* XI, no. 2 (1968), 128–40, which analyzes the common rationale in Indian and expansionist policy; George Lictheim, "The Concept of Ideology," *History and Theory,* IV, no. 2 (1965); 165–95; Thomas A. Bailey, "America's Emergence as a World Power: The Myth and the Verity," *Pacific Historical Review,* XXX (Feb. 1961), 1–16, which suggests early emergence of American power and imperialism; Leon Baritz, "The Idea of the West," *American Historical Review,* LXVI (April 1961), 618–40, which traces the "imperial idea of the west" from antiquity to the United States; William A. Williams, "The Age of Mercantilism: An Interpretation of the American Political Economy, 1763 to 1928," *William and Mary Quarterly,* 3rd ser. XV (Oct. 1958), 419–37, which argues that the Louisiana Purchase stimulated an expansionist philosophy; J. G. de Roulhac Hamilton, "The Pacifism of Thomas Jefferson," *Virginia Quarterly Review,* XXXI (Autumn 1955), 607–20, which explains that Jefferson would use force to attain policy objectives; Julian P. Boyd, "Thomas Jefferson's

'Empire of Liberty,' " *ibid.*, XXIV (Autumn 1948), 538–54; John C. Parish, "The Emergence of the Idea of Manifest Destiny," in his *The Persistence of the Westward Movement and Other Essays* (Berkeley, Calif., 1943), pp. 47–77; Lauro A. De Rojas, "A Consequence of the Louisiana Purchase," *Louisiana Historical Quarterly,* XXI (April 1938), 362–66; Julius W. Pratt, "The Ideology of American Expansion," in *Essays in Honor William E. Dodd,* ed. Avery Craven (Chicago, 1935), pp. 335–53; Pratt, "The Origin of 'Manifest Destiny,' " *American Historical Review,* XXXII (July 1927), 795–98, which traces use of the phrase; Frederick J. Turner, "The Significance of the Mississippi Valley in American History," in his *The Frontier in American History* (New York, 1920), pp. 177–204, "The Ohio Valley in American History," in *ibid.*, pp. 157–76, "The Diplomatic Contest for the Mississippi Valley," *Atlantic Monthly,* XCIII (May 1904), 676–91, (June 1904), 807–17, and "The Significance of the Louisiana Purchase," *Review of Reviews,* XXVII (May 1903), 578–84; Charles M. Harvey, "The Louisiana Expansion in Its World Aspect," *Atlantic Monthly,* LXXXIV (Oct. 1899), 549–57, which says Americans won Louisiana because they "belonged to a world conquering race"; Samuel M. Davis, "Some of the Consequences of the Louisiana Purchase," in *Annual Report of the American Historical Association for the Year 1897* (Washington, D.C., 1898), pp. 151–60; C. F. Robertson, "The Louisiana Purchase in Its Influence upon the American System," *Papers of the American Historical Association,* I, no. 4 (New York, 1885), 253–90; and Albert C. Ramsey, ed., *The Other Side: or Notes for the History of the War between Mexico and the United States Written in Mexico and Translated from the Spanish* (New York, 1850), in which the introductory essay analyzes the Louisiana affair and the roots of the United States expansionism.

Index*

Adams, Henry, 37, 166, 249
Adams, John: as expansionist 35, 46, 68, 70; on Spanish boundary conflict, 65; on peace emissaries, 139; and implied powers of presidency, 254
Adams, John Quincy, 190, 254
Adams, Samuel, 35
Addington, Henry (British Prime Minister), 143–144
Adet, Pierre Auguste (French minister to U.S.), 82
Aix-la-Chapelle, Treaty of, 19
Albany plan of union and expansionism, 23
American Geography, 247
American Revolution: 33, 35, 75, 108, 122; and expansionism, 36, 41, 46, 245
Amiens, Peace of (1802): 97, 101, 111; collapse of, 153, 154, 174
Anglo-American expansion. See Expansionism; Imperialism
Anglo-American imperialism. See Empire; Expansionism; Imperialism
Aranda, Pedro Pablo Abarca y Bolea, conde de (Spanish ambassador to France), 37
Aranjuez, Convention of (1801), 96, 104, 111
Armstrong, John (U.S. minister to France), 222, 230, 231, 233–234
Arroyo Hondo, 227, 235, 236
Atlantic States, 66
Aubry, Charles Philippe de (French governor of Louisiana), 31
Austria: war with France (1795), 80

Bacon, Francis, 243
Barbé-Marbois, Marquis François de (French minister of the treasury): favors cession of Louisiana, 162, 163, 164; and Livingston and Monroe, 167–171; and Floridas, 169, 170–171, 174, 213, 216, 221
Baring, Alexander (British banker), 173, 188
Baring Brothers (English banking house), 172
Basel, Treaty of (1795), 60, 61, 80, 81

Baton Rouge, 32, 34, 66, 220, 221, 228, 239
Bayou Pierre, 229, 236
Beckwith, George (British agent), 77
Bernadotte, Jean Baptiste Jules (French minister to U.S.): 150–151; in France, 179–180
Berthier, Louis Alexandre (envoy to Spain), 92, 93, 94–95
Bienville, Jean Baptiste Lemoyne, sieur de (governor-general of Louisiana), 12, 13, 16, 17–18
Blacks, disturbed by French repossession of Louisiana, 151. See also Santo Domingo; Toussaint
Blainville, Pierre-Joseph de Cèleron de (explorer), 21
Blount, Senator William, 63, 72
Blount Conspiracy, 63
Bonaparte, Joseph: signs Treaty of Amiens, 101; and Livingston, 119, 130, 164, 250; and Louisiana sale, 119, 164, 165, 166
Bonaparte, Lucien, 96, 165–166
Bonaparte, Napoleon. See Napoleon
Boone, Daniel, 198
Boston Independent Chronicle, 178
Bourbon Family Compact, 27
Bowdoin, James (U.S. minister to Spain), 234, 235
Braddock, Edward (British commander), 24
Breckinridge, Senator John, 140, 191
Brevil, Villars de (French trade commissioner), 76
Britain. See England
Burr, Aaron, 237, 238

Cabeza de Vaca, Álvar Núñez, 4
Cabildo (municipal council New Orleans), 45
Cabot, George, 178
Cadillac, Antoine de la Mothe (governor of Louisiana), 11
Cambacérès, Jean Jacques Régis de (second French consul), 216
Canada: 17, 26, 81, 131, 212; claimed by U.S., 35–36, 210; Directory's scheme on, 109; Franklin's plans for, 245; Jef-

*Prepared by Terry W. Strieter

INDEX

Canada—*(Continued)*
ferson's plans for, 254
Carlos III of Spain, 26, 28, 46
Carlos IV of Spain: creates "Prince of the Peace," 61; and Napoleon, 92, 93, 96, 223; cedes Louisiana, 95, 104–105, 148–149, 193–194, 200, 201; instructions to Morales, 120; declares war on England, 223
Carondelet, Barón Francisco Luis Héctor (Louisiana governor): revives Indian alliances, 54, 59; and U.S. expansion, 54, 55, 57, 59, 63; British Canada aid, 59–60; and Pinckney Treaty, 62
Casa Calvo, Sebastián (boundary commissioner), 204, 209, 220–221
Cevallos, Pedre de (Spanish minister of foreign affairs): 96–97, 104, 158; and Louisiana transfer, 105, 142, 194, 199; and U.S. demands, 142, 220; and Floridas transfer, 142, 224
Champlain, Samuel de (governor of New France), 5
Channing, Edward, 120
Cherokee Indians, 25. *See also* Indians
Chickasaw Indians, 17, 44. *See also* Indians
Choctaw Indians, 44, 132. *See also* Indians
Choiseul, Duc Étienne François de (French foreign minister), peace negotiations of (1761), 26, 27, 28; refuses aid to Creoles, 30, 31
Chouart, Médard, sieur des Groseilliers (explorer), 5
Civil War (U.S.), 241, 254
Claiborne, William C.C. (governor of Mississippi Territory): 121, 132, 181, 200; commander of troops, 132, 227–228, 234–235; occupies Louisiana, 201, 204, 205; and Creoles, 206, 211, 236; as Jefferson's proconsul, 210; and claims to Floridas and Texas, 217; governor Territory of Orleans, 227–228; cooperates with Wilkinson, 234; occupies West Florida, 239
Clark, Daniel, Jr., 66, 67, 68, 200, 201
Clark, General George Rogers, 34, 36, 79, 137
Clark, William. *See* Lewis and Clark expedition
Clay, Henry, 198–199
Colbert, Jean Baptiste (French minister of

finance), 5, 6
Collot, Georges Henri Victor (French official), 82–83, 88, 94, 147, 159
Colorado River, 231
Commerce. *See* Trade
Commissioners (U.S.), in Louisiana, 201, 204, 205, 206
Compagnie des Indes of John Law, 14–15, 16, 17
Compagnie de la Louisiane ou d'Occident, 13
Congress, U.S.: 35, 45, 46, 48, 50; and war issues, 87, 116, 127, 139–140, 190, 200, 229; Jefferson and, 127, 187, 207, 210, 229; and Louisiana treaties, 134, 181, 182, 183–184, 189–192, 207, 211, 251; and West Florida, 134, 231, 232, 233, 234, 239; authorizes Lewis and Clark expedition, 137; Ross resolutions, 157; and expansionism, 187. *See also* House of Representatives; Senate
Conquistadores, 4
Constitution (U.S.): 171, 191, 211, 249; Jefferson's views on, 181–185; and expansion issue, 182–183, 184, 192, 246, 252–253
Consulate (French): 91, 117, 161, 195; U.S. relations with, 112–113, 125, 172, 180; view of deposit suspension, 142, 143
Continental Congress, 35
Continental destiny, 245. *See also* Expansionism; Imperialism
Contraband commerce, 19, 55
Coxe, Daniel, 9, 10
Creek Indians, 44, 49–50. *See also* Indians
Creoles (Louisiana): and French and Indian War, 25; relations with Spanish, 26, 31, 45, 71, 72; affection for France, 30, 31, 45, 57, 78, 92, 196; fear of slave uprising, 98, 151; dislike of U.S., 196, 206, 211, 212, 236, 237, 253
Crèvecoeur, J. Hector St. John de, 245
Crozat, Antoine (French merchant), 11, 12, 13
Cuba, 29, 222, 254

Dearborn, Henry (secretary of war), 132
Declaration of Independence, 249, 253
Decrès, Denis (French minister of navy and colonies): organizes occupation forces for Louisiana, 103, 104, 149, 150, 152, 154; favors retention of Lou-

Index

isiana, 162–163; Napoleon's confidant, 164

Delacroix, Charles (French minister of foreign relations), 82, 84, 86

Deposit crisis. *See* New Orleans

De Soto, Hernando, 4–5

Dickinson, John, 233

Dinwiddie, Robert (lieutenant-governor of Virginia), 23

Directory (France): 82, 84, 85, 88–89, 92, 109; relations with Spain, 82, 83; fear of U.S. and Britain, 82, 86; overthrow, 91

Doctrine of discovery, 8

Drayton, William Henry, 21

Du Pont de Nemours, Pierre Samuel: 114, 134; views on Louisiana, 115, 130, 142, 155, 161, 173, 251

Duquesne, Ange de Menneville, marquis de (governor of Canada), 22–23

East Florida, 131, 136, 213, 214, 239. *See also* Floridas; Expansionism

Eastern Louisiana, 27, 28, 37, 66. *See also* Louisiana

Egypt, Napoleon and, 155

Ellery, William, 35

Empire, x, 210. *See also* Expansionism; Imperialism

Empire for liberty, 248. *See also* Expansionism; Jefferson

England: and Louisiana territory, 12, 33, 77, 112, 113, 143, 153, 154, 172, 173, 174, 186; and French rivalry, 15, 18, 24, 25, 70, 109, 143, 148, 153, 164, 166, 172, 174, 203; opposes Albany plan, 23; notes American expansionism, 38, 53, 70, 245; Nootka Sound crisis, 53; Spanish alliance, 60; holds Gibraltar, 83–84; attempts to bribe Joseph Bonaparte, 119; encourages U.S. alliance, 135; opposes cession of Floridas, 148; protests annexation of West Florida, 240

Erving, George W. (*chargé d'affaires*, Madrid), 230

Etruria, Kingdom, 98, 104, 105, 148, 194

Executive power, 187–188, 212

Expansionism (U.S.): ideology of, ix, 250, 255; as sense of mission, x, 242; and trade, 8, 17, 19, 32–33; expressions of, 10, 12, 15, 19, 21, 22, 24, 32, 34–35, 40, 41, 42, 45–46, 52, 57, 64–66, 71,

73–74, 82, 116, 121–122, 146, 156, 170, 177, 192, 200, 204–205, 208, 210, 214, 217, 219, 220, 223, 239, 245–246, 251, 253, 254, 255; and Spain, 28, 32, 36–37, 39, 40, 42–44, 50–55, 64, 66, 71, 93, 193, 219, 228, 240–246; and France, 37, 71, 76–77, 80, 86, 87, 93, 97, 147, 149, 156, 159, 197, 214, 221, 245; and Constitution, 182–183, 192; popular support of, 225. *See also* Empire, Imperialism

Falkland Islands, 33

Family Compact (Bourbon), 27

Fauchet, Jean Antoine Joseph (French minister to U.S.), 79, 80

Federalists: pro-British attitude, 58, 138; favor war, 68–69, 71, 116, 122, 138, 139–140, 179, 214, 247; fear of French, 69, 81, 85, 138; and Mississippi crisis, 69, 116, 118, 122, 133, 139, 141, 178–179, 185–186, 189, 250; Ross as spokesman, 139–140; and Republicans, 179, 187, 207, 250; oppose Louisiana incorporation, 190–191; and Jefferson, 212, 213, 229

Fernando, Duke of Parma, 92, 148

First Consul. *See* Napoleon

Floridablanca, Don José Moñino y Redondo, conde de (first minister of Spain), 46–47

Floridas: Spanish control of, 8, 34, 39, 49, 202, 203, 208, 215; and France, 8, 148, 155, 213, 239; British possession of, 29, 34, 39; U.S. views on, 35, 36, 49, 59, 155, 170, 215, 217; plot to revolutionize, 51; desired by Jefferson, 53, 61, 224, 254; expected U.S. occupation of, 59, 68, 178, 198, 203, 247; U.S. attempt to acquire, 110, 111, 129, 134, 215, 231, 245; settlements attacked, 239

Folch, Vicente (governor of West Florida), 198, 221

Fontainebleau, Treaty of (1762), 28

Fort Adams, 132, 201, 204, 234

Fort Duquesne, 23, 24

Fort Rosalie, 12, 16

Fort Saint Louis, 7, 10, 11

Fort Stoddert, 217–218

Founding Fathers, 242, 246

Fox Indians, 16, 17. *See also* Indians

France: relations with Spain, 3, 7, 8, 57,

France—*(Continued)*
58, 59, 71, 78, 79, 81, 92, 144, 202, 223, 230; settles Mississippi Valley, 5; government at Versailles, 6, 13, 37; and Louisiana, 7, 9, 20, 45, 66, 71, 75, 78, 79, 80, 81, 82, 84, 87, 91, 92, 108, 117, 122, 147, 151, 204, 205, 207, 217, 249; rivalry with England, 5, 6, 9, 12, 22, 25–26, 85, 174; relations with Indians, 15, 16, 18, 24–25, 149; alliance with U.S., 35, 75; and American expansionism, 37, 87, 125, 147, 214, 221, 245; strained relations with U.S., 58, 85, 87, 101, 122, 125, 180; and Floridas, 75, 82, 84, 87, 213; and U.S. acquisition of Floridas, 87, 216, 221, 222, 224; in Santo Domingo, 103, 203

Franklin, Benjamin, 22, 35, 36, 244, 245, 249

French and Indian War, 23, 244. *See also* Seven Years' War

French Revolution: Louisiana and, 55, 78

Frontenac, Louis de Buade, comte de (governor of New France), 6

Frontiersmen (U.S.), 58, 63

Gage, Thomas (British commander), 33

Galissonière, Roland-Mîchel Barrin, comte de La (governor of Canada), 21, 22

Gallatin, Albert: opposes conquest of Floridas, 70–71, 225; as secretary of the treasury, 137, 182, 218; expansionist, 138, 182–183, 187; on occupying Louisiana, 199–200; and Mobile Act, 218–219, 225

Gálvez, Don Bernardo de (governor of Louisiana), 33–34

Gálveztown, 41

Gardoqui, Don Diego de (Spanish envoy), 46, 47, 48, 50, 51, 77

Gayoso, Manuel Luis de (governor of Natchez district), 64, 65, 71

Gazette de France, 102

Genêt, Edmond C. (French emissary to U.S.), 57, 58, 79

George III, 153

Gibraltar, 34, 83

Girondins (France), 78–79

Godoy, Manuel de, duque de la Alcudia (Spain's first minister of state): views on relations with U.S., 60, 61, 62, 64, 65, 80, 84, 88, 142, 194–195, 202, 230;

Louisiana as bargaining tool, 60, 80, 83, 85, 88–89; and French pressure for Louisiana, 80, 83, 84, 88; influence on Spanish policy, 86, 88–89, 96, 104; view of Louisiana cession, 88–89, 194, 202; and Napoleon, 104, 158, 194, 217; intent on keeping Floridas, 148, 158, 202, 217

Government of Louisiana Law (1804), 212

Great Britain. *See* England

Grenville, William Wyndham (British foreign minister), 70

Griswold, Gaylord, 189, 190

Griswold, Roger, 133–134

Guillemardet, Ferdinand Pierre (French ambassador), 87

Gulf of Mexico, 29, 152, 227

Hakluyt, Richard, 243

Hamilton, Alexander: on control of Mississippi, 53; commands provisional army, 68; and Wilkinson scheme, 68, 72; on expansion, 68, 128, 139, 247; advises John Adams, 70; favors Louisiana Purchase, 179

Hamiltonians. *See* Federalists

Harrison, William Henry (governor of Indian Territory), 133

Havana: British capture of (1762), 28; Spanish military base, 34, 201, 228–229

Hawkesbury, Lord (British foreign secretary), 88, 109, 111, 113

Helvoët Sluys, 149, 150, 152

Hennepin, Louis (explorer), 9

Henry, Patrick, 247

Herrera y Leyva, Simón de, 236

Holland, 97, 154, 157, 174

Hope and Company (Dutch banking house), 172

House of Representatives (U.S.): Federalist war measures, 133; resolution on Louisiana (1803), 134; and Jefferson, 134, 231, 232; authorizes exploration of Louisiana, 219. *See also* Congress; United States

Hudson Bay, 11

Humphreys, David (American minister to Spain), 85, 93

Iberville, Pierre Lemoyne, sieur de (founder of Louisiana), 9–10, 12

Idéologues, 173

Index

Illinois: French views on, 15, 18, 21, 25; English control of, 26, 34; trade of, 32; conquered by G.R. Clark, 36
Illinois River, 6, 7, 132
Imperialism, x, 241–255. *See also* Expansionism
Imperialists, 3, 8, 17, 187. *See also* Expansionism
Indians: and expansionists, 3, 44, 57, 59, 237, 243, 245, 246, 248; and Europeans, 4, 5, 6, 10, 15, 16, 18, 22, 24–25, 32; sought as allies, 10, 17, 18, 22, 39, 44, 59, 149, 198; and racism, 22, 185, 243, 246; conquest of, 37, 57, 59, 133, 237, 243, 248; as allies against U.S., 44, 49, 50, 54, 62, 63, 103, 198; and Lewis and Clark expedition, 137, 138; Jefferson view of, 185
Iroquois, 19. *See also* Indians
Irujo, Carlos Martinez de (Spanish minister to U.S.), 63, 65, 69, 124; quarrel with Pickering, 65; fears U.S. invasion of Louisiana, 69, 124, 203; and deposit crisis, 124, 142, 144; and Jefferson, 124, 144, 199, 203, 208, 230; opposes U.S. scientific expedition, 136; view of French cession Louisiana, 193, 194, 199; defensive measures, 198, 199, 200; protests Louisiana purchase, 199, 203–204; and Floridas, 198, 204, 218, 223

Jackson, Andrew, 180, 199, 238
Jacobins (France), 79
Jay, John (U.S. peace commissioner), 37, 47, 48, 49, 61, 79
Jay-Gardoqui Treaty, 46, 47, 48, 59
Jay Treaty (1794), 79, 80
Jefferson, Thomas: governor of Virginia, 35–36; expansionist policy of, 36, 49, 53, 78, 79, 107, 112, 115, 117, 129, 132, 143, 145, 182, 194, 202, 203, 213, 214, 219, 232, 248, 249, 253, 254; secretary of state, 52, 61, 78; on migration to Louisiana, 52, 132–133; threatens force, 79, 124, 127–128, 129, 132, 135, 138, 144, 145, 193, 200, 201, 202, 203, 204, 220, 229; and New Orleans, 110, 129, 135, 136, 145; and the Floridas, 110, 129, 135, 136, 144, 145, 178, 214, 215, 216, 217, 220, 223, 224, 229, 238; presidential messages, 127–128, 187, 253
—and Congress, 229, 231, 233, 234

—and the Constitution, 181, 182, 183–184, 185, 252, 254
—diplomacy of, 53, 113, 129, 134, 219, 224
—and England: threatens alliance with, 110, 112, 114, 117, 135, 144, 224; and seizure of northern Louisiana, 137; distrust of, 143; and joint Louisiana invasion, 144; European war and, 145; maritime troubles with, 238
—and Federalists, 138, 141, 212, 250
—and France: Santo Domingo, 99, 101, 129; repossession of Louisiana, 99, 101, 112, 114, 115; and Toussaint, 100, 101, 107, 113, 133; assumes Floridas ceded to, 136; conciliatory attitude of, 142; friendly gesture towards, 181; Rochambeau, 203; requests funds for, 232
—Indian policy of, 132, 133
—and Louisiana: 41, 108, 110–111, 112, 122; purchase of, 170, 185; as U.S. possession, 210, 211; government of, 211, 212, 253; boundaries of, 213, 215, 238
—pacificism and truculence of, 115, 116, 128, 129, 132, 220, 225, 231, 248
—Politics of: dilemma over deposit crisis, 123, 128–129; deflates critics, 135; re-election (1804), 208
—Spain, attitude towards, 49, 53, 110, 124, 129, 136, 193, 194, 200, 203, 213, 215, 223, 224, 229
Jeffersonians: 132, 143, 174, 181, 198, 227, 253; expansionist policy of, 138, 191, 200, 208, 217, 219, 220, 223, 247, 248, 249, 254
—and Floridas: use of frontier ambiguities, 213, 219; attempt to buy, 214; Mobile Act, 219; seek Napoleon's aid, 217, 223, 225; war scare, 228, 230; negotiations fail, 235
—and Louisiana cession: 145, 192; and Spain, 199, 200–201, 202; benefits of, 207; governing of, 210; and France, 251. *See also* Republicans
Jesuit missionaries, 5
Jolliet, Louis, 6
Josephine (wife of Napoleon), 98
Jubilee: Louisiana, 207; national, 208

Kemper, Nathan and Samuel, 220, 228
Kentuckians, battle with Spanish troops, 52

Kentucky, Spain and, 39, 42, 50, 51, 198, 224

Kentucky Palladium, 113

Kerlérec, Louis Billouart, chevalier de (governor of Louisiana), 25, 26

King George's War, 18

King, Rufus (minister to England), and Miranda plan, 70; on French possession of Louisiana, 101, 107, 109, 111; favors buying Louisiana and Floridas, 113, 154; on British possession of New Orleans, 143, 154; and news of Louisiana agreement, 178; replaced, 216

King William's War, 9

La Galissonière, Roland-Mîchel Barrin, comte de (governor of Canada), 21, 22

Lake of the Woods, 37, 209

La Salle, Robert Cavelier, sieur de, 6–8

Laussat, Pierre Clément de (prefect for Louisiana), 103, 145, 146, 150, 151, 180, 196, 197, 201, 204, 205, 206, 217

Law, John, 13–14

Lebrun, Charles François (third French consul), 130, 168

Le Cap François, 100–101, 102

Leclerc, Charles Victor Emmanuel (commander of Santo Domingo forces): attack on Toussaint, 100, 101, 102; notes American hostility, 116; death of, 149, 151, 152, 155

Le Moniteur, 153

Létombe, Joseph Philippe (French consul general), 87, 88

Lewis, Meriwether, 137, 138

Lewis and Clark expedition, 137, 198

Liguest, Pierre Laclède, 29

Lille, France, peace negotiations (1797), 85–86

Lincoln, Levi (attorney general), 182, 212

Livingston, Robert R. (minister to France): 110–111; view of Talleyrand, 112; on U.S. desire for New Orleans and Floridas, 111, 130, 131, 164, 165, 213, 219, 221; on Napoleon's power, 118, 123; and Louisiana sale, 117, 118, 119, 123, 141, 142, 155, 161, 162, 164, 165, 167, 171, 184, 250–251; solicits French help, 125; and expansionism, 131, 173, 213–214, 219, 251; and Monroe, 142, 162, 167, 169, 222

Loftus, Arthur, 29–30

Louis XIV, 5, 7, 10–11, 13

Louis XV, 17, 28

Louisiana: extent of territory, 3, 7, 11, 169, 209, 214; as barrier to Anglo-American advance, 12, 26; settlements in, 14, 43, 71, 209; agriculture of, 14, 72–73; lower, 18, 25, 26, 40, 41, 44, 45, 51, 58, 62; upper and Illinois country, 18, 25, 209–210; exploration, 20; broken up by Treaty of Paris (1763), 29; transfer to Spain, 30, 228; Americans dominate economy, 45, 55, 66, 73, 159; transfer to U.S., 51, 71, 72, 73, 169, 170, 171, 172, 193, 203, 247, 250; transfer to France, 77, 78, 83, 105, 107, 111, 149; as key to America, 94; Napoleon and, 148, 195; government of, 210

Louisiana Company, 9

Louisiana, District of, 212

Louisiana Jubilee, 207

Louisiana Purchase: treaties (1803), 170–172, 179, 187, 190, 212; effects on U.S., 189, 254; congressional debates on, 189–192; as bargain, 251; states formed from, 253–254; as part Anglo-American imperial tradition, 255

L'Ouverture. *See* Toussaint L'Ouverture

Luis, Prince of Parma, 96, 104, 105

Lunéville, Treaty of, 96

Madison, James: and Blount conspiracy, 63; on French desire for Louisiana, 91, 101, 117, 124–125, 130, 131, 155; and Toussaint, 99; on expansion, 108; fear of British, 109; and Louisiana payment, 115, 116, 188, 192, 206; and Floridas, 215, 217, 218, 223, 224, 235, 239; view of deposit issue, 121, 124, 129, 155–156; on Ross resolutions, 140; Livingston-Monroe hostility, 162, 169; pleased with Louisiana negotiations, 177, 180; view of Spanish protests, 188, 199, 200, 202; favors swift transfer, 200, 201; favors territorial status for Louisiana, 212; and Mobile Act, 218; orders Monroe to Madrid, 220; as interpreter of Constitution, 246; as expansionist, 246, 249

Mallet, Pierre and Paul (explorers), 17, 18

Malmesbury, Lord James Harris (English negotiator), 85

Index

Malone, Dumas, 184
Malta: cause for war, 154, 155, 166
Manifest Destiny: as imperialism, 241, 242; Jefferson and, 248; development of, 255
María Luisa, Queen of Spain, 84, 148
Maritime grievances, U.S. and Britain (1807), 238
Marquette, Père Jacques, 6
Matagorda Bay, Texas, 7
Mather, Cotton and Increase, 243
McGillivray, Alexander (Creek chieftain), 49, 50
Mediterranean, possible hostilities in, 220
Merchants (U.S.), and Santo Domingo, 152. See also Santo Domingo
Mexico: American schemes and, 54, 59, 94, 140, 239; Americans on borders, 74, 193; and French, 81; Louisiana as a barrier to, 86; defense of, 202; Burr plan to invade, 237; and Andrew Jackson, 238; Jefferson's desire for, 254
Miranda, Francisco, 69, 70
Miró, Esteban (acting governor of Louisiana), 42, 50–51
Mission, idea of. See Expansionism
Mississippi Bubble, 14
Mississippi River: navigation of, 3, 6, 8, 29, 38, 45, 58; as U.S. boundary, 37, 38, 209; Spanish control of, 39, 40, 45; American use of, 51, 58, 62; deposit crisis, 119–142 passim; possible blockade of, 198, 229; closed to Spanish ships, 239
Mississippi Territory, 65, 81, 140, 201, 213, 220
Mississippi Valley: commercial revolution of, 66; Anglo-American imperialism in, 78, 245, 247
Missouri country, Americans in, 73, 137, 198
Mobile Act (1804), 216, 218, 219
Mobile Bay area, 34, 43, 44, 213, 216, 219, 239
Mobile River, 17, 155, 218
Monroe, James: view of deposit suspension, 121, 143, 156; and Federalists, 134–135, 139, 156, 223; instructions, 136, 144, 220; and French, 156, 163, 171, 193, 216, 222, 224; Livingston's hostility, 161, 162, 167, 169; as expansionist, 195–196, 213, 215, 251; minister to England, 216; mission to Spain, 220, 222, 223, 224
Monroe Doctrine, 81
Montcalm de Saint-Véran, Marquis Louis Joseph de, 24–25
Montesquieu, Charles Louis de Secondat, Baron de, 109, 190–191
Morales, Juan Ventura (acting intendant of Louisiana), anti-American regulations, 71; view on deposit, 119–120, 122, 124, 142, 145; Jefferson view of, 128–129
Morris, Gouverneur, 177, 191, 210
Morse, Jedidiah, 41, 247
Môrtefontaine, Treaty of (1800), 95, 96, 99, 108, 172
Moustier, Comte Éléonore François Élie (French minister to U.S.), 77, 78, 86, 97

Nacogdoches, U.S.-Spanish confrontation at, 198, 235
Napoleon Bonaparte; 91, 92, 96, 97; contempt for Godoy, 105, 158; and Santo Domingo, 98, 100, 129, 151, 152; and Anglo-American alliance, 131; and western empire, 95, 111, 147, 148, 149, 151, 250; suspension of deposit, 122, 125; prepares Louisiana occupation forces, 148–149, 150–152; and Peace of Amiens, 153, 154, 174; and American expansionism, 158, 173; Florida negotiations, 170, 217, 222, 223, 230–235, 239; as emperor, 222, 223
—and Louisiana cession: 113, 122; reasons for, 154, 156–157, 158, 162–163, 194–196, 249, 251; and promise to Spain, 158, 194; sale negotiations, 161–166, 172, 174, 184, 186–187, 188; flawed title to, 193–194, 199, 203
—and Spanish retrocession of Louisiana: desire for Floridas, 92; and U.S. reaction, 93, 97–98, 108–109; plans for occupation, 103, 104; and British objections, 109
Narváez, Pánfilo de (explorer), 4
Natchez Indians, 4, 16–17
Natchez, Mississippi: 12, 15, 16, 32, 42, 57, 64, 65; Spanish control of, 34, 64; American rebellion, 64, 65; agitation in over deposit suspension, 121; approves Louisiana Purchase, 180; receives arms, 200; Burr arrested in, 238
Natchitoches, 12, 228, 235

INDEX

National Intelligencer, 178, 207

Native Americans. *See* Indians

Navarro, Martín de (Louisiana intendant), 40, 50

Negroes. *See* Blacks; Toussaint; Santo Domingo

Neutral Ground Agreement (1806), 236, 238

New Englanders, 190

New Manifest Destiny, 242

New Mexico, 18, 19

New Orleans: French rule, 13–14, 16, 163, 205; Spanish rule, 28, 30–31, 32, 197, 228; Creoles, 31, 78, 151, 211; economic life, 33, 42, 44, 45, 65–66, 72, 120, 197, 209; and American Revolution, 34; Americanization of, 42, 145; U.S. deposit rights, 51, 62, 119, 195; U.S. desire to buy, 53, 110, 116, 129, 134, 138, 249; Collot in, 83; threat of conquest, 109, 124, 133, 140, 143; and Jefferson, 113; reaction to U.S. possession, 197, 204; statehood request, 211, 212; and Wilkinson, 221, 238

Newspapers (U.S.): and Louisiana Purchase, 180, 208; possible U.S.-Spanish war, 201

New York Evening Post, 127, 138

Nicolet, Jean (explorer), 5

Nootka Sound crisis, 53, 61

Northeast, 46, 49, 73

Nouvelle Découverte (1697), 9

Nuestra Señora de Los Adaes, 228

O'Fallon, James, 54

Ohio River, 16, 23, 39, 54, 57

Ohio Valley, 12, 15, 19, 21, 25, 26, 42, 58, 62, 83, 246

O'Reilly, Alexander (Spanish general), 31–32, 33

Orleans, Territory of, 212, 229, 237

Ottawa Indians, 30. *See also* Indians

Otto, Louis Guillaume (French *chargé* in U.S.), 49

Pacific Ocean, 38, 136, 137, 219, 240

Paine, Thomas, 129–130, 185

Paris, Treaties of: (1763), 29; (1783), 38, 39, 245

Parkman, Francis, 30

Parma, Duke of, 84, 92, 95, 148. *See also* Fernando

Parma, Prince of, 96, 104, 105. *See also* Luis

Pensacola, Florida, 32, 33, 34, 43, 44

Perdido River, 214, 216, 217, 220, 223, 224, 240

Périer, Étienne de (governor-general of Louisiana), 16–17

Pérignon, Dominique Catherine (French diplomatist), 86

Philadelphia, 63, 208

Philippe II, duc d'Orleans, 13

Philippines, 29

Pichon, Louis André (French *chargé*): 99, 101, 108; notes possible clash with U.S., 110, 112, 117, 118, 141, 155, 157; view of Jefferson, 118, 128, 207; on Federalists, 118, 141; and deposit suspension, 131, 142–143; and Louisiana transfer, 180, 188, 192, 199, 200, 201, 206, 207

Pickering, Timothy: fear of French in Louisiana, 62, 65, 69, 84, 85, 86; quarrel with Irujo, 65; Miranda plan, 70; in Senate, 190

Pinckney, Charles (minister to Spain): 121, 142, 202, 230; Spain restores deposit, 142; warns of U.S. force, 202, 208, 220; and claims settlement, 217; works with Monroe, 224; recalled (1805), 230

Pinckney, Thomas (diplomatist), 60, 61, 62

Pinckney's Treaty. *See* San Lorenzo, Treaty of

Piñeda, Alonso Alvárez de (explorer), 4

Pitt, William, 53, 70, 85

Pollock, Oliver, 33, 35

Pontalba, Joseph Xavier Delfau de, 94–95

Pontchartrain, Louis de Phélypeaux, comte de (French minister of marine), 9, 10

Pontiac (chief of Ottawa Indians), 30

Potomac River, 122, 198, 229

Presidential authority, 187–188, 212

Presidential campaign of 1804, 208

Public opinion (U.S.), in 1803, 229

Puritans and expansion, 243

Quasi-War (1797–1800): 68, 69, 71, 89, 99, 108, 216; and Talleyrand, 87, 88; negotiations, 93, 95

Queen Anne's War, 10

Racism, Anglo-American, 185, 243, 246.

See also Expansionism; Indians; Spain

Randolph, John (majority leader of House), resolutions of, 128, 189; bill on Louisiana revenue laws, 216; quoted, 227; opposes Jefferson, 232, 233, 234

Ratisbon, Treaty of, 7

Red River, 12, 20, 43, 227

Reinhard, Karl Friedrich (French minister of foreign relations), 91

Republican government, theory on size, 191

Republicans (U.S.): and Federalists, 133, 140, 186, 247; as expansionists, 140, 190, 232; praise Jefferson's foreign policy, 145, 207; dominate Eighth Congress, 187, 190; and western immigration, 210. *See also* Jeffersonians

Revolutionary War. *See* American Revolution

Rio Bravo. *See* Rio Grande

Rio Grande, 12, 214, 217, 224

Rochambeau, Donatien de (Santo Domingo commander), 152, 157, 203

Rocky Mountains, 209, 219

Ross, Senator James, 140, 167

Ryswick, Treaty of, 9

Sabine River, 198, 227, 229, 235, 236, 238

Saint-Cyr, Laurent de Gouvion (French ambassador to Spain), 105

St. Denis, Louis Juchereau de (explorer), 11–12

Saint Domingue. *See* Santo Domingo

Saint Louis, 29, 34, 43, 83, 206n., 210, 234, 237

Salcedo, Don Manuel Juan de (governor of Louisiana), 120, 124, 129, 204

San Ildefonso: first treaty (1796), 84; second treaty (1800), 95, 138, 169, 189

San Lorenzo, Treaty of (1795), 61–62, 64, 66, 80, 119, 121, 189

Santa Fe, New Mexico, 17–18, 198

Santo Domingo: British desire for, 70; French rule in, 85, 104, 111, 129, 149, 151, 152, 154, 203; slave revolt, 98; commerce, 233

Sébastiani, François Horace Bastien (French officer), 153

Secessionist sentiment, 51, 59, 68, 123

Seigneley, Marquis de, 3

Senate (U.S.), 140, 187, 216. *See also* Congress; United States

Seven Years' War, 24, 25, 29, 32, 75, 109. *See also* French and Indian War

Sevier, John, 51

Shawnee Indians, 30

Shirley, William (governor of Massachusetts), 18

Simcoe, John G. (British governor of Upper Canada), 59 60

Smith, James, 161

Smuggling, 45, 72–73, 140

Soldiers. *See* Troops

Southerners: as expansionists, 35, 49; and Mississippi issues, 45, 46, 48; fear of possible slave revolt, 112

Spain: feebleness of, 49, 63, 71, 87, 158, 159, 174, 192, 194, 196, 200, 203, 215
—and American expansion: 36–37, 43, 50, 54, 76, 83, 193, 219, 245; and Western secessionists, 51; and Nootka Sound crisis, 53–54; inability to stop, 159, 202; and racism, 246; empire dismantled, 254
—American views of: 185, 215, 224; role of trustee, 129, 249
—and Floridas: 12, 208, 215, 216, 228; loss of West Florida, 239–240
—Indian policy of: 32, 39, 44, 49, 198
—and Louisiana: 5, 32, 34; defense of, 36, 39, 44, 49, 50, 51, 52, 54, 61, 64, 71, 72, 227, 229; and Mississippi, 40, 43, 44–45, 67; immigration, 52, 71; transfer to France, 105; oppose U.S. purchase, 184, 192, 193, 202, 203, 206; yields to Americans, 202, 208, 245
—relations with Britain: war with, 27, 34, 67; backs down in confrontation with, 33, 53; aids American Revolution, 36; Nootka Sound crisis, 53, 54; allied with, 58
—relations with France: La Salle expedition and, 8; colonial rivalry, 19; hazy claim to Louisiana, 26; protests ceding eastern Louisiana to England, 28; war with (1793), 54; peace with (1795), 60; allows French troops in Louisiana, 88; cedes Elba to, 96; and cession of Louisiana to U.S., 158; treaty obligation to, 196; seeks help of, 220; occupied by, 239
—relations with United States: 36, 38, 51, 60, 72, 120, 143; economic influence of Americans, 44, 66, 67; abandons claims to Old Southwest, 61–62; Nat-

INDEX

Spain—*Continued*
chez rebellion (1797), 64; expects war with U.S., 198; appeasement of, 208; and Quasi-War claims, 216, 217; and Florida revolt, 221; and Texas, 227–228, 229, 236; resigned to war with U.S., 230; refuses cooperation with U.S.. 235
"Spanish Conspiracy," 51, 62
Spotswood, Alexander (lieutenant governor of Virginia), 15
Stoddard, Amos (U.S. Army officer), 206n

Talleyrand-Périgord, Charles Maurice de (French minister of foreign relations); and Spanish cession of Louisiana, 75, 86, 87, 91, 93, 98, 108, 109, 112, 130, 131, 195; and American expansionism, 75, 86, 87, 222; key figure in Quasi-War, 87, 89; bribes to, 89, 166, 195; deposit question and, 118, 125, 141, 195; sale of Louisiana and, 111, 112, 141–142, 153, 156–157, 164, 168, 172, 173, 195; on U.S. Floridas claim, 221, 222; suggests French arbitration, 230
Talon, Jean (intendant of New France), 5–6
Tardiveau, Barthélemi (French trader), 76
Tariff (Spanish) of 1788, 51
Tatooed Serpent (Natchez chief), 3
Texas: Spanish desire to hold, 8, 17, 193, 198, 202, 208, 235; Anglo-American penetration, 33, 73–74; Spanish troops in, 198, 229, 236; U.S. claim to, 214, 217, 219, 231; Jeffersonians favor seizure, 224, 229; confrontation over, 228, 229, 235, 236; Burr invasion, 237
Thornton, Edward (British *chargé*), 112, 116, 131–132, 135, 207
Times of London, 157, 222
Tonti, Henry de (explorer), 7, 8
Tonty's Fort, 8
Toussaint L'Ouverture, 98–99, 102
Trade (U.S.): contraband, 19, 55; with Spain, 42, 46–47, 72; smuggling, 45, 72–73, 140; in New Orleans, 121, 197. *See also* United States
Treaties. *See* by name
Troops (French and Spanish). *See* France; Spain
Troops (U.S.): in Louisiana, 121, 132,

181, 200, 201, 204–205, 227–228, 235, 253; and crisis of 1805–1806, 228–229, 236; occupation of West Florida, 239. *See also* United States
Turner, Frederick Jackson, 37
Turreau, Louis Marie (French minister to U.S.), 221, 223, 225
Tuscany, 96
Two Million Dollar Act (1806), 233

Ulloa, Antonio de (Spanish official), 30, 31
United States: expansionism, 35, 44, 155, 225; depression, 47; idea of mission, 49; possession of Natchez region, 65; Spanish and Louisiana retrocession, 81, 84; and French seizure of ships, 101; population growth, 110–111; union threatened, 123; and rights deposit, 136; and Floridas, 155, 198, 217, 224; possible French war, 195, 252–253; and New Orleans, 204, 206, 208, 212; power of, 215, 248, 254; threatened use of navy, 220, 234; and spoliation claims, 224; war crisis of 1805, 227; maritime problems, 230; and Mobile uprising, 239. *See also* Expansionism; Louisiana
Unzaga y Amezaga, Don Luis de (first Spanish governor of Louisiana), 33
Urquijo, Mariano Luis (Spanish secretary for foreign affairs), 72, 92, 95
Utrecht, Treaty of (1713), 11

Vaudreuil-Cavagnial, Pierre de Rigaud, marquis de (governor of New France), 18, 19
Vergennes, Charles Gravier, comte de (French minister for foreign affairs), 37, 75, 76
Victor, Claude P., duc de Bellune (captain general of Louisiana): 103, 217; rumors about deposit suspension, 144; instructions, 149, 150; expedition of, 150, 152
Volney, Constantin François de Chasseboeuf, comte de, 79

War: threats of, 33, 131, 133, 145, 174, 225, 228, 233. *See also* American Revolution; Quasi-War
War Hawks, 122, 123. *See also* War
War of the League of Augsburg, 9

324

War of the Spanish Succession, 10
Washington, George, 23, 53, 60, 139, 254
West Florida: 34, 35, 39, 235; Americanization of, 42, 64, 73, 228, 245; economic and strategic importance of, 43, 213; U.S. ready to buy, 110, 136, 218; U.S. claim to, 169, 170, 213, 214, 215, 216, 218, 220, 222, 223, 229; uprising, 220, 239. *See also* Floridas
West Indies, 66, 76, 86, 102
Westerners: favor expansion, 36, 58, 71, 123, 129, 180; and Mississippi, 42–43, 46, 48, 58, 67, 73, 121–122; favor economic growth, 42–43, 70, 76; secession sentiment, 48, 50, 59, 116, 237; and Spain, 59, 64, 70–71, 110, 120, 235, 237; and France, 68, 70, 76; and Jefferson, 68, 70, 123, 129, 145, 250; threaten New Orleans, 124; Monroe and, 135
White, James, 50
Whitworth, Lord (British ambassador to France), 154
Wilkinson, General James: 50, 67, 68, 210, 217, 221; plot for Floridas and Louisiana, 51, 62, 67; commander of army in west, 67, 201, 234; receives Louisiana, 201, 204, 205; governor Louisiana Territory, 234; and Burr scheme, 236–237, 238; occupies West Florida (1813), 240
Wilson, Woodrow, 241
Wolcott, Oliver, Jr., 82
Wolfe, James (British general), 244

Yazoo Strip, 39

OTHER LOUISIANA PAPERBACKS IN HISTORY

The Napoleonic Revolution Robert B. Holtman

The Marble Man: Robert E. Lee and His Image in American Society
Thomas L. Connelly

The Stonewall Brigade James I. Robertson, Jr.

I'll Take My Stand: The South and the Agrarian Tradition
Twelve Southerners

To Die Game: The Story of the Lowry Band, Indian Guerrillas of
Reconstruction W. McKee Evans

The Forgotten People: Cane River's Creoles of Color Gary B. Mills

Latin American Diplomatic History: An Introduction
Harold Eugene Davis, John J. Finan, F. Taylor Peck

Slave Testimony: Two Centuries of Letters, Speeches, Interviews,
and Autobiographies Edited by John W. Blassingame

Gentleman in a Dustcoat: A Biography of John Crowe Ransom
Thomas Daniel Young

The Rise and Fall of Black Slavery C. Duncan Rice

The New South Creed: A Study in Southern Mythmaking
Paul M. Gaston

The Wild Man from Sugar Creek: The Political Career of Eugene
Talmadge William Anderson

The Radical Republicans: Lincoln's Vanguard for Racial Justice
Hans L. Trefousse

Southern Negroes, 1861–1865 Bell I. Wiley

Lanterns on the Levee: Recollections of a Planter's Son
William Alexander Percy

Darwin and the Modern World View John C. Greene

Bricks Without Straw Albion W. Tourgée. Edited by Otto H. Olsen

The Barber of Natchez Edwin Adams Davis and
William Ransom Hogan

Bourbonism and Agrarian Protest: Louisiana Politics, 1877–1900
William Ivy Hair

Epidemics in Colonial America John Duffy

The First South John Richard Alden

The Earl of Louisiana A. J. Liebling

The South and the Sectional Conflict David M. Potter

And the War Came: The North and the Secession Crisis, 1860–1881
Kenneth M. Stampp

Twelve Years a Slave Solomon Northup. Edited by Sue Eakin and
Joseph Logsdon

The Suppression of the African Slave Trade W. E. B. Du Bois

F. D. R. and the South Frank Freidel

The Supreme Court from Taft to Warren Alpheus Thomas Mason

Reconstruction in Retrospect: Views from the Turn of the Century
Edited by Richard N. Current

Reconstruction: An Anthology of Revisionist Writings Edited by
Kenneth M. Stampp and Leon Litwack

Reconstruction in Mississippi James W. Garner

Origins of Class Struggle in Louisiana Roger W. Shugg

The Slave Economy of the Old South: Selected Essays in Economic
and Social History Ulrich Bonnell Phillips. Edited by
Eugene D. Genovese

The Burden of Southern History C. Vann Woodward

Jim Crow's Defense: Anti-Negro Thought in America, 1900–1930
I. A. Newby

Civil War in the Making, 1815–1860 Avery O. Craven

The Politics of Reconstruction, 1863–1867 David Donald

Look Away from Dixie Frank E. Smith

The Cold War: Retrospect and Prospect Frederick L. Schuman

Writing Southern History: Essays in Historiography in Honor of
Fletcher M. Green Edited by Arthur S. Link and
Rembert W. Patrick

Romanticism and Nationalism in the Old South Rollin G. Osterweis

The Mind of the Old South Clement Eaton

Pitchfork Ben Tillman Francis Butler Simkins

Hoke Smith and the Politics of the New South
Dewey W. Grantham, Jr.

Religion and the Constitution Paul G. Kauper

American Negro Slavery Ulrich Bonnell Phillips

The Meaning of Yalta: Big Three Diplomacy and the New Balance
of Power Edited by John L. Snell

Southern Legacy Hodding Carter

Edmund Ruffin, Southerner: A Study in Secession
Avery O. Craven

Romance and Realism in Southern Politics T. Harry Williams

Plato Eric Voegelin

A HISTORY OF THE SOUTH

The Southern Colonies in the Seventeenth Century, 1607–1689
Wesley Frank Craven

The South in the Revolution, 1763–1789 John Richard Alden

The South in the New Nation, 1789–1819 Thomas P. Abernethy

The Development of Southern Sectionalism, 1819–1848
Charles S. Sydnor

Origins of the New South, 1877–1913 C. Vann Woodward

The Emergence of the New South, 1913–1945 George B. Tindall